Jew vs. Arab

Sibling Rivalry of the Ages

Ivan C. Scott

LOST
COAST
PRESS

JEW VS. ARAB: SIBLING RIVALRY OF THE AGES
Copyright ©2001 by Ivan C. Scott

Lost Coast Press
155 Cypress Street
Fort Bragg, CA 95437
(800) 773-7782
www.cypresshouse.com

Cover design and illustration: Charles Hathaway,
Mendocino Graphics

LIBRARY OF CONGRESS CATALOGING-IN PUBLICATION DATA

Scott,Ivan, 1928-
    Jew vs. Arab : sibling rivalry of the ages / Ivan C. Scott.
    P.cm.
    Includes index.
    ISBN 1-882897-60-9
    1. Jewish-Arab relations. 2. Jewish-Arab relations--History--1917-
1948. 3. Palestine--Ethnic relations. 4. Arab-Israel conflict.
5. Judaism--Relations--Islam. 6. Israel--Ethnic relations.
I. Title: Jew versus Arab.
II. Title.
    DS 119.7 .S3797 2000
    956.04--dc21   00-046154

Manufactured in the U.S.A.
First edition
2 4 6 8 9 7 5 3 1

The conflict is, in a certain way,
a family affair between two Semitic peoples
who are characterized by stubbornness and lack of flexibility.

—Nahum Goldmann

Contents

Jew vs. Arab

Sibling Rivalry of the Ages

Introduction

The Bible of the Christians and the Jews has been called the greatest story ever told. But it is not a greater story than that of the rivalry between Jews and Arabs. Like all family quarrels, it is so old that one cannot say who started it; one cannot say, to paraphrase Jesus of Nazareth, who cast the first stone.

In a given generation, the general public almost always views the conflict between Jew and Arab as a current event. Since the struggle between the antagonists has been continuous over centuries, it is easy to forget that continuity. At any given moment, it is not the event that is so important, but the antecedents of present strife. Each party to this enduring and seemingly insoluble conflict forgets that they are all victims of their own history.

The story of world Jewry is the story of dispossession, dispersal, and alienation; whether as a result of their own faults or simply by becoming incidental victims in great events that overwhelmed them, cannot be said. The story is easily told in outline: how they lost territory over time, were driven or transported out of their own land over long periods; the insensible, anonymous migrations over ages and vast spaces of territory at the same time (the famous Diaspora), leaving behind land virtually unoccupied by their own kind. And just as nature abhors a vacuum, in the world of mammals, open territory is but a niche to be filled by the hungry and the restless. Arabs moved in as Jews moved out, over centuries, and again insensibly, so that no one in a given generation might mark any one event as being significant in what was in fact a human continuum: Jews departing and Arabs entering into what was deemed one of the fairest of lands: that land of milk and honey which, in ancient times, wandering Hebrews took for their own from those weaker than themselves, and over succeeding centuries lost to those stronger than themselves.

The story of the Jews' outward migration is not more interesting than the reverse tide when, still once more almost insensibly, beginning in the last half of the nineteenth century, a trickle of humanity seeking the lost motherland became ever larger. Finally, a day would come when one could speak of a torrent of dispossessed Jews descending upon a land that they fancied was still theirs despite more than a thousand years' absence.

The background to the nineteenth-century migrations was a great moving force of social protest when the ideal of political democracy became joined to another ideal: social justice. After World War One, Russian communism, the most virulent manifestation of social democracy, was implanted in the collapsing Czarist empire. It was the work of a few zealots who entertained a fantastic vision of the future: the end of poverty, the attainment of human equality, the realization of social justice; a society freed at last from the capitalist way of life; a society, they imagined, so perfect that it would be harmonious and self-regulating; in brief, a classless society. And since this species of society would appear everywhere in the world, they supposed, sovereign states would, in the classic prediction of the Marxists, "fade away."

How unlikely it seems in retrospect that Zionism, with its parochial view of the world, should have been another extreme manifestation of the same social democratic movement. Yet, an examination of the welter of ideas generated by Zionism reveals a movement of Jewish thought as chiliastic as that of the Marxist socialists. Traditional Judaism, emerging Jewish nationalism, and theories of social alienation and class conflict, did finally combine to produce what was called at the time Labor Zionism. That particular ethos became implanted by force and violence in Palestine; as communism was being established in Russia at the same time, by force and violence also.

As communism in Russia became eventually an unworkable experiment, so did Labor Zionism fail to realize its promise in the new state of Israel. Both movements were propelled by dedicated elites who, like all zealots, had not the slightest doubt about the rightness of their respective causes. Their ruthless disregard for others' rights in pursuit of their fancied higher ones gave them the qualities required of heroes: courage, resolution in adversity, dedication and single-mindedness, which allowed them, as a small minority in the presence of an inert majority, to have their own way. But what they created at great cost could not be bequeathed to succeeding generations.

It may be argued that communism failed in Russia because it did not get a fair chance. The need to answer a continuous resistance from the world of capitalism caused Russian communism's eventual collapse, the result of those exertions. Energies that should have been expended on the system envisioned were instead spent in defense of that same system. Communist aggression outside Russia could be called a defense, in the sense that if the world did not become communist, Russian communism (an imperiled island in a sea of capitalism) would perish—and so it did. Likewise, the Zionist dream faltered and failed in a sea of angry Moslems.

In retrospect one can say that the attempt of alienated social reformers to establish a heaven on earth in Russia should not have taken place. The Russian people suffered from it, as did those of many other countries who resisted the attempt. Likewise the ambitious plan to establish a homeland in Palestine for world Jewry became an impossible dream. Wise voices counseled against it at the outset, but were scarcely heard in the storm of enthusiasm and faith that the dream engendered. As it was not possible for the world's humanity to be shaped in the communist image, so too it was not possible for the Jews of the world in their many millions to settle down on a territory so small as Palestine. In its actual development modern Israel became a refuge for the few desperate ones among them. Supported by contributions from world Jewry as well as massive aid from the patron state, the United States, Israel imposed upon the international community an incalculable cost in lost lives, human misery and wasted treasure. Once committed to maintaining the State of Israel, the United States could not, out of the irrational requirements of pride and honor, abandon its client state. In the end, the client, by surviving, became other than what Zionists had hoped for. The Zionist dream became a nightmare, quite literally a bleeding ulcer on the face of the earth.

The sovereignty of a state is a two-edged sword. It gives the state complete freedom of action, answerable to no one, subject to nothing except the power of others. It also leaves the state wholly responsible for its own existence. In a supreme crisis, if it is small and weak, only its allies and perhaps the charity of the international community can save it. Great Britain, the first patron, soon regretted its pro-Zionist policy and abandoned its creature; this being "The Great Betrayal," as the Jews characterized it. Since then, the United States, as the current mediating power in the Middle East, has regularly disappointed the Israelis (more betrayals). The contradiction in American foreign policy vis-à-vis the Middle East is the same as that experienced by Great Britain: to defend Israel is to insult Moslem sensibilities while injuring Arab interests. To abandon the Israelis to their fate is to invite the prospect of another Holocaust—unthinkable to the patron state and unacceptable to the international community.

In the last analysis, the support of Zionism by Great Britain, then continued by the United States, imposes upon all peoples of the world an insoluble riddle, giving point to Karl Marx's inscrutable remark: "History is a conundrum resting on the brow of mankind."

iv

CHAPTER ONE

The Religious Background

ANCIENT ISRAEL

ews believe that the origins of their people are found in the creation of the world: the simultaneous genesis of themselves and their religion; for they believe that they are God's "chosen people." In the beginning, as the story goes, there was a void and darkness, and God said, "Let there be light." And there was light. On the second day He parted the waters and drew together the dry land. In the days that followed He created a multiplicity of life forms, which crowded into every ecological niche on the planet. The sixth day He made man, in His own image, "from the dust of the ground and breathed into his nostrils the breath of life." God called him Adam (man) and placed him in a garden called Eden where he might till the land and live forever, and therefore one may suppose that Adam, like his Maker, was immortal.

But Adam became lonely and God made him a mate from one of his ribs. "This is now bone of my bones," said Adam, "and flesh of my flesh." He called her "woman," for "she was taken out of a man." When the woman gave Adam an apple from the Tree of

1

Knowledge and both did eat, they lost their innocence and were ashamed of their nakedness. Angrily, God cast them out of the Garden of Eden and cursed them. Metaphorically speaking, this was the Jews' first trespass against their Maker, their first defiance, which resulted in their exile; there would be more.

Henceforth Adam would earn his livelihood by the sweat of his brow, and his wife would bear their children in pain. Their immortality was taken from them. "For dust thou art, and unto dust shalt thou return." Their equality as man and woman came to an end: "Thy desire shall be to thy husband, and he shall rule over thee."

Adam named his wife Eve, "because she was the mother of all living." They had two sons, Abel and Cain. The latter would murder the former. This tragedy may be taken as a metaphor for the conflict between a settled agriculture and a pastoral life. When the two boys grew up, Cain became a tiller of the soil; Abel a keeper of sheep. When the fruits of their labor were offered to the Lord, He received Abel's favorably (with respect), "but unto Cain and his offering he did not respect," suggesting that this was a desert deity who valued the pastoral life and disapproved of farming; thus the cause for Cain's unbounded rage and the murder of his younger brother.

The common origin of Arab and Jew is the desert, the word "Arab" meaning just that. Hebrew is a corruption of the word *Habiru* (wanderer). Migratory people organized primitively in tribes, they could never make more than a fanciful claim to Canaan, legendary land of milk and honey, which they coveted. These mythical claims to the Promised Land resulted in the final mythology: they were relatives all, Arab and Jew, descended from Abraham, their most distant ancestor, and all claimed the same land.

Abraham (born Abram) and his two brothers, Nahor and Harran, were Arameans (Syrians, in modern parlance), living in Ur of Chaldee (better known in history as Babylonia). At God's urging, Abram took his wife, Sarai, along with Lot (the grandson of Harran, who had died) into the land that belonged to Canaan. Like Abram and his brothers, Canaan was descended from Noah, as was presumably all humankind after the Great Flood, that agency by which God had destroyed the whole of His unsatisfactory creation except for Noah and his family, who had found favor in their Maker's eyes.

When Abram reached the age of ninety-nine years God talked with him about his inheritance. Henceforth Abram would be called Abraham and Sarai would be called Sarah. There would be a covenant between God and Abraham, who could expect to be the "father of many nations." His posterity would receive "all the land of Canaan, for an everlasting possession; and I will be their God."

There was a hard condition attached to God's beneficence. "Ye shall circumcise the flesh of your foreskin and it shall be a token of the covenant betwixt you and me." Henceforth every male in Abraham's line would have to be circumcised or else be expelled from Abraham's ever-growing family. Thus was established a peculiar fetish that would never die out: the circumcised Jewish male. [1]

Thirteen years earlier, when Abraham was eighty-six, he "had gone unto Hagar," Sarah's handmaiden, and the result was the birth of a boy. An angel of the Lord predicted that he would grow up to be a "wild man: his hand will be against every man and every man's hand against him..." The angel also gave the boy a name, Ishmael.

In order that Abraham might have a legitimate heir, God promised that Sarah, though barren all her life, would bear a child, to be called Isaac. "Then Abraham fell upon his face and laughed." Sarah was ninety years old and he nearly one hundred. God simply replied, "Sarah, thy wife, will bear thee a son indeed." The next day Abraham, Ishmael (now thirteen), "and all the men of his house, born in the house, bought with money of the stranger, were circumcised with him."

Sarah bore a son, Isaac, as foretold. As time passed, Isaac's wife, Rebecca, though barren also, conceived twins. Even in her womb the twins struggled with each other. God reassured Rebecca, saying, "two nations are in your womb...the one people shall be stronger than the other people; and the elder shall serve the younger."

The firstborn was reddish in color and hairy, so they named him Esau. The other boy grasped Esau's heel as he slipped out of the womb, so they called him Jacob, which means "the grappler." It is the fable of Cain and Abel repeated. When they were grown, Jacob talked his older brother into selling him his birthright. Then he deceived his father Isaac, who was now blind, into giving him his blessing, which should have gone to Esau, the eldest son. Realizing that he had been deceived, Isaac was greatly saddened, but felt that what had been done could not be revoked.

Learning of Jacob's treachery, Esau vowed to kill his brother. Jacob fled. After years away from home, and having married two Canaanite sisters, he returned to confront Esau. Still fearing his brother, Jacob lagged behind his traveling companions. One night, alone, he was confronted by a man (probably an angel) who wrestled with him throughout the night. In order to bring the contest to a close, the man touched the socket of Jacob's hip, laming him. "Now," said the man, having wrestled Jacob to a draw, "your name from this day forward will be Israel, for as a prince hast thou power with God and with men."

When Jacob arrived in the land of the Canaanites, God appeared and said to him, "Your name is Israel. The land I gave to Abraham and Isaac I now give to you."

Like his younger brother, Esau had taken Canaanite women for his wives, as his father had desired. Settling in the hill country of Seir, he waxed mightily in herds and retainers, calling himself Edom; his followers known as Edomites. "Kings," says the Bible's narrator, "reigned in Edom before any Israelite king reigned." [2]

It is the separation of the brothers and the fortunes of their descendants that allow Abraham's heirs to claim the land of Canaan. Esau's line becomes obscure. His descendants, the Edomites, appear only sporadically in the Hebrew Bible, but always as enemies of Israel. [3]

Of course, the gist of the quarrel between the siblings is now clear: Esau, the eldest, the rightful heir to Abraham's legacy through his father, Isaac, was despoiled by his dishonest younger brother

Jacob (Israel). Thus, the Land of Canaan, stolen by Israel's line, belongs rightfully to Esau's heirs. But it is to be noted that this species of theft is aided and abetted by God, who favors the wily Israel over the good-hearted Esau.

Ishmael, Abraham's bastard, is promised nothing, as is usually the case with illegitimate heirs. The Jews would never allow the Arabs to forget how unworthy as a consequence their claim to Canaan. Ishmael, "who was born according to the flesh," observed St. Paul [writing in this context as a Jew and not a Christian], "persecuted the one [Israel] who was born according to the spirit." Ishmael, illicit product of Abraham's lust for Hagar (Sarah's serving girl), did not rank with Israel, who issued from the aged Sarah's virtuous loins. "What does the scripture say?" asked Paul. "Drive out the slave and her child; for the slave's child will not share the inheritance with the free woman's child." [4]

When later the Arabs began to consult the Hebrew sources in order to legitimize their new religion, Islam, they could not decide between two ancestors able to connect them to Abraham's legacy. They could choose Esau, the eldest son of Isaac and Rebecca, or Ishmael, Isaac's half–brother. But the descendants of the former, calling themselves Idumaeans, had become Yahweh worshippers, leaving the Arabs only Ishmael as their claimant. To the Jews, either choice would have to be considered irrelevant. Yahweh had disinherited both Esau and Ishmael by promising the land of Canaan to Israel.

The mythical claims of the sibling rivals, Jew and Arab, is complicated by the claims advanced by another relative: the Arameans (modern Syrians), who could trace their descent back to Abraham's brother Nahor. This triangular contest between the uncle and the nephews best explains the family quarrel, and has a particular relevance for modern times. In the period when the Hebrews were taking possession of a part of Canaan, the Arameans had approached a zenith in wealth and influence. The most important of them were the Chaldeans, from whom had sprung the legendary Abraham and his lesser-known brother

Nahor. So great was Aramaic influence and prestige that in a short time their language (a Semitic tongue) would become the lingua franca of western Asia. For centuries, much of the religious literature, both Jewish and Christian (Syriac), would be published and read in the vernacular tongue of the Arameans. By the time of Jesus of Nazareth it would be the popular tongue of much of future Palestine.

To follow Israel's line a little further, Joseph became the favorite son of Jacob, i.e., Israel. Coveting his coat of many colors, Joseph's jealous brothers sold him into bondage. He was eventually carried into Egypt, where his wit and abilities allowed him to become an important figure, surpassed in power only by the Pharaoh. Later his brothers arrived in Egypt with their flocks and were forgiven their iniquities. Their descendants prospered, but when they asked to leave Egypt, the Pharaoh refused to let them go.

The drama of the twentieth century Holocaust is foreshadowed in the sad fate of Israel's descendants. A new Pharaoh, as reprehensible as the modern Hitler, enslaves them. [5] But a savior arrives when the Pharaoh's daughter plucks the baby Moses from the river Nile. Raised as an Egyptian prince, Moses learns only when he is grown that he is an Israelite, of the house of Levi.

Exodus is perhaps the most widely known of the Bible stories: Moses one day saw an Egyptian beating a Hebrew slave. Enraged, he killed the man. Fearing the consequences, he fled into the desert. There he encountered God. The two agreed upon a plan to force Pharaoh to let the Children of Israel go. In order to persuade the enslaved Hebrews that Moses was God's *bona fide* spokesman, God taught Moses some magic tricks that would mystify not only the Children of Israel but the Pharaoh too: turning a shepherd's staff into a serpent; making his hand appear palsied and then abruptly healed. If these "signs" did not have their desired effect, Moses would take water out of the river and allow it to run onto the dry land where it would turn to blood.

To make Moses still more impressive God would cause the Pharaoh to become inflexible in his resolve to keep the Children of Israel in bondage. "I will harden his heart that he should not let the people go." Since Moses admitted that he was not very articulate, his brother Aaron would be let in on the plan so as to serve as Moses' assistant. The rest of the story is well known: how inflexible the Pharaoh became, causing Moses to work his wonders. Despite the devastation caused by a succession of miracles: turning all the waters of Egypt to blood, killing all the Egyptian cattle (the cattle of the Israelites were unaffected), bringing down plagues on the land, — including an inundation of frogs followed by a virtual flood of lice (—"all the dust of the land became lice"), then hail and "fire mingled with hail"— still, the Pharaoh hardened his heart and would not let the Children of Israel go. God therefore prepared to kill the firstborn of every Egyptian, including the Pharaoh's own. Only the Children of Israel might be saved from the Angel of Death by smearing the blood of a freshly killed lamb on the lintels and doorposts of the house. This would be the "Passover," a holy event, to be memorialized forever after, as the Holocaust in later times is to be forever memorialized.

On the frightful night of Passover, 600,000 Israelites, as well as others ("a mixed multitude"), began streaming out of Egypt. There is the famous line, "And the Lord went before them by day in a pillar of a cloud to lead them the way; and by night in a pillar of fire to give them light; to go by day and night." Even so, the Egyptian pursuers caught up with them at the Red Sea. But then another miracle occurred; the protecting God of the Hebrews parted the waters, making a dry highway that allowed for their final escape.

By such a dramatic exodus did the Children of Israel regain their freedom, but thereafter, too weak and divided to enter the land of Canaan, they wandered for forty years in the desert. Moses died without seeing the Promised Land. His chief lieutenant, Joshua, led the Israelites across the River Jordan into Canaan (today commonly referred to as the West Bank), where further fabulous events would give them control of a part of the country.

Historically speaking, Canaan was always vulnerable to invasion, yet exceptionally resistant to outright conquest. One of the earliest cradles of civilization in the Middle East, characterized by walled and fortified cities, its origins can be traced back at least five millennia before Christ's time; a civilized condition of life as ancient as that of Egypt. But Egyptian towns and cities were forged into an imperial unity very early, giving the rulers irresistible sway over many peoples far beyond Egypt's frontiers. Canaan, to the contrary, and rather like the Greek peninsula somewhat later, experienced a different development. A rivalry of many city-states created an equipoise among them that did not allow the strongest to absorb the rest; at least not for long. But this disunity created a weakness so great that they often fell under the rule of a foreign power. Indeed, the history of ancient Canaan foretells the pattern of events in modern Palestine: incessant rivalry, and often warfare, between petty states that are perpetually under the influence, and sometimes the domination, of great powers beyond their own borders.

Historians, philologists, and archaeologists together cannot reconstruct the actual development of events in Canaan around 1200 B.C. There is a consensus, however, that the Canaanites, a very mixed population both ethnically and culturally, faced a double danger: semi-nomadic invaders coming in from the deserts on the one side, and in the other direction a veritable flood of migrants, the so-called "Sea People," who were pouring out of the Aegean basin and settling along the coast of Asia Minor. While Hebrews were taking over the hill country, the Sea People (Philistines in the case of Canaan) were occupying the coastal areas and building fortified cities.

The conquest of the hill country seems to have been the cooperative work of three groups: Hebrew tribes already settled in Canaan for perhaps two centuries; incoming Hebrews who, in Judaic tradition, were fleeing from Egypt; and certain indigenous Canaanites who began to join the Hebrews. Social historians believe it was the classic example and one of the oldest, of social warfare: the hungry and desperately poor immigrants overwhelming the rich and contented, ensconced behind their fortified walls.

The documentary evidence is compelling enough to make one think the Hebrews arrived in Canaan in two waves, separated by about two hundred years. The earliest migrations, including Edomites, Moabites, Ammonites, and Leahites (Jacob among this group), began to appear in Canaan about 1400 B.C. The later migration, around 1200 B.C. (a concurrent movement with the Sea People), included the Rachel-tribes, Ephraim, Manasseh and Benjamin (Moses and Joshua the famous names in this migration). It is interesting to note that while Moses was appealing to the Pharaoh to let his people go, the Canaanites were pleading with the Pharaoh to save them from these same barbarians.

If their ancient legends, embedded in the theological language of the Torah, have a kernel of historical truth, Hebrew tribes wandered into a land called Canaan and after a time wandered out again. Thereafter they wandered into Egypt and become slaves. Escaping from the heartless Pharaoh, they wandered in the wilderness under Moses' leadership for forty years, then wandered back into Canaan again. Over the next couple of generations, and after much fighting, they established themselves with some certainty in what someday would be called central Palestine.

The mixed horde of people who overran the hill country were as violently disposed toward each other as toward those they had come to dominate. Eventually, authority was imposed upon most of them by a military commander of genius, a man both imperious and criminal by nature: the famous King David. Over a period of forty years his driving ambition and ruthless abilities united the contentious Hebrew tribes, allowing for a stable monarchy with Jerusalem as its capital. But this same unity was undone in the next forty years (the length of King Solomon's reign). In less than three generations the independence and prosperity of the Israelites came to depend upon close relations with the superpower of the region, Egypt; a relationship so close it could be called a client-patron arrangement, not unlike the one established between modern Israel and the United States.

The ascendancy of the Hebrews in Canaan was as fragile and

ephemeral as their unity. After Solomon's death in 933 the tribes divided again, those in the north establishing a separate kingdom. The history of this monarchy, under a succession of rulers, was unrelieved fratricidal conflict. Soon both the quarreling tribes and the patron-state Egypt succumbed to Assyria, a rising power in the Middle East. In a three-year campaign, King Sargon occupied the whole territory north of Jerusalem, transforming the country that would henceforth be known as Samaria. "I besieged and conquered Samaria," Sargon boasted, "led away as booty 27, 290 inhabitants of it … The town I rebuilt better than it was before and settled therein people from countries which I myself had conquered." [6]

Judah, the small Hebrew kingdom in the south, survived much longer, from 933 to 585. But it too succumbed to the power of the next imperial master, Babylonia. Nebuchadnezzar did to the southern Hebrew tribes what Sargon had done to those in the north, taking the Jewish king captive and transporting Jerusalem's upper classes to Babylon: the famous Babylonian Captivity.

This was the time when Hebrew (henceforth Jewish) scholars set down in their exile an account of their people; a compilation of what had already been written, but also a recapitulation of legends, oral traditions and, not least important, the liturgical legacy of many generations of Hebrews. [7]

In 586 Nebuchadnezzar ordered the Temple at Jerusalem torn down and part of the city's walls razed. With the fall of Judah, the Jewish Diaspora, which had begun with the dispersal of the ten tribes of Israel, became accelerated.

The Biblical account of these events explains the tragedy in supernatural terms. From the time that Moses led the people of Israel out of Egypt, God had empowered exceptional men (prophets) to give warnings of the errant ways of His chosen people, promising dire retribution if they should rebel against His will. But they did so repeatedly, and the final disasters are owed to their "stiff-neckedness" (read "overweening pride"). Failing to obey Yahweh, they were punished, exile their sentence. It would last 2,000 years.

A secular account of these same events would give a more

complex explanation. A petty state in the ancient land of Canaan, Israel had been unified with difficulty, survived thereafter only briefly as either a client of Egypt or by paying tribute (a form of extortion), first to Assyria, then to Babylonia. The result of all this was the dispersal of the Hebrew people. Some were taken into captivity, but most migrated to other countries over succeeding centuries, seeking employment and a better life; preserving their religion and customs wherever they went; always clinging to the largely fanciful memory that they had once been a united, prosperous people, but above all a great people.

The hope that this condition of independence and greatness might return came to them briefly with the appearance of still another dominant power, the Persian Empire. King Cyrus, adopting a policy of religious toleration for the heterogeneous populations under his control, allowed the Jewish exiles to return to their native land. This had a profound impact on Judaism. For not only did the Torah, or more exactly the Pentateuch, take form in this period, the exiles brought back, as a result of their Babylonian experience, new ideas, new concepts about Heaven and Hell; especially the notion spreading throughout the Middle East of a savior begotten by God, i.e., the Son of God. [8]

Returning to Jerusalem, the Jews (now clients of the Persian king) rebuilt the Temple the Assyrians had destroyed sixty-six years earlier. For Jewish chroniclers this served as a significant date for a new period of their history: the era of the Second Temple. The oldest conditions persisted, however: foreign domination — galling to the proud Jews — and continuous disputes. Invariably these were debilitating religious issues.

Earlier, the Assyrian ascendancy in Canaan had produced far-reaching consequences for the future of Israel, the Jews in general, and for Christianity later. The policy of forced transportation by the Assyrians, in order to control the different peoples under their power, literally transformed the northern regions of Canaan, especially Samaria. A large influx of eastern ethnic groups, either as a result of Assyrian forced transport or simply as a result of a natural migration of uprooted people, caused a severe diminution of the autochthonous Hebrews. Perhaps as many as 200,000 of them were carried, driven, or harassed out of the country in less than twenty-five years. An equal number of immigrants moved in to replace them. By the time Jesus was born, the Hebrew population in Galilee and to a large extent Samaria as well, was a distinct minority, "a dispersion among the heathen," as the historian Emile Schurer called it.[9] The Hebrew language disappeared almost entirely, replaced by Aramaic, which became the lingua franca for what was now a multicultural, multi-ethnic area. Finally, the ancient, simple desert religion of the wandering Hebrews began to disappear. By the time of Christ's advent, radical ideas with their roots in the East predominated. A Galilean, speaking Aramaic and imbued with new ideas, Jesus entered upon his short-lived ministry. Journeying to Jerusalem he found the old-time religion in force and full vigor. That Jerusalem had been Hellenized to a degree cannot be doubted, but it is equally certain that Judaic fundamentalism had remained untouched by these outside influences. The Sadducees, a very narrow class of Jerusalem's citizenry, had felt the impact of Hellenistic culture. Highly secularized, middle-to upper-middle-class Jews, they were, collectively speaking, that kind of conservative type one finds in any urban society: religiously conservative, socially progressive.[10] Graecophiles, they were open to modern ways and innovation. In religious terms, they were opposed to oral law, too popular, too democratic for them. They favored a strict adherence to the written law, Mosaic Law, the law as old as the Hebrew nation itself. In religious terms, therefore, the Sadducees saw eye-to-eye with the other dominant social class, the Pharisees, who were ultra-orthodox in both social and religious matters. While the Sadducees rejected the popular belief in Heaven, salvation, the resurrection of the dead, and the immortality of the soul, the Pharisees accepted all of these. The Pharisees resented Hellenistic influences and were rabidly anti-Roman (the latest bearers of foreign ways). The Sadducees were disposed to cooperate with the Roman power, and took little interest in supporting the spirit of national revolt, which promised not only revolutionary changes for society, but retribution by Rome, a power infamous for savage reprisal.

The dissolving influences of Hellenism, brought into Canaan by Alexander the Great and his successors, the Seleucids, were necessarily destructive of orthodox Judaism. The Egyptian Ptolemies, who followed the Seleucids, promoted Hellenism as well. Their successors, the Romans, who were as Hellenized as any other progressive people in the Middle East, continued to establish what might be called a modern way of life.

From the time of the Prophet Ezra, the dominant trend in Judaism had been conservative if not reactionary; a pious resolve to recover the past and to repel heathen influences. In brief, the conservative forces in Jerusalem society sought to establish the preeminent rule of the priestly class. The Pharisees, more than a sect, as often thought, but a party with political ramifications and an agenda, were the moving spirit of reaction. Their agents and sympathizers operated effectively outside and well beyond Jerusalem, wherever Judaism appeared to be threatened by what could be called, in contemporary parlance, liberal ideas. [11] For them the Torah served as the sole rule of conduct for all Jews, Mosaic Law being the foundation of Hebrew life. "In the form of a law given by God Himself [Mosaic Law], the Jew was told what he had to do as a faithful servant of Jehovah, what festivals to celebrate, what sacrifices to offer, what tribute to pay to the priests who conducted the services, and generally what religious ceremonies to perform." [12]

Jesus' intrusion into Jerusalem's politics (which were inherently religious) was aggravated by his open contempt for the Pharisees. An outsider from Galilee, a region characterized by one historian as populated by "a mongrel race," Jesus encountered the indigenous Hebrew stock. [13] It can be suspected that its leaders would not tolerate what they imagined was his racial impurity; nor could they accept the alien ideas he brought with him.

Jesus' brief career occurred in a period of intense speculation about the afterlife. Contacts with Mesopotamia during the Babylonian captivity had enriched a simple desert religion with Zoroastrian ideas about good and evil, the eternal struggle between the force of light, Ahura Mazda, and of darkness, Angra Maihyu; a belief also in demons and angels; and super angels, the archangels most frequently mentioned: Raphael, Michael, and Gabriel. Paradise, a Persian concept, had been taken into a growing body of Hebrew apocalyptic writings. Shoel, which for the nomadic Hebrews had signified no more than a final resting-place for the dead, became elevated in importance. Some apocalyptic writers believed it was not only "the bourn from which no traveler returns," but actually a stage in the ascent to paradise; a place of judgment also, perhaps a final judgment: some would be resurrected, others condemned to damnation. Those whose lives had been wicked would go to the "black recesses of Hell," but "the godly shall live again on earth." [14]

More than is usually realized, and more than can be demonstrated with precision, Jesus was (like the real founder of Christianity, Saul of Tarsus), a Hellenized Jew. [15] It is generally believed that he could speak three languages: Greek, Aramaic and Hebrew. He grew up among a people who were profoundly religious and just as profoundly superstitious. His mother's fascination with the Book of Daniel was fastened on his mind at an early age, as was true for his brothers and sisters also. In the Galilee, miracle workers abounded (Jesus only one among many), and no doubt charlatans were just as numerous. The main elements of his teachings are found in the apocalyptic writings of the time: Salvation of the Elect, redemption, resurrection, Hell for the blasphemer and the abominable, the coming of the Messiah (not to be confused with the Son of Man). [16] The evangelical faith that the despised, despoiled, uprooted Jew would be reborn spiritually and become the herald for all mankind was still another part of Jesus' complex, personal mission. Presenting himself as a teacher, willing and able to dispute with the learned rabbis, Jesus revealed that he had a good knowledge of the oral and written traditions of his religion. He did not hesitate to proclaim himself the Son of Man, who sat on the right hand of the Father. He would not claim to be the

Messiah, however, his message not concerned with this world but the hereafter. It appears that he did consider himself to be the Righteous Teacher, a notion (like baptism) he probably gained from John the Baptist, who had baptized him. It is likely that John had learned of these ideas and practices from the Essenes, a small, exclusive Hebrew sect that had taken up a secluded life in the hills northwest of Jerusalem. Always vague, always evasive in his replies, preferring to speak in parables, Jesus let his disciples think pretty much what they wished about him. When Peter asserted that Jesus was indeed the Messiah, the latter turned his response into confusion by implying that the Messiah and the Suffering Servant of the Lord were one and the same.

Over the centuries, the concept of a Messiah had evolved into diametrically opposed notions: that of a secular, military figure (House of David) and a sacerdotal figure (House of Levi). The origin of these perceptions is usually traced to the "joint leadership of Joshua and Zerubella, the two 'sons of oil,' in the early days of the Second Temple." [17]

It would seem that Jesus in his saintly mission should have been in the line of Zerubella. But no, since he claimed his descent from the House of David, he should have more properly presented himself as a military figure. Inexplicably, he could not be the one; he would not be the other.

How Jesus ran afoul of the law is well known. His tendencies not to defend himself are equally well known and always puzzling to the secular mind. To the Christian, however, the explanation for this is in the teleology developed after his death. As Jesus said, he was alpha and omega, implying that he had been born to play a predetermined and passive role in God's plan for human salvation. He seemed to think of himself as a necessary sacrifice for what he believed in, remarking, while walking in the Garden of Gethsemane on the eve of his execution, that he was resigned to his fate ("The spirit is willing but the flesh is weak"). This became clear the next day in his interview with the Roman procurator, Pontius Pilate, when with a little candor he could have saved himself.

15

The execution of Jesus of Nazareth, carried out as the will of the citizens of Jerusalem, possessed, as it turned out, universal significance. Within a decade this tragic affair, deprecated by the Jews as nothing more than the death of a convicted felon (crucified along with two other miscreants), took on unexpected dimensions. It is recorded that Saul of Tarsus, a Hellenized Jew belonging to the Pharisee party, who for nearly ten years had regularly participated in the persecution and sometimes the execution of those few who followed Christ's teaching, experienced a profound religious insight, perhaps a revelation. The story is told how, on one of his journeys to Damascus, "the Risen Christ" appeared and demanded to know why Saul was persecuting those who believed in Him. One may presume that Saul did not have a ready answer, because he accepted Christ as his savior at once, and a little later changed his name to Paul. For the rest of his life he gave witness to Christ's saving mission. The message was simple and unequivocal: one must confess with his mouth and believe in his heart that only through Christ may one save his soul and enter into Heaven. It was indeed a powerful and thought-provoking message from which a truly religious individual might turn away with hesitation and perhaps with considerable worry: What if Paul's, i.e., Christ's, message was true?

Paul's contribution to the rise of a new religion, Christianity, was of manifold significance. By preaching that Jesus' message should be carried to the Gentiles, he would cause Christianity (still a Jewish sect) to escape its parochial origins. By renouncing the ritual of circumcision, the original bond established between God and Abraham, he made it manifestly easier for mature Gentiles to embrace the religion of the Nazarenes, soon to be called Christian. [18]

Judaism was an exclusive religion, fashioned over many generations for a relatively small, relatively pure ethnic group, possessing as much a national character as a theological import for the believer. [19] By contrast, Pauline Christianity was cosmopolitan, recognizing no limitations, no barrier to the conversion of the unbeliever; neither racial nor national qualifications were required. All could believe in Christ and be saved.

16

Paul's second contribution to the faith of the Nazarenes was the introduction of Hellenistic influences, such as Greek philosophical precepts, Greek humanism, Greek ethics, and Greek epistemology (the Logos) Once started down this rational and latitudinarian road, Christian believers—especially their spiritual leaders—would be disposed to borrow from diverse cultural matters deemed to be an enrichment of the new religion. For example, when the question of Jesus' birth date (unknown in fact) could not be estimated satisfactorily, an arbitrary date was selected. [20] It happened to coincide with the twenty-fifth of December, the day when, over many centuries, Romans had prayed annually for the return of the sun as the winter solstice approached; also the day when the people exchanged gifts in order to propitiate the gods.

Competing religions would discover that their chief ideas, and sometimes even their fetishes, were being absorbed by their rival, Christianity, as for example the vicarious ingestion of Christ's blood and body. Such a religion, syncretistic as it is termed technically, produced in a few generations a synthesis of so many things that it will not be adequately resumed in less space than a book can provide.

In contrast to the proselytizing Christian faith, Judaism borrowed nothing. Indeed, the rabbis tended to repulse all innovations that threatened the traditional and narrow practices of an exclusive religion. Christ's personal tragedy may be considered the direct result of this desire to keep Judaism pure and undefiled by any outside influence.

ISLAM

Both Jews and Arabs were (and are) Semitic speakers. The dress and customs of the desert Semites were universally the same over immense spaces of North Africa; virtually unchanging over centuries, so simple and unvarying was the lifestyle, so few the needs of both nomads and villagers. With the progressive desiccation of the Middle East, after 10,000 B.C. a settled agriculture in most places gave way to customary habits of foraging for pasture. A meager agriculture was possible, but in only a few places, notably the widely scattered oases and along the river valleys. Commerce was as primitive as the other aspects of the economy: trade and barter in the necessities of life, and luxurious items for a few favored individuals. This meant that both nomads and villagers lived at the subsistence level. The close familial relations between villager and nomad were constant. Relatives moved back and forth regularly between the town and hinterland. Mohammed, for example, born in a relatively large town situated on a main trading route, was sent as a small child to live with Bedouin relatives for a few years.

The evolution of Arab tribal life was not different from that of the Hebrew. The Bedouins in Mohammed's time were what they had been for ages, barbarians by any usual criteria. Illiterate, their devotion was no more than a simple animism. In the Arabian Peninsula there were myriad deities to be propitiated, but all tribal gods were considered to be secondary to a superior god, Allah, the rain god. [21] The trading towns that had sprung up along the caravan routes from Syria to southern Arabia exhibited the same polytheism.

The Jewish migrations after the destruction of the Second Temple had resulted in Jewish colonies being established in the larger Arab towns. Christians too had arrived in Arabia by the seventh century C.E. [22] A pronounced monotheism, well rooted in the northern half of the peninsula, commonly called the Hedjaz, impacted profoundly on those few special ones who were known as *hanifs* (truth seekers). It appears that Mohammed was one of these, perplexed and dissatisfied with the contradictions he found in Judaism and Christianity, and the inadequacies of the Arabs' traditional henotheism. It is unlikely that he became a student of Judaic and Christian Scriptures until he was well into his middle years. The little that is known about his early life is fragmentary, presenting at most an outline of events. He was born in what today would be called middle-class circumstances, to a family that had some repute and influence in Mecca. Orphaned early, he was raised by his relatives, the influential and materially well-off Hashemite clan. As a young man he engaged in trade; probably accompanied caravans both to the north and south of the peninsula. While still relatively young he married a well-to-do widow, fifteen years his senior, giving him security for the rest of his fairly long life. He sired a number of children by his first wife. The sons died early while the daughters lived long. In his thirties he became a self-appointed, self-advertised wise man, holy in his outlook and behavior. At about age forty, he may have experienced that trauma which is called in contemporary society a mid-life crisis. Seeking solitude, he got into the habit of walking several miles out of town to a prominent elevation called Mount Hira. On more than one occasion he stayed overnight in a cave. It is possible that he was epileptic; consequently Western writers doubt his claim to have experienced revelations, though Mohammed might have thought so. On one of his nocturnal stays in the cave the Angel Gabriel appeared, asking him to read a message he had brought. Illiterate, Mohammed replied, "I can't." "Read!" commanded the angel. Again Mohammed said, "I can't." After that he went several times to the cave and memorized what the angel was charged to tell him. These revelations he caused to be written down in short verses *(suras)*. When he had experienced his seventy-fourth revelation he became convinced that he was a prophet. His wife, Khadijah, believed that he had received an authentic calling and sought the opinion of her cousin, a learned Christian. The savant agreed, thinking Mohammed's experience on Mount Hira was not unlike Moses' encounter with God on Mount Sinai.

To Mohammed, what he had heard was the word of God, and he evidently concluded that his mission was to deliver the message. Thus the famous line: "There is no God but Allah and Mohammed is His Messenger," or alternatively, "Mohammed is His prophet."

In the next ten years Mohammed had little success in spreading God's word, aside from converting some of his friends and relatives to his religious point of view. In the meantime, his activities aroused the resentment of rival families in Mecca who suspected the worst about his ambitions, especially the threat he posed to the established order.

Over many centuries Mecca had become a religious sanctuary for the Arab tribes. Its chief shrine, the Kaaba, a small cuboidal building, contained a large number of effigies. A black stone (probably a meteorite) fixed to the outer wall was the abode of the god Hubal.

Mohammed became increasingly outspoken in his disapproval of idol worship, as did his few followers. He gained some converts among the Umayyah clan, who accepted his increasingly strong statements on monotheism. They remained faithful to their idols nonetheless; no contradiction, after all, in a society that was at once polytheistic and henotheistic. Allah, the rain god, held first place in rank and devotion. [23]

Those who agreed to follow Mohammed were dubbed Moslems (*mu'adhdhin*), i.e., those who have submitted, for which the word Islam was used, but submission to whom or what? To Mohammed, or to Allah, the chief god? Submission to both Allah *and* Mohammed, evidently, for the latter's authority was unquestioned by the mu'adhdhin. Still, his following was small, consisting mostly of young people and the poor of Mecca. For the most part the important families ignored him, or jeered him, or took him seriously as a potential threat; therefore they thought how they might dispose of him.

Aware of the danger, Mohammed sent a trusted agent to Ethiopia, where Coptic Christianity was long established. His motives in this case are uncertain, but irrelevant since these overtures came to nothing. He was perhaps saved by the timely arrival of envoys from Yathrib (later to be called Medina), an oasis town north of Mecca where tribal warfare had become endemic. Asked to mediate, Mohammed accepted the invitation. Secretly, he and a devoted companion fled Mecca on the night of 15 July 622. This flight (*Hegira*) was a milestone in Mohammed's career and later would serve as the starting date of the Moslem era.

Until Mohammed moved to Yathrib he had had little or no contact with Jews, for there were few in Mecca. Three Jewish tribes lived on the Yathrib oasis. How long they had been there is unknown. Some evidence suggests since the time of the Babylonian Captivity. Over the ensuing centuries they became closely affiliated with the Arab tribes, following the urban-nomadic pattern of Arabia: Jews in town living in houses, Jews beyond the towns living in tents; and a regular intercourse between the two. The Jewish tribes were drawn into the constant warfare all the Semitic tribesmen knew. Jews and Arabs made pacts against others and against each other. Shifting allegiances and blood feuds constituted the acme of this existence. Mohammed had been invited for this precise reason: to resolve disputes, but his evolving religious ideas became a part of his work as a pacifier.

Some of Mohammed's revelations were contested by the Jews, perhaps forcing him to take in more and more Judaic lore. The conventional explanation that he chose what appealed to him from both Judaic and Christian doctrines is probably too static a concept to explain the evolution of his doctrines. It became a practice on Friday—market day in Yathrib—for Mohammed and the other hanifs to criticize each other and pit their learning against one another. Mohammed's eventual supremacy over his rivals and his domination of the whole community came from this simple social activity, just as his religious beliefs finally crystallized as a revision and a synthesis of Judaic oral traditions. As Christianity, denounced as a heresy by the Jews, had evolved out of Judaism, so did Islam begin to emerge in the same way. Mohammed did not think (like Jesus in this regard) that he was creating a new religion. Rather, as a prophet he believed he was "restoring and reforming the Abrahamic heritage among the Jews and Christians of Arabia." [24] Contemptuous of Arab idolaters and aware of how often the Hebrews had relapsed into paganism, he intended to draw them not into a new religion but to introduce them to what was true in the old religion, i.e., traditional Judaism. In brief, he had no quarrel with the People of the Book, though he doubted some parts of both Christian and Judaic doctrines. On the other hand, like all who are sure they have been enlightened by revelation, he could not think of himself as being other than the single repository of truth.

This dogmatic and inflexible will was evidently not apparent at the beginning when he was welcomed as a mediator. In fact, he chose to live almost like a recluse for the better part of the first year. Eventually, presenting himself ingenuously as a prophet in the Judaic tradition, he received a poor welcome from the Jews. Henceforth he attempted to persuade both Jewish and Arab tribesmen to acknowledge his personal faith. The Jews resisted his efforts vigorously. Eventually, failing to persuade his Jewish rivals, he and his Arab allies killed a good many of them and expelled the rest from Yathrib. Thereafter, to the degree that he won over some Arab tribes, others came his way.

Preaching, raiding, looting (in the Arab tribal tradition), and winning idolaters to his side, Mohammed waxed mightily in both wealth and influence. Yathrib was renamed Madinat an-nabi, the City of the Prophet, becoming henceforth what was quite common in Arabia, another Holy Town (*harum*). From this base he would extend his operations, and in the next five to seven years make his political and theological powers absolute. Those in Mecca who had taken him for a fool and forced him to flee to Yathrib now recognized him to be a danger. They sent armed troops against him but were almost always defeated. After several battles, Mohammed prepared to march on Mecca, but his enemies had no heart for further fighting. Tradition relates that an agreement was reached whereby Mohammed and his forces would camp outside Mecca for a year, then be allowed to visit the Kaaba. After entering Mecca the next year, Mohammed chose not to leave. By the unspoken assent of those who had opposed him, he made his control of the town as complete as the mastery he had enjoyed at Medina. In the two years of life remaining to him, he established a vigorous, albeit short-lived, theocracy. As with all theocracies, the leader's charismatic personality harnessed the inimical forces of religious certitude and the panoply of political power. His spiritual aura sustained his political power; his political power protected his sacerdotal pretensions.

One of his first acts after setting himself up in Mecca was to have the idols removed from the Kaaba. Allah could not be disturbed, however, nor did Mohammed dare to remove the sacred stone implanted in the wall of the Kaaba. That fetish was as imperishable as the stone itself. (It is revered to this day, the gleaming brilliance of its surface the result of literally billions of lips caressing it over many centuries.)

After long reflection Mohammed concluded that Abraham and Ishmael together had built the Kaaba. He accepted the widespread belief held by learned Jews that Ishmael, the son of Abraham, had fathered the Arab people. He believed also that the Hebrew people in their long wandering and frequent contacts with the Canaanite idolaters had produced a false religion: Judaism. But Islam, Abraham's original and uncorrupted religion, had now been recovered by Mohammed himself, and this truth he was charged to give to all the world.

In his final two years Mohammed refined what was in fact a personal theology. During the eight years at Medina, he had sat many hours with others around campfires or in the market places. Some of those present could recall his words, which were now cast in the form of verses (suras). Arranged as a book, they were called "Readings," i.e., *Qu'ran* (Koran). It is sometimes debated whether the compilation of these verses occurred in Mohammed's last years or after his death. It may be presumed that there is some truth in either version. The suras were of various lengths and of uneven quality, without unity, ranging from poetic and philosophical thoughts to prescriptions on how to behave, what to eat and drink, and above all what to believe. Some were written rather like parables, others were little homilies. All were considered the word of God sent to the faithful through an inspired Messenger, Mohammed.

As for doctrine, the Christian notion of the Trinity, Father, Son and Holy Ghost, he judged to be a disguised polytheism. Like the Jews, he denied the divinity of Christ. He rejected the doctrine of Original Sin. In disobeying God, Adam had not sinned; he committed a grievous error, but it did not taint mankind. [25]

In his view, Jesus of Nazareth had been merely a prophet; only one among many in a long line of prophets, and there had been many. After Mohammed's time, Moslem scholars estimated there had been 124,000 prophets. (The Hebrews referred to less than two dozen.) To Mohammed, Jesus of Nazareth was, like all those who came before him, an inspired man. Yet he was special, for Mohammed accepted the Christian doctrine that the martyr had not died on the cross, but through a faultless life had earned immortality. [26]

The belief in a Messiah, the essential element in both Judaism and Christianity, did not interest Mohammed, though he had no doubt that Jesus was born as the "promised Messiah;" moreover, that his mother was a virgin, "purified above all women." [27] Unlike the Jews, the Arabs were not a beleaguered people who yearned to be saved. The Christian belief that the Messiah had come as the Son of God under miraculous circumstances in order to save Mankind for a life in the hereafter—this was for the shrewd and practical Prophet too far-fetched to be believed. Salvation for the individual, he believed, is to be gained through right conduct and moral rectitude, which saves one from the fires of Hell and promises the delights of Paradise.

The doctrines of the Last Judgment and resurrection had an important place in Mohammed's theology. Meditating upon this he arrived at the question of free will vs. predestination, as would Calvinists almost a millennium later. God, omniscient and omnipotent, has arranged the future, but leaves to each individual the hard task of finding his way by an exercise of free will. Only by being virtuous can one be sure of which way he is moving in life toward his predestined end.

Mohammed reached his predestined end in 632, dying at the age of sixty-two or sixty-three. It is thought that the essential articles of his faith had by then been translated to the Moslem believers: that there is no God but Allah and Mohammed is his Messenger; and the Koran is the revealed word of God. The Old and New Testaments are the result of revelation too, but unreliable because of human tampering.

The duties of a Moslem were few but firm: pray five times daily; fast for a month each year in commemoration of the flight to Medina *(Ramadan)*; make the pilgrimage to Mecca once in a lifetime (if possible); give alms; and join the Holy War *(jihad)* when required. *Sunna*, the righteous path the prophet had followed, is the prescribed path for every believer, much as Christians believed a faithful servant of Christ should follow in the Savior's footsteps and imitate his saintly life.

Mohammed's death left his newfound religion without a leader, and the movement established in his name without direction. Like most despots he had not thought of a successor, at least not enough to name one. In any case, it is the singular character of all theocracies, so rare as a form of government, that a leader of such magnitude cannot easily be replaced by a lesser figure. His preference for a successor, had it been sought in his last hours, probably would have been his cousin, Ali, who was his son-in-law also, by reason of having married one of the Prophet's daughters, Fatima. "I am the city of knowledge," Mohammed remarked at one point, "and Ali his gate." This is not unlike the remark attributed to Christ: "Peter, thou art a rock and on this rock I shall build my church." However, in the aftermath of the Prophet's death, Ali was passed over. The military and political power came into the hands of Mohammed's second-in-command, Abu Bakr, who was chosen by acclamation. This would set a lasting precedent: that the successor to Mohammed (the Caliph) should be elected. [28]

Hardly had the Prophet died and a successor been found when the Arab tribes began to fade into the desert. Western skeptics would say that their defection was in keeping with tribal traditions. Not religion, but military success under Mohammed's leadership, and booty from war, had drawn them to him. Indeed, shortly after his death widespread disaffection commenced. This, the Great Apostasy *(Ridda*, i.e., "backsliding") threatened to undo everything the Prophet had accomplished. Not least of all, it could be considered the death knell for a religion still essentially formless: there was no priesthood, no body of teachers, no sacraments, and no rituals—in short, no institutional structure.

Almost on the eve of his death Mohammed had been planning a military campaign into Syria. His spies had regularly reported the disorganization and weakness they saw in the marginal provinces of the Byzantine Empire, leaving the Prophet to believe that both booty and converts could be gained by a bold campaign. In 632, the year of the Prophet's death, Abu Bakr, now the Caliph, set in motion a fateful action against the Byzantines.

The usual explanation offered by western historians is that Abu Bakr undertook this campaign in order to entice defecting Arabs back into the Islamic fold; certainly one of several motives. However, it is to be seen as a continuation of Mohammed's original design, that is, Holy War against the unbelievers. The campaign, an unexpectedly easy conquest of a good part of Byzantium in the next few years, was not undertaken merely to satisfy the cupidity of simple tribesmen, but to carry the one true religion far out into the world—Mohammed's most enduring legacy.

Each year thereafter, under a succession of Caliphs, Islam expanded. Syria fell in a three-year campaign; Egypt was defeated and occupied in less than two years; the Persian Empire was more tenacious in its defense, but it too fell in less than six years.

Once in control of the Middle East, the Arab host pushed on across Eurasia, and westward at the same time, reaching China by 750 and the north of Roman Gaul (present-day France) by 732. The extent and consequences of the Moslem conquest can hardly be overstated. "Few events in human history," observes one writer, "have transformed the face of such a large part of the globe as rapidly and as decisively as did the expansion of early Islam and the conquest by Moslems of much of the ancient world." [29] Remarkably, in only a few decades Arab warriors had overrun and occupied ancient, powerful civilizations. Wherever they conquered they imposed their religion on the defeated people. But there is evidence that suggests that imposition is too strong a word. Rather, in many cases the conquered peoples adopted Islam because it seemed superior to the traditional religions. There were other reasons too. The methods of conquest, consolidation, and control went back to Mohammed's earliest campaigns against both Jewish and Arab tribes at Medina. Intimidation was tried first; if that failed, conquest followed. Thereafter the defeated were offered treaty terms. The alternatives were either to accept Islam, thereby becoming a member of the Moslem Brotherhood *(Umma)* with all its advantages, or accept a second-class status, relying on the sufferance of the Arab conquerors (but the price for this would be to pay a tax for the privilege of being tolerated). This economic fact, as much as the popularity of the new religion, caused many Jews and Christians to convert to Islam. [30]

Whatever the explanation, large parts of the Middle East that had been predominately Christian for centuries became Moslem in a short time. Judaism in these same regions had never been a significant religion, in the sense that it possessed few adherents (because in part it was an exclusive religion and in a way a national devotion). Also, many Jews in the past centuries had begun their long exile, traveling to nearly all parts of Eurasia, to become finally a worldwide Diaspora.

Within a century Islam had become much more than a religion: it was an enormous empire, stretching from northern India and China in the East to the Pyrenees Mountains in Spain to the west. The conquest of this vast area by no more than 100,000 warriors in the space of three generations is no more astonishing than the fact that Arabia, a poor, underpopulated, essentially barbaric region of North Africa, could furnish administrators enough to manage the innumerable peoples who had fallen under Arab rule. The answer to what seems a puzzle is perhaps self-evident. A new and complex culture grew up as a complement to the newly established Arab authority. The uncomplicated Islam of Mohammed's devising, appropriate for a desert people both illiterate and superstitious, did not correspond at all to the Islam that developed in the Middle East during a hundred years of warfare punctuated by nearly continuous rebellion and savage infighting among the conquering Arabs themselves. The integration of ancient religious traditions in a part of the world already civilized for 5,000 years with the precepts of a new religion was not, as often thought in the West, the work of cruel, fanatical warriors imposing their faith on the vanquished at the point of a sword. Nor was it the work of zealous missionaries taking orders from a distant spiritual office, as in the case of Christian proselytization. There was, to adopt Toynbee's thesis, neither a universal church nor a universal empire to offer resistance at the time of Islam's advent. Instead, the Arabs found great disorder, approaching chaos, as the two great contending powers, Byzantium and Persia, had, in their ceaseless struggles, reached a point of near exhaustion. It was into this cultural and political vacuum that the Arab invaders came, filling the void with their energy and purpose. Scorning and at the same time fearing the great cities (much as the German barbarians had behaved in their conquest of the western half of the Roman Empire), the Arab conquerors lived in large encampments outside the cities, sticking to their tents; apart and alien from the regions they dominated. Their lasting supremacy did not come through direct rule, there being too few of them in the midst of too many subjects. They maintained their control by a visible presence and the promise of retribution, as by horse and camel they could swiftly reassert their authority if it were tested. If one thinks about it, this kind of authority could not have lasted more than a generation or two, but that was enough time for the new symbols of faith, order, and obedience to be joined with the oldest ruling symbols. This conjunction of many cultures over a vast area produced, in a relatively short time, not only a new syncretistic religion, Islam, but a cultural uniformity as well, creating a visible unity on the secular plane while not disturbing the earlier diversity. And this was Islam, at once a cultural phenomenon and a spiritual reality that permeated the souls of millions of believers.

The life of a Moslem was (and still is, in principle) a narrow pathway (Sunna) that signifies the customary way of behaving. A very few things informed Sunna: the Koran, the Prophet's sayings, and his manner of living. He abjured pork and alcohol, liked honey, had the habit of tinting his beard with henna, and always wore green clothing. He spoke softly, ate moderately, and slept little (this last perhaps not unusual for an old man). He also had a taste for women, and once he had acquired wealth and power began to accumulate a harem. *Purdah*, the Moslem practice of concealing its women from public view, probably began with Mohammed's habits. He remained a lusty old man almost up to the end. [31] But his exceptionally sensual appetite was not the cause for those suras that give a religious sanction to traditional Semitic polygamy. His several marriages (an estimated ten) and a large troop of concubines were for the most part the result of political actions. His youngest wife was deflowered when she was nine (he had married her two years earlier.) He took his oldest concubine in her fifty-eighth year.

For Moslem scholars the reliability of the Koran was no more certain than was the New Testament for Christian scholars. Yet, the development of Islamic theology and a juridical code for everyday living depended upon Koranic scriptures as well as traditions. Some part of the Koran was probably written down in Mohammed's lifetime; the remainder by scribes who relied upon the recollections of reliable people. The tradition of memory and recitation was common to all Semitic people, as was storytelling. Inevitably, these tales received embellishments in the retelling. The Koran, therefore (like the Jewish Torah), was to some degree an historical document, but it was also an assemblage of myths requiring several generations for its compilation. Arab historians were not unaware of this problem. That is to say, some things must be taken on faith. It is just as certain that Jesus walked on the water of the Sea of Galilee as it is that Mohammed leapt from the Dome of the Rock for an overnight visit to heaven (by a ladder, it was sometimes said; other times on the back of his favorite horse, which, unlike Pegasus, needed no wings).

The Prophet's sayings, or table talk, were compiled after his death. In his lifetime, it was thought that he had uttered one million. After long studies, and some agreement among Islamic scholars, the number was reduced to 260,000—still too many to be useful. Consequently, there arose what was termed the "science of sayings." There emerged a "chain of translators" *(Isnad)*, the purpose being to trace the sayings back to their source and separate the authentic from the spurious.

Never has a faith been subjected to more conscious science than the revealed truth of Allah. On the grounds of an unshakable faith in the Hadiths and the undoubted supernatural truth of the Koran as revelation, a law code was devised, appropriate for all cultures, all peoples, nations, classes and races. Wherever the local law was adapted to the religious law, there one found the spiritual law for regulating one's life, called *Sharia*. For a long time theology and law were considered to be one and the same, both characterized as *fiqh* (insight), "which embraced right action and right belief."[32] (A Westerner would call this attitude "common sense.")

The union of theological truth and secular law corresponded exactly to the Islamic outlook, always surprising to any Moslem that it could even be questioned. Indubitably, the good society is grounded in religious truth. The time would come when the example of the West would be presented to the world of Islam and would fail to meet this test. In the West almost every country separated the state from the church, either formally by law (as for example in France and the United States) or as a practical matter. The result in all cases had been to produce an amoral society, stimulating the natural wickedness of people and destructive of religion. This conviction would never die out, whatever a Moslem's factional or sectarian loyalty might be.

Sunni Moslems were from the beginning the overwhelming majority, but a significant minority arose in Iraq and Persia, beginning with some certainty in 740. Far more influential than their small numbers might suggest, the Shi'a (Party of Ali), became concentrated in Persia (modern Iran), as it is today. This schism occurred most basically over the matter of succession to the Caliphate. The Sunnis stood for election, the candidate having to be related to the Meccan tribe of Quraysh. The Shi'ites, much more mystically, believed the succession to the Caliphate was determined by God, who would always choose a candidate from Ali's line, or more exactly the descendants of Ali's children borne by his wife Fatima.

This irresoluble quarrel over the question of legitimate power, which was at once political and spiritual, would in time destroy the integrity of the Arab hegemony. Prolonged strife caused the ruling capital to be moved several times, from Mecca to Jerusalem to Damascus and, finally, to Baghdad. There the Arab domination finally came to an end, as did the empire itself.

But Islam did not decline. Rather, it revived under the harsh but beneficent blows it received from still another wave of barbarians, the Turks, coming off the steppes of Asia. Adopting Islam, Turkish adventurers and mercenaries finally made the Caliphate their own. In a further evolution the ancient office was eclipsed by a new one: the Sultanate. With the final death throes of Byzantium in 1453, the spiritual and political capital of Islam was moved to Constantinople. In 1517 the Arab regions of the Middle East came under the rule of the Ottoman Turks. Like the Jews before them, the Arabs became a subject people, scarcely remembering when they were great and their achievements had been of a kind to transform not only the Middle East, but vast reaches of the planet, far into southeast Asia and the Pacific islands in one direction and deep into darkest Africa in another.

NOTES

1 Unlike some Semitic tribes, the Hebrews did not circumcise their females.

2 Genesis 36:38.

3 In Hellenistic times they became known as Idumaeans.

4 Galatians, 4:29-30.

5 The Egyptian captivity, a tragedy in the Judean-Christian tradition, is in the Islamic tradition merely God's just punishment of an errant people "because they had disbelieved the signs of God...because they disobeyed, and were transgressors." Koran, 2:60-62.

6 J. A. Thompson, *The Bible and Archaeology*, (Grand Rapids, Michigan,1965), p. 135.

7 The completion of the first five books of the Old Testament (or Torah) often called the Pentateuch and proclaimed as the "Priestly Code" by Ezra in 444 B.C., actually transpired during the Persian domination, Babylon having fallen to King Cyrus in 539.

8 It was reputed, for example, that Alexander the Great had been sired by a god.

9 Emile Shurer, *A History of the Jewish People in the Time of Jesus*, ed. Naham V. Glatzer (New York, 1961), p. 16.

10 Adin Steinsaltz, *The Essential Talmud* (New York, 1976), p. 21.

11 The current scholarly concensus is, contrary to the traditional interpretation found in the Four Gospels, that the Pharisees only became a significant force in Jewish politics after Christ's time.

12 Shurer, *A History of the Jewish People*, p. 17.

13 Albert A. Trever, *History of Ancient Civilization*. Vol. I, *The Ancient Near East and Greece* (New York, 1936), p. 96.

14 D.S. Russell, *The Method and Message of Jewish Apocalyptic. 200 B.C.-A. D. 100* (Philadelphia, 1964), p. 371.

15 Saul (his given Hebrew name) was changed to Paul after his conversion to the Nazarene belief.

16 T.W. Manson, *The Teaching of Jesus* (New York, 1931), p. 227.

17 Ibid., p. 321.

18 The term "Christian," (from Christos, "the anointed one") was first used by Greek converts at Damascus and Antioch, probably before Paul's conversion. See Trever, *History of the Ancient World*, II, p. 471.

19 A traditional Jewish exclusiveness was not typical of the Diaspora Jews in antiquity. Abandoning the strict tenets of the Mosaic Law, they became "zealous propagandists for their religion" (i.e., Judaism, not that of the Nazarene believers). Trever, I, p. 524.

20 The year of his birth was also unknown, not calculated until the Middle Ages (and then erroneously). The general opinion now is that he was born sometime between 7 and 4 B.C.

21 Joseph Heniger, "Pre-Islamic Bedouin Religion," *Studies on Islam*, ed., Merlin L. Swartz (Oxford University Press, 1981), pp. 10-12.

22 Ibid., p. 12.

23 Gordon Darnell Newby, *A History of the Jews of Arabia. From Ancient Times to their Eclipse under Islam*, (University of South Carolina Press, 1988), p. 85.

24 Raphael Patai, *The Seed of Abraham. Jews and Arabs in Contact and Conflict* (University of Utah Press, 1986), pp. 18-28, passim.

25 Koran, 7:1-24.

26 The Prophet's words are nonetheless ambiguous: "Yet they did not slay him, neither crucified him, only a likeness of that was shown them...they have no knowledge of him, except the following surmise; and they slew him not of a certainty...no indeed; God raised him up to Him." Koran, 4:154-159.

27 Koran, 3:42-47.

28 Not immediately, however. Abu Bakr lived only two more years and before dying appointed his own successor, a colleague named Omar.

29 Fred McGraw Donner, *The Early Islamic Conquests* (Princeton University Press, 1981), p. 3.

30 It is always remarked that the Muslims were especially considerate of their arch religious rivals, the Jews and Christians, calling them the People of the Book.

31 William E. Phipps, *Muhammed and Jesus. A Comparison of the Prophets and their Teachings* (New York, 1996), pp. 142-43.

32 *Islam*, John Alden Williams, ed. (New York, 1962), p. 173.

CHAPTER TWO

The Jewish Diaspora

THE ILLUSION OF
JEWISH NATIONALISM

t the beginning of the Christian era an estimated one million Jews lived in the Roman province of Palestine. Another three or four million were dispersed throughout the empire, from Asia Minor (modern Turkey) to Spain.[33] After the destruction of the Second Temple in 70 C.E., an immense migration commenced, accelerating a movement already several centuries old. Those Jews who remained in the former Judea fell more completely than before under Roman rule. The few who resisted Roman rule took a last stand on a massive mountain plateau, Masada, and after a long siege committed suicide rather than surrender. In a way, their sacrifice betokened the death of Hebrew civilization itself, becoming, as Arnold Toynbee termed it, a "fossilized relic" of Syriac Society. [34]

The remnants of this lost civilization began to wander ever further into the world, preserving their identity by a complete devotion to their religion. So distinctive was that identity that in whatever country they settled, they were readily recognized by their customs, their dress, their exclusive spirit and, not infrequently, their distinctive physiognomy. To the degree that they resisted acculturation in any country, they experienced discrimination and often persecution. To the extent that they were persecuted, the greater became their determination to maintain their unique identity. Their solidarity, their tenacity, resulted from what Ernest Renan called "a patriotism of merchants scattered in every locality, each one acquainted with the other, a patriotism which does not found states, but autonomous communities in the midst of other states. They lived in their own districts separated from the general jurisdiction, in havens of peace and happiness, and regarded by the rest of the population with resentment and hostility." In these circumstances, the Jew "was able to bear poverty easily. What he was able to do even more was to combine his most lofty religious feelings with an outstanding business sense." [35]

There were few civilized places that did not receive an alien intruder, the displaced Jew, from South Africa to China, from Arabia to Australia. It is probable that the Jewish exodus reached China via the Silk Road not later than 200 C.E. [36] Like the Parsees, a Persian people also victimized as a result of resisting Hellenistic influences, the migrating Jews settled in the coastal towns of India. There, like the Parsees also, they survived to modern times, as has been noted, "through a combination of ecclesiastical discipline with business enterprise." [37]

The fate of the Jews in China is unknown. By the time of the Yuan Dynasty, Jews were dispersed over northern China, and by Sung times were settled south of the Yangtze River. For many centuries Jewish communities flourished in China, but the normal vicissitudes of Imperial China, which entailed the rise and fall of dynasties, barbarian invasions, civil wars, and long interregnums, had an inevitably destructive effect on an alien people. Eventually, it is thought, they "forgot their own traditions and were culturally and physically assimilated into the overwhelming mass of Chinese society." [38]

Frequently subjected to discrimination and violent mistreatment, the alien Jew was never trusted and often exploited by the host country. This was especially true in Europe, a part of the world profoundly affected for over 2,000 years by Christ's tragic death. The Jews began moving into the West from the earliest times, migrating family by family into what would one day be called Europe, advancing almost imperceptibly northward with the conquest and settlement of Gaul by the Romans.

The transformation of Gaul over the succeeding centuries into a distinctive ethnic polity, *Île de France*, paralleled developments among the Germanic tribes. In this same period of time, each tribe would become a distinctive people living on a particular territory, which would ultimately earn some of them the status of nation-state.[39] In this geopolitical environment large numbers of tiny Jewish nuclei underwent their own metamorphoses. Ceasing to be oriental, the Jews became occidental to some extent, but without abandoning most of the culture, which left them being something other than European. No single individual in any given generation could bear witness to the transformation of a whole people.

By the eighteenth century, historians, whose function is to serve the collective memory, found the Jews a fascinating subject for study. How had they arrived in the heart of Europe, so far from their native land? Why did they persist, after so many centuries, in living apart from the community in which they found themselves? Why did they cling to strange dietary habits, preserve peculiar customs, and maintain a manner of dress and comportment that set them aside from the rest? Why did they prefer to be different, perpetuating their social obloquy, thereby inviting the inevitable persecution that the normative majority imposes as if by a law of nature on the deviant minority? Why indeed did they not become Christians in a part of the world that was overwhelmingly Christian in both belief and practice? Why did they stubbornly insist that Jesus had been a false Messiah, and wait for their deliverance by the true Messiah?

Both religions possessed a messianic tradition, the emergence of Christianity being, in fact, the result of a widespread messianism in the last century before the advent of Jesus Christ. The universal redeemer to the Christians was Christ; but to the Jews he was a false Messiah, which had sealed his fate: crucified with the consent of the Jerusalem populace. Thereafter, those who believed in the martyred

Christ waited for his Second Coming, when the faithful would be carried to Heaven and given everlasting life.

The Jews waited also, but for a different kind of Messiah. In the beginning they had believed in a redeemer who would lift the Roman oppression, restore their independence as a people, and unite the quarreling Hebrew tribes. In brief, they had waited for a military chieftain, another King David. In their long exile after the destruction of the Second Temple, they continued to wait, but with a changed expectation. The Messiah would deliver them from the alien condition in which they found themselves nearly everywhere in the world, and return them to the lost homeland, *Eretz Yisrael* (the Israel of David's and Solomon's time). It should be stressed, however, that this was not a national yearning but, indubitably, a religious fixation. For ages, well into the nineteenth century, world Jewry did not have a sense of close affiliation other than a common religious identity. Too diverse by reason of their dispersal, they lacked ethnic solidarity. For Jews in the Western world that feeling would finally evolve almost imperceptibly after 1815, just as the sense of nationality was coming to many subject peoples in Europe. But in the absence of a collective national sentiment, Jews in their majority clung to a supernatural conception of redemption.

Toward the middle of the nineteenth century, a Polish Rabbi, Hirsch Kalischer, argued that once Jews began to settle in Turkish Palestine, the Messiah would appear and complete their return to Eretz Yisrael. In order to realize this dream, Kalischer persuaded a wealthy Jew, Asher Meyer Rothschild, a citizen of Frankfurt, to finance the establishment of a colony near Jaffa in 1870. It was called *Mikveh Israel* (the Ingathering of Israel). The project did not attract many Jewish settlers, but more important than this, the Messiah failed to appear. And therefore, a purely religious motivation, the oldest part of the Jewish tradition, did not seem effective in the case of Mikveh Israel. Shortly, a better motivation was found in the Jewish national idea.

By this time a generation of Jewish intellectuals had written abundantly on the several problems facing world Jewry; *viz.*, were they a nation or merely a religious community? Could they become assimilated to a given national entity in Europe (or anywhere else in the world, for that matter) without losing their distinctive quality as Jews? Could a homeland for Jews be found anywhere that would, or could, accommodate the many Jews of the world? Would a Messiah bring about their redemption? Would it be accomplished in the sense of a national movement?

The French Revolution gave a decided fillip to the sense of nationhood in Europe, i.e., the fraternity of a kindred people. During his campaign in the Middle East, Napoleon visited Jerusalem, the name as bewitching to a pagan like himself as to the believers, whether Christian, Jew or Moslem. There, in a speech, he pronounced the Jews to be a nation, calling them the "rightful heirs of Palestine" and praising them for their fortitude in preserving their identity, however dispersed they had become. [40]

The effects of Napoleon's remarks, one may imagine, did not go very far beyond Jerusalem; certainly would not have penetrated the consciousness of a people as scattered and diverse as world Jewry had become by the nineteenth century. His intuition merely reflected the general movement of thought and action in his time. Many nationalities had begun to stir after 1815. Aware of their distinctive culture, which set them aside from others, they were nonetheless passive; subject nationalities, it was said, suggesting their docility and the permanent authority of their masters, *viz.*, the Italians submitted to the Austrians, the Irish to the English, the Poles to the Russians, the Norwegians to the Swedes, almost *ad infinitum*. All this would change over the next few decades, from which Jewish nationalists would take an exceptional profit. But the fact was that World Jewry, living on many national territories for centuries, always nativized to some degree, did not in the aggregate exist as a nation. There was no territory distinctively Jewish. Jews were without a unifying language in the vernacular sense. [41] Hebrew was for the educated few, not a medium for everyday use. Joseph Stalin, in his *Marxism and Nationalism* (1903), reiterated this well-worn thesis. Jews lacked the attributes of a nation: no common language, no territory, ergo no national identity. "What sort of a nation", he wondered, "is a Jewish nation that consists of Georgian, Daghestanian, Russian, American and other Jews, the members of which do not understand each other (since they speak different languages), inhabit different parts of the globe, will never see each other, will never act together, whether in time of peace or in time of war?" No, concluded Stalin, such is a "paper" nation. [42]

It was with difficulty that one could think of a Jewish "type," a distinctive physiognomy, though the hooked Semitic nose was frequently the preferred stereotype. The existence of a pure Jewish ethnicity is to be doubted. Despite a natural and perhaps necessary clannishness, as well as their exclusiveness, which was an essential part of their history; despite all these forces leading toward inbreeding, the Jews experienced miscegenation as much as any other people might. The distance between a Jewish cobbler in Yemen, for example, and a Jewish banker in New York City, was not a matter of a few thousand miles; it was the distance between race and culture that is measured in light years.

Jewish ethnicity, as much as the term may be admitted, was that of a shared experience, usually termed by the Gentiles as "Jewishness." But this was enough to form the idea of a nation-in-exile. Whether a Jew lived in Arabia, India, Europe, or America, he had only to be literate (and if illiterate had only to listen to his rabbi) to know that his fellows around the world existed as a nation. Such was the myth, but also the growing reality, as more and more Jews began to believe that which could not be proved. [43]

Intellectual history is marked by distinctive phases, measured by sudden insights that serve as milestones in the evolution of thought. One of these was the work of a relatively obscure Jewish scholar, Heinrich Graetz, who argued that Judaism was more than a literary genre for self-absorbed and mystical rabbis. More than a religious tradition, it was a unique historical migration, which could make the boast that throughout a millennium or more the religious beliefs of a people had remained intact. [44]

Graetz's seminal work was followed by a more influential book, Moses Hess's *Rome and Jerusalem*, published in 1862. His message was clear: Jews could only realize their destiny fully, become fully emancipated, by returning to Zion. [45]

Hess was a product of the eighteenth century Jewish Enlightenment *(Haskalah)*. Coeval with the Enlightenment of the Gentiles, Haskalah possessed the same rationale: a reliance upon reason, a distrust of the emotions; less similar, however, in that while Gentile philosophies doubted and often rejected revealed religion, the men and women of Haskalah could not break away cleanly from the faith of their fathers. They were disposed nonetheless to submit a revered religion to reasonable investigation, based, as was often said, on the exercise of right reason for the purposes of removing an extraneous mythology. Typically, they would be deists in the Jewish manner, not different from their skeptical Gentile counterparts.

The European Enlightenment made Jewish emancipation possible. While a natural sympathy may arise in any human breast for the suffering of the Jews in an alien world, it should not be forgotten that the rabbis, guardians of the Judaic tradition, did not hesitate to insist upon the error of the Christians in believing that Christ was the universal redeemer. Such blasphemy, in their view, could not go unchallenged. The intransigence of the two faiths, stemming from a common source, would not fade away until most Christians in the West had become so secularized that the issue seemed finally to have no relevance in a modern world. It was judged to be an arcane debate about the past; one that had lost its significance. Most educated Jews in the West were becoming so well assimilated by the host countries that they too were becoming indifferent to the Messiah question.

The transition from the secular and, one may say, humanistic Haskalah to what has been called "positive-historical Judaism" occupied a long period from around 1780–1850. Moses Hess may be considered representative of the Jewish intellectuals of that era. His early life reflected the most general pattern of the Jewish middle class: a conventional childhood, his intellectual formation the result of university training. His further education and subsequent career drew him away from the close-knit Jewish communal life. He became, in his own words, "estranged," and would not return until he was a mature man, perhaps even embarrassed by his long absence. "Here I stand," he wrote in 1812, "after 20 years of estrangement, in the midst of my people..." [46] In a way, Hess became in his middle years a born-again Jew. Having come home, as it were, he wished to find his roots.

Generally speaking, the recovery of faith for a believer is a more profound experience than the original discovery of its truth. Besides a return to his roots at a point in his life when he had the intellectual capacity to examine them, Hess had been greatly influenced by the socialist movement. His association with Karl Marx, an apostate Jew whose estrangement would be permanent, was instructive to Hess, but mainly in spiritual terms. In his early years he had favored an assimilation of Jews into the host country. Almost a Gentile in his predilections, he considered the typical Jew to be money-mad, grubbing, and materialistic; an unwitting contributor to a predatory capitalism.

The stigma attached to the Jews, not much less reprehensible than the murder of Christ, was their propensity to profit by charging usurious interest on loans. It was a fault too great to be forgiven. "The Jews have been punished severely from time to time," admitted a certain German citizen, Peter Schwartz, "but they do not suffer innocently; they suffer because of their wickedness, because they cheat people and ruin whole countries by their usury and secret murders, as everyone knows. There is no people more wicked, more cunning, more avaricious, more impudent, more troublesome, more venomous, more wrathful, more deceptive, and more ignominious." [47]

Marx, in his alienation, went much further than Hess in condemning capitalism, considering it an iniquitous institution created by greedy Jews. On the foundations of the earliest protests against personal privilege and great wealth, Marx built a towering intellectual structure, a critique that dissected and dismissed historic capitalism. In its coming demise he imagined the last stages of decadent capitalism to be rather like a chrysalis out of which would emerge socialism. After that, communism (a well-formed idea by his time) would proceed to its inevitable end. All social classes would disappear, as well as private property (the ultimate cause of all injustice, as Rousseau thought). Equality of persons, equality of possessions through collective living, would become a universal norm. And, because harmony and justice would arise in a world so ordered, the sovereign state, which behaved like an animal (behemoth) in an environment that resembled a jungle, would in the classic Marxist phrase, "wither away." All forms of coercion would disappear also. Social alienation would vanish. Police and magistrates would be no more necessary to a truly egalitarian society than would armies to protect the savage states from each other.

This chiliastic view of a world past and a world to come was consonant with the emerging Zionist fantasy of creating a utopia in Turkish Palestine. Therefore it is not surprising to know that many young Jewish intellectuals subscribed to Marx's idealism, especially his attempt to organize the world's working people. This, the so-called First International, established in 1964, would cease to function in less than ten years' time, [48] but it would be reborn in 1874 as the Second International, and it too would appeal to many Jews.

Hess and Marx parted company after a time, the result of two personalities in conflict, the friction intensified by a profound philosophical difference between them. Hess, the older man, had discovered that socialism led him to a compassionate regard for religion (both Christian and Jewish) and a fascination for his own origins as an alienated Jew. Marx, to the contrary, reviled religion, the "opiate of the people." He became an outspoken atheist and, in academic terms at least, an apostle of violence. His vaunted "scientific socialism" stood in stark contrast to the pacific ideals entertained by the "socialist rabbis," Hess to be counted among these.

After his break with Marx, Hess remained a socialist, but of the seraphic variety, attracted to the ideals of the French utopian socialists whom Marx attacked so bitterly. It seemed, however, that Hess could not escape from the effects of his personal assimilation. Eretz Yisrael, he wrote, was not for every Jew. Most Jews, he believed, would not return to Palestine in the future (a correct prediction, as it turned out). "Even after the establishment of a Jewish state, the majority of the Jews who live at present in the civilized occidental countries will undoubtedly remain where they are." [49]

Among the rabbis of western Europe, the urge for emancipation and integration into Gentile society had become stronger than the age-old hope of redemption, namely that a Messiah would appear and lead His people back to the Chosen Land. The mainstream of Jewish thought very much doubted the Zionist idea, the attitude summed up by an Austrian rabbi, Adolf Jellinek. "We consider ourselves German," he wrote, "French, English, Magyar, Italian, to the marrow of our bones. ... We have lost the sense of Hebrew nationality." [50] At a rabbinical conference held at Frankfort in 1845, the meaning of the Messianic idea was debated. Did it mean a literal transfer of world Jewry back to Palestine or did it simply mean a mystical union of the collective Jewish soul with God, "a substitute for the idea of immortality," as one rabbi said? The resolution adopted by the majority was: "The Messianic idea should receive prominent mention in the prayers, but all petitions for our return to the land of our fathers and for the restoration of a Jewish state should be eliminated from the litany." [51] At mid-century, therefore, rabbinical opinion held that emancipation promised no more than salvation in this life for all Jews; the idea of returning to Eretz Yisrael was neither feasible nor necessary.

Abandoned by the orthodox Jews, as they always would be in the future, the secular Zionists promoted the Zionist idea with vigor. [52] Alienated and often persecuted, Jews required a haven that only Eretz Yisrael could provide. They thought of it as the ancient homeland.

It is at least ironic that the erroneous notion of a pure Jewish ethnicity was forwarded by a man who was a Jew in his imagination only, one Joseph Salvador. A French citizen, his antecedents on his father's side were Jewish; on his mother's side he was a Catholic. By the strict requirements of the Jewish legal code *(Halakah)* he was not a Jew. But Salvador considered himself to be one. Half-Catholic, half-Jew, he carried the nameless guilt so many Christians were beginning to experience: how they had wronged the innocent Jew, forcing him into his ghetto, shutting him out of the mainstream of national life, reviling him for his peculiarities. "Children of Israel," wrote Salvador, "whom we have oppressed and slandered for so long, we offer you with joy the corner of the earth inhabited by your ancestors." [53] That would be Eretz Yisrael, or "Zion," as it was called a little later in the century.

The road to Zion ran through Russia, where more than five million Jews lived in a virtually sequestered state: the Pale of the Settlement, separated from the Russian Gentiles on the one hand, and on the other, largely isolated from the rest of world Jewry. The Pale of the Settlement: the term fastened itself on the collective mind of world Jewry in the nineteenth century with the same emotional intensity that the word *holocaust* would have for Jews in the next century. A vast territory, it consisted of fifteen Russian provinces and ten Polish ones (that part of Poland attached to the Russian empire in 1815, called Congress Poland). It is reckoned that 98 percent of the Jews in this area spoke Yiddish, the vernacular of all Jews living in central Europe.

For centuries in Russia, as in the rest of Europe, Jews had lived in relative isolation, and seemed less civilized than the general population around them by reason of two conditions of their lives: their tendency to live apart from the host society, their uniqueness as seemingly inassimilable strangers; and secondly, in Russia as elsewhere, the restrictive laws that encumbered their activities and their movements. The Pale of the Settlement was for all practical purposes a closed-off area in which Jews might live with reasonable security, and grow rich and successful, as often happened over a number of generations, suffering no more than the normal kinds of disadvantages that the majority of a given society will impose upon a minority perceived not to be not only different, but politically dangerous if allowed too much freedom.

For centuries Jews in Russia had lived in relatively comfortable circumstances, profiting from a salubrious neglect that was quite common among the world's traditional empires. The ultimate authority was distant, remote, and inefficient, its power felt only periodically when taxes were collected or the exigencies of empire demanded an exceptional conscription of troops. But all this changed early in the nineteenth century, the result of the Napoleonic invasion of Russia, and the reform movement that followed upon those wars, especially with the advent of Nicholas the First, a determined Russifier and unifier of his far-flung domains. [54]

A severe Russification had the effect of intensifying Jewish separateness, further accentuating their peculiarities. "There is a people that dwells apart," wrote an English journalist in the late 1800s, "not reckoned among the nations." [55] One saw them at the railroad stations," he reported, so distinctive in appearance, "as in America you can distinguish Negroes. This is more a matter of dress—of hair and beard and cap and caftan—than of physiognomy. But even more still is it a matter of demeanor. They seem never for an instant to lose the consciousness that they are a race apart. It is in their walk, in their sidelong glance, in the carriage of their sloping shoulders, in the curious gesture with the uplifted palm." Nicholas the First, he thought, had "solidified [them] into a dense, hard baked and endlessly resistant mass." [56]

As the European Enlightenment (Gentile variety) had passed into Russia, affecting the educated classes markedly, so had the Jewish Enlightenment *(Haskala)* penetrated Russian Jewry. Leo Pinsker, a Jew living in Odessa, was perhaps only typical of the Russian intelligentsia in this regard, but was destined to be more influential than most of the Russian Jewish writers. Three influences had a profound effect on him: the terrible pogroms of 1881–82; the emigration to Palestine *(First Aliyah)* that attended these persecutions; and last but not least, the secular critique of the Enlightenment, whose ideals, however denatured in Russia, represented a high standard to which every progressive Jew and Gentile could subscribe.

Pinsker repudiated the traditional messianic vision entertained by orthodox Jewry. In his entirely secular view, the Jewish people would have to help themselves because no one else would, thus the title of his book: *Auto-Emancipation: An Admonition to His Brethren by a Russian Jew*, published anonymously in 1882. [57]

In order to escape the alienation that was the life experience of all Jews in the Diaspora, they would have to organize. An activist as much as a writer, Pinsker established a committee for action, calling it the Society for the Support of Jewish Agriculture in Syria and Palestine.

Auto-emancipation was widely translated, representing a milestone in the early formation of Zionism. The real turning point, however, was the pogroms, a direct result of the assassination of Czar Alexander II in March 1881. Those among the ruling circle concluded at once that the murder represented another proof of the oft-repeated charge that Jewish conspiracies abounded in Russia. The latent anti-Semitism of the Russian public was only too easily aroused, and once unleashed was not to be checked until the lust for violence had been satiated. Mobs that needed no direction descended upon Jewish quarters throughout the Pale of the Settlement.

A harbinger of the next century's Holocaust, these government-inspired atrocities drove many poor and defenseless Jews out of their shops and houses into the streets and onto the roads. Finally, those who could afford it boarded trains for the West. Shortly, the legendary generosity of the Rothschilds came into play. Rumors became rife that those who could get out of Russia would be transported, cost-free, all the way to America, and so began the panic that turned into a flood of Russian exiles. Most would indeed reach the United States. There the established Jewry welcomed them badly. Besides the almost insupportable expense of housing and maintaining the destitute immigrants, borne almost entirely by the Hebrew Immigrant Aid Society, there was the fear among American Jewry of an adverse Gentile reaction. Moreover, social exclusiveness permeated migrant Jews, each wave of immigrants establishing isolated, self-sufficient communities, unwilling to yield an inch to the next arrivals. The oldest of American Jewry, Sephardic Jews, present almost from the beginning of the republic, behaved like a Jewish aristocracy, reluctant to consort with those arriving from Germany. Both Sephardic and German Jews looked askance at the poor rustics flooding in from Russia. "To suggest," editorialized the *New York Jewish Messenger*, "that three million of them settle in America evidences more enthusiasm than common sense. A better way, perhaps would be to send American Jewish missionaries to Russia to civilize them there rather than give them an opportunity to Russianize us in the event of such colossal emigration. ... the task of Americanizing them is too difficult for one to view the advent of three million more with anything but trepidation." [58]

In brief, American Jews practiced their own variety of anti-Semitism; imposed on their own kind the same social slights and little persecutions that the Gentiles perpetuated against them.

In the emergency created by the pogroms, tremendous sums were collected for relief in Europe by various eleemosynary organizations. But money was not enough. The word went out that the Russian Jews were no more wanted by their brethren in the New World than in the Old World. [59] "Human nature does not change," wrote one of the émigrés. "In the Middle Ages the sign of an alien was religion and now it is nationality." But it was more than that. The transition from religious bigotry to social antipathy can be almost pinpointed: 1862, when the term "anti-Semitic" was coined. William Marr, a German pamphleteer, brought the term into general usage by founding in 1879 the *AntiSemiten-Liga*. Where before Christians had reviled Jews as "Christ killers," they now considered them to be an inferior breed of people who by their pernicious presence had corrupted a pure European population. The racist Aryan doctrines of the twentieth century began at this point.

Christian ambivalence toward the Jew was so intense one can speak of a collective neurosis. Christians studied the Jewish holy book (Old Testament), tracing their origins back to the mythical Abraham, with as much devotion as either Jews or Moslems. The sticking point was Christ's Passion, his sacrifice making him the true Messiah for all Christians, but to the Jews a false one. Balanced scholarship, such as that published by Moses Hess, could not resolve this impasse. A policy of emancipation of the Jews, adopted by several of the Western countries, had been no more than marginally successful.

The emancipation of the Jews in Western Europe and America owed much to Napoleon's example. He and his advisors believed that a kind of vicious cycle had produced Jewish alienation, their persecution, and a restricted life in the ghetto as citizens *déclassé*. "Their customs and their practices kept them from society," wrote Count Molé, "by which they were in turn rejected." [60] In February 1807, the ancient Jewish council, the *Sanhedrin*, was revived, meeting under Napoleon's chairmanship. Yielding to the imperial will, the delegates renounced rabbinical jurisdiction and independent corporate status, implicitly giving up any hope of returning to Israel. They agreed also to the marriage of Jews and non-Jews, but refused to give such unions a religious sanction. "We are no longer a nation within a nation," said one of them. France is our country . . ." Thus Napoleon's solution for age-old Jewish alienation prevailed, which meant unqualified assimilation. But this was no solution to the many Jews who considered that assimilation on this basis meant eventual loss of their religion, the only shield for their unique identity.

With the failure of Jewish emancipation by the late nineteenth century, some Jews believed that a general exodus from Europe was required. However, Palestine did not appeal to the great majority of them. Between 1881 and 1914, an estimated one and a half million Jews left Russia. Along with those who had emigrated earlier, a total of more than two million chose to live in New York City, making it what was called humorously, but not without truth, a Jewish city. Only about thirty thousand took the hard and dangerous road to Palestine. [61]

Entry into Palestine was difficult in any case. The country belonged to the Ottoman Empire, and the Turks controlled emigration with some rigor. The solution of this problem seemed simple: the Jews would simply buy Palestine, the authors of this plan certain that the Sultan would cooperate. "It was," wrote one of them, "a matter of a million more or a million less . . . only a matter of price." [62]

The thought that the Turkish Sultan, wealthy almost beyond measure and in possession of vast spaces and immense resources, would deign to negotiate with the hard-pressed Jews on this basis is almost amusing. The most sanguine of these daydreams are mainly instructive for revealing the Ashkenazic mentality: they believed they could buy anything; money could correct any wrong.

Along with the illusion that Palestine could be purchased easily and cheaply, there was another misconception. To the early Zionists, Eretz Yisrael seemed to be a vast and almost empty space, more than adequate for the totality of world Jewry. The fact that Arabs had lived there for many centuries did not enter seriously into their thinking. To the Russian Jews especially, Palestine seemed like a pioneer country, unsettled, romantic in its aspect, calling for heroic settlers. The attitude was not different from the way European Gentiles viewed the American West at about the same time: lightly populated by Indians, judged an inferior people with no good reason for being there; to be supplanted by others who knew how to develop the land. By the mid-eighties, ardent pioneers in Russia, almost all young Jews, had organized expeditionary groups. Among these was *Am Olam*, which, significantly enough, did not look to Palestine but to the United States. These pioneers did in fact succeed in establishing colonies in America, the most remarkable of these being New Odessa, in Oregon.

Another pioneer group, called *Bilu*, looked to Zion. While the affluent Jews thought of buying Palestine, these Zionists would colonize it. Their ultimate goal: "the establishment of colonies of farmers and artisans in Eretz Israel," in order to "place all of the land and its productivity in the hands of the Jews. Then there will come the glorious day whose advent was prophesied by Isaiah," when the Jews "with arms in their hands, if necessary, will publicly proclaim themselves masters of their ancient homeland." [63]

THE RISE OF POLITICAL ZIONISM

For more than a century world Jewry had been distracted by the question of its collective identity. Were Jews citizens of a given nation, thus identified by culture and language, as say, German, French, Russian, American? Or were they a unique people who, in the aggregate, transcended national boundaries?

If a Jew chose to emphasize his legal nationality, he accepted his eventual absorption into the host country to which he belonged as a matter of law. This meant assimilation over time; ultimately in two or three generations a disappearance of the family's Jewishness. The use of Hebrew would fall into disuse. The practice of elaborate rituals would lapse as each member of the family became a more secular and less religious Jew. Kosher food would give way to any given national cuisine. The plaintive cry, "Lest I forget thee, Oh Jerusalem," would most certainly be forgotten.

If a Jew chose to remain orthodox in his attachments and outlook, and avoided assimilation with all of its corrupting influences, he chose necessarily a life of isolation. Thus, a pure Jew would be persecuted for what the Gentiles termed his "clannishness," his exclusiveness, so much a deviant from the societal norms that otherwise embraced him that he seemed to deserve the harassment and sometimes outright abuse that comes to those who insist upon being different.

Throughout the nineteenth century, Western European Jews had become more and more assimilated to the host country; always distressed by the evidence of continuing persecution despite this absorption, the pogroms in Russia, for example, the scurrilous anti-Semitic literature that circulated late in the century, and the continued persecution of Jews on religious grounds. Racial theories arose, widely disseminated by various anti-Semitic writers, teaching that an inferior people from the Middle East had entered the Western world and polluted the pure races already there.

It seemed a Jew could never be a loyal citizen of his country. The proof of this was thought to be seen in the large number of Jews who became active members of the Second International, an organization dedicated to the destruction of capitalism, the overthrow of bourgeois governments; run (as it was said) by and for the interests of the dominant middle class. The most sensational proof of all seemed to be confirmed by the alleged treachery of an Alsatian Jew, Captain Dreyfus, a French citizen accused of passing military secrets to France's hereditary enemy, Imperial Germany.

The Dreyfus Affair is so well known in outline that it scarcely needs to be told again; the Captain was court-martialed, found guilty as charged, publicly stripped of his rank and sent to the iniquitous penal colony, Devil's Island, to serve a life sentence at hard labor. Those who believed in his innocence, among them the celebrated French author, Zola, commenced a defense action that went on for years. Finally, after conclusive evidence showed that others than Dreyfus had been guilty of espionage and that high military figures had intentionally framed Dreyfus, he was released from Devil's Island. But even after that, the politics in the case were such that he was not fully exonerated until 1906.

The moral to the story was not hard to find. A French Jew, loyal to his country, had been falsely charged, humiliated, incarcerated, and only reluctantly released, all because he was a Jew. Jewish intellectuals drew the necessary conclusion: to be an emancipated Jew in Europe, even an enlightened Europe, was no guarantee against discrimination and injustice. One could only be a Jew, free and whole, in his own country. But the Jews did not have a country.

The dénouement of the Dreyfus Affair served to draw together the ideas to be found in *Haskalah* literature, the restive and bitter rebellion of the international socialist movement, and the primordial fantasies of orthodox Jews who yearned to return to their homeland, Eretz Yisrael. The conventional telling relates how the injustice done to Dreyfus so enraged an Austrian Jew, Theodore Herzl, that he sat down and propounded Zionism in sheer reaction, entitling his work *Das Judenstaat*. But this gives Herzl too much credit. It almost goes without saying that his "role in the history of political Zionism was primarily in the creation and organizational propulsion of the movement and in dramatically publicizing it rather than in formulating its ideology," [64] that he "was no more aware of the semantics of the term Zionism than he was of the ideological and programmatic formulations that had preceded him..." [65]

Herzl had definite opinions nonetheless. Like Moses Hess, he had been almost completely assimilated to the host country, Austria, thereby losing an emotional tie with Judaism. He lived, as has been observed, in "an acculturated but socially Jewish milieu." [66] He was, in brief, a Jew in name only, a false position of which he took periodic note—and he suffered from it. The ambivalent existence of the Jew who cannot quite accept his Jewishness and yet is not quite able to be accepted by the Gentile society in which he has succeeded in every way except by social integration, created for Herzl a perpetual distress. *Das Judenstaat* was, one must suppose, a personal catharsis. It is not so much that his book offered still one more gloss on the now long-discussed possibilities of a Jewish state, but that it appeared at the right moment. Jews in both Western Europe and North America had arrived at that point where they could no longer advance; yet, having enjoyed the results of emancipation in most places, they could not accept the possibility of falling back into the old condition of the ghetto. To go further in the betterment of themselves, they would have to give up all but a nominal attachment to their ancient religion. Yet, they were blocked in any case by an invidious anti-Semitism that would never die out. In the Middle Ages, a fundamentalist Christianity, intolerant and often cruel, had made an assimilation of the Jews impossible. Now, ironically, emancipation produced a new, equally virulent anti-Semitism. The advances the Jews had achieved in business and finance, education, and professional callings, made them, Herzl thought, "fearful rivals of the middle class." Thus, Jews found themselves being divided three ways: those who accepted complete assimilation and ceased to be Jews in any meaningful sense; those who remained rigidly orthodox, down to dress, customs, rituals, and values, choosing a self-imposed isolation from Gentile society; and, between these extremes, the rest, the majority it may be thought, whose lives were spent in a social limbo. By the compromises they made, such Jews lived in two worlds at once, perhaps neurotic as a consequence. And this would explain Herzl's psyche.

At the beginning of the twenty-first century it is difficult to imagine how deep was the gulf between Jew and Gentile, or how reluctant the Jew was to relate to, much less integrate himself into, a society he perceived to be an alien world. A commentator in the eighteenth century put it this way:

> As long as Jews keep the laws of Moses, as long as for instance they do not take their meals with us, and at mealtimes or with simple folk over a glass of beer are not able to make friends, they will never (I do not speak of individuals but of the greater part) fuse with us like Catholics and Lutherans, Germans, Italians (Wende) and Frenchmen living in the same state. [67]

Herzl's attitude reflected what Zionism finally became by the end of the nineteenth century: a repudiation of assimilation, for it promised over time a loss of Jewish identity. Where Moses Hess had imagined a future condition when Eretz Yisrael would become a homeland for Middle Eastern Jews (because they were still essentially Semitic people), but not for the advanced Jews of the West, Herzl looked upon Eretz Yisrael (Zion) as the redemptive home for all Jews. His was not a religious obsession, however, but merely a personal conviction; and this really corresponded to the nameless, perhaps unconscious, will of millions of Jews. Hence *Der Judenstaat*, a book without distinction, became a literary icon because it announced a critical turning point.

To popularize his ideas Herzl next wrote a novel, *Altneuland*, the title itself suggestive of an image: ancient Israel would be recovered to become a new Israel. The country lost in antiquity would arise from its ashes, like the fabled phoenix, to become a modern country of industry, finance, science, labor and capital. There could be no end to such an image because Western society itself is endless in its progression and its changes. In the state he imagined, a utopia despite his denial, Herzl pictured a nearly uniform material comfort for the citizens: no rich and no poor, humane laws, public relief for the destitute and the unlucky. A highly centralized government would be balanced by local self-help, cooperative farms for example. Tolerance (could a Jew neglect this attribute?) would be a guiding principle. Jews, Christians, Moslems would respect each other and live together in peace.

What Herzl described for his readers was not a state but uniquely a society; a "New Society," declared David Littwak, one of his characters. "We have no state, like the Europeans of your time. We are simply a large cooperative association which is called the New Society." [68] Such a society, almost self-governing, would require little management, and therefore the institutions of government would be few, even rudimentary. The legislature would be in session only a few weeks each year. The president would be a figurehead. For such affairs as the state had to deal with there would be a small, well-trained and, of course, incorruptible bureaucracy.

In its principles the Old New Land seemed to evoke Rousseau's idea of the General Will, that is, the basic impulse of the people's needs and desires to be realized by a universal legislator. And therefore, as Rousseau's ideas have often been judged to be totalitarian, in implication at least, Herzl's ideas also promised a totalitarian state and society. Indeed, the concept of a corporate society exercised the imagination of Herzl's generation, and would evolve into a full expression in the Fascist, Nazi, and Communist experiments after World War One. In his *Judenstaat*, Hertzl advanced the oldest thesis for justifying dictatorship, namely, a weak and divided people who cannot help themselves require the help of those few who are strong. From his knowledge of Roman law he borrowed the concept of *gestor*, the collective entity that ministers to those who cannot care for themselves. [69] "At present," he wrote, "the Jewish people are prevented by the Diaspora from conducting its own political affairs, yet is in a condition of more or less severe distress in a number of places. It needs, above all things, a gestor." [70] Accordingly, he proposed one, calling it the Society of Jews, a term so close in name to another authoritarian organization that one is compelled to reflect: Society of Jesus. Herzl's Society of Jews would act rather like a directorate with both political and diplomatic functions. Negotiations with the Great Powers would commence in order to secure sovereignty over a territory (not, in Herzl's first thoughts, necessarily Palestine). At the same time, education of the Jewish masses would be undertaken so that they might become aware of their nationality (their true identity as Israelites). This process was not unlike Karl Marx's efforts to make the workers of the world class-conscious so that they might be aware of the revolutionary role that history imposed upon them.

Equally imaginative was Herzl's plan to create a "Jewish Company." Its function would be to transfer Jewish funds from the many host communities for the purpose of building the infrastructure of the new Jewish state. He thought it would be a sort of joint stock company, incorporated in Great Britain, the original subscriptions coming from wealthy Jews.

In 1897 Herzl created an international body composed of influential Jews, calling it the Zionist Organization. Since the Jewish Diaspora was worldwide, the Zionist Organization could bring its influence to bear on every continent and every important country. Established as cooperating federations, the Zionist Organization, through its political and financial connections, would become a machine with incalculable influence.

At the first Zionist Congress, convened at Basle in 1897, communication for the delegates would have been difficult, and often impossible. A Jew from the United States and a Jew from Hungary, for example, could only stare at each other. If both were (and very likely so) middle-class Jews, they probably would not have known French, still the elegant lingua franca of the well educated. They would not have known Hebrew, virtually a dead language. The Hungarian Jew would probably have spoken fluent Yiddish (the vernacular of Eastern European Jews), but the American Jew would not have known Yiddish well enough to use it. And therefore one of the first goals set by the delegates was the restoration of Hebrew, which they believed was their native language.

Religious matters had no place at the congress for delegates who were political Zionists *par excellence*. Highly secularized, they knew the Torah little better than the average American at the end of the twentieth century knows the New Testament. The myths entertained by their forefathers probably bored them, and they could only be amused, if not mystified, by the mumbling gyrations of the dark-garbed, broad-hatted, fanatical Hasidic Jews.

Delegations from Europe, the United States, and Palestine established an agenda for the first congress. The main points were: world Jewry would be encouraged to finance those Jews who wished to move to Palestine; Hebrew would be revived as the language of the Jews; and organizations would be established to promote the Zionist cause. All this was a recapitulation of Herzl's personal program, already published. In 1902 two important organizations were formed: the Jewish Colonial Trust and the Jewish National Fund.

Herzl was both a visionary and a very practical man. What he dreamed of could never be realized by Jews alone. They were scattered, possessed no territory and, despite the protestations of their intelligentsia to the contrary, did not share a sense of nationality. When the Zionists used the pronoun "we," signifying world Jewry, they really spoke for themselves; a small clique composed of middle-class, acculturated Jews who entertained a bewitching vision, but without the means to realize it. With almost prophetic insight Herzl discerned the key that would give success: Zionists would have to cultivate the cupidity of Western imperialists (a single patron would be enough); secondly, they would call upon some part of the vast wealth accumulated by world Jewry over many centuries. Accordingly, he approached Kaiser Wilhelm of Germany, his entrée accomplished by a "Christian Zionist," Reverend Hecklin. Kaiser Wilhelm's Middle East aspirations were well known. [71] Herzl proposed two fantasies at once: The establishment of a German protectorate in Palestine (presumably the Sultan would be powerless to prevent this); and the formation of a Jewish Land Development Corporation so as to facilitate Jewish emigration.

The Kaiser agreed with Herzl, but diplomatic exchanges thereafter informed him that the great powers, Great Britain, France, and Russia were opposed. Herzl's plans were stillborn.

The German gambit having failed, Herzl approached the Sultan directly. (Pourparlers extending over nearly two years were required before Abdul Hamid, the "mad Red Sultan" defamed by Gladstone, would receive him.) Herzl's proposition was simplicity itself: the Sultan could escape from his French and British creditors by accepting a loan from Jewish bankers. In exchange for the Jews refunding the Turkish debt, the Sultan would grant the Zionists a charter that would allow them to settle in Palestine. With the Zionists rooted in this fashion, Herzl supposed the Jewish state would materialize in a matter of years. [72] Negotiations with the Sultan (or more exactly the Sultan's minions) went on fruitlessly for several years, up to Herzl's death in 1904. The talks died as Herzl expired, at about the same time that the Second Aliyah was dying in Palestine for another reason.

It has been stressed that the secular Zionists, Herzl only typical of these, did not attach a religious significance to the problem of a Jewish state. It could be Palestine or Syria, or almost any part of Africa—even Argentina had been taken into consideration as a site for the future Jewish homeland; finally, Uganda, a British protectorate, was considered and rejected. [73]

Sentiment and practical politics, not Hebrew prophecy, were the deciding factors. Having settled upon Palestine as the natural and necessary haven for world Jewry, Herzl had to consider the demographic facts. Perhaps as many as 650,000 Arabs, almost entirely Moslem, occupied the country, most families having been there for generations. Nevertheless, Herzl confided to his diary, the mass of the Arab peasantry could be moved out. He imagined how the Jews would "spirit the penniless population across the border by procuring employment for it in the transient countries, while denying it any employment in our own country, i.e., the future Israel." As for the big Arab landowners, the elite called *effendi*, money would manage them too. They could be "had for a price." [74]

The ethos of Zionism was, as one sees, tinctured from its inception by Western capitalist values; the mentality of the stereotypical used car dealer who does not scruple to exploit the frailties of a poor and ignorant customer. The long tutelage Jewry had experienced in the competitive world of capitalism girded them for what in all appearances must have seemed an enormous undertaking: 650,000 Arabs possessed, as a right, lands that some of them had occupied continuously since at least the seventh century, enriching them by hard labor and enduring every alien regime imposed upon them for over a thousand years. But from the Jewish point of view Palestine had always been theirs, granted to them by Yahweh.

Herzl had no doubt that a Jewish conspiracy to deceive and dispossess a simple people who were only too easy a target for sophisticated Westerners could cause a black page to be written in Jewish history. Should this "involuntary expropriation" take place, he wrote, "people will avoid us. We are in bad odor." But, he predicted, by the time that odor should befall them they would be in possession of the land and immune to world opinion. "We shall be firmly established in our country, no longer fearing the influx of foreigners, and receiving our visitors with aristocratic benevolence and proud amiability. [75]

In the critical years that preceded the formation of Herzl's Zionist Organization, the international socialist movement had brought the interests of organized labor into play. Rural self-sufficiency, a dream out of the past like the Zionist dream itself, was now confronted by a present reality and still one more dream: the brotherhood of man could be realized by overthrowing capitalism and establishing a new social order for the world. From the beginning Zionism was linked to a revolutionary whirlwind that took enthralled labor for its child. Rapid industrialization in the Western world, from which Jewish financiers and entrepreneurs had profited, also produced a growing mass of workers (skilled and unskilled) no longer relying on the land for a living, but dependent on the wages offered them by capitalists, both Jew and Gentile.

Jewish socialists who took Marxism as a basis for their ideology (and most did) accepted the doctrines Marx had laid down for interpreting the course of all human history. Nationalism, they believed, was a vanishing force in European life. Those Jews who expressed theories about Jewish nationalism were therefore in error. Moreover, the goal of the Zionists, acquisition of Eretz Yisrael, was a chimera. In 1901 the Fourth Conference of the Jewish Bund repudiated political Zionism, declaring that "the acquisition of a territory for the Jews was an objective of little value, because such territory would be able to support but a fraction of the whole people, and thus would be incapable of solving the Jewish question." [76]

The Political Zionists, an elite group who presumed to lead the Jews back to their homeland, were professional people, distinctively middle class and capitalist in their most basic values. They represented everything Marxist Socialists deplored. Social Zionism, as it developed, had to find some new and original basis for the development of its ideology. This feat was accomplished by a Russian Jew, Nahman Syrkin, who was acutely aware of this dilemma. He understood, he wrote, "the thankless task of being a socialist among Zionists and a Zionist among socialists." [77] In 1907 he moved to the United States and joined the American branch of the World Confederation of *Poaeli Zion* (Workers of Zion), a labor-oriented group that had grown up within the Zionist organization. The next year he published a book, *The Jewish Question and the Socialist Jewish State*. A seminal work, it could be seen in retrospect as a harbinger for a movement that later would be called National Socialism. Syrkin's argument was very simple: one could be a socialist, a nationalist, and a Jew. The Marxists were wrong; socialism and nationalism were natural allies, not antagonists. The loyalty of the worker would not be to his class, as Marx had predicted, but to his nation. Later, Mussolini and Hitler would take this idea very far.

Poaeli Zion first organized Jewish dissidents in Russia, then grew in numbers and sophistication during the period of the second migration to Palestine (Second Aliyah). By 1907 it had been established rather like a caucus within the Zionist organization, calling itself the World Confederation of Poaeli Zion. Syrkin became its chief ideologue, arguing that while class antipathy, proletarian versus bourgeois, divided Political Zionism, a common sense of Jewish nationalism held them together for the great work of emancipation. "Why," he asked "should the Jewish proletariat, which will be the first to be helped by Zionism in the material sense, reject it merely because the other classes of Jewry have also adopted Zionism for national and ideological reasons?" [78]

Retaining the Marxist rhetorical language, Syrkin saw the world revolution envisioned by the Second International enthusiasts and the redemption of the Jewish people as only parts of the whole. He foresaw "the blending of all the nations into a higher unity, the creation of a humanity with a common language, territory and fate." [79]

By the time World War One broke out in 1914, the World Confederation of Poaeli Zion had become a rival to both the Jewish Bund and the Zionist Organization. Its most extreme members fraternized with the Second International and would later collaborate with Lenin's Communist Third International. Marxist dialectical theories conditioned their thoughts so completely that one may say they were Jews in name only. In this far-left wing of the international socialist movement, communism and Labor Zionism would be compatible, sharing the vision of a redeemed mankind; Jews truly emancipated from the superstitions of the old religion, but equally saved from the cupidity of their capitalist middle-class fellows. In the fantastic vision entertained by Poaeli Zionists, class warfare would erupt in Palestine once the bourgeois-dominated Zionist Organization had gathered sufficient capitalist resources from world Jewry. In brief, only bourgeois Zionists, necessary instruments of history, could carry out the first stages of Jewish emancipation. But then, the Jewish proletariat would take charge of the last phases, ushering in the Age of Man.

Meanwhile, and in reality, the steady infiltration of Turkish Palestine, in both legal and illegal ways, promised over time the realization of a Jewish homeland. A collectivist agriculture, rural socialism so to speak, was the underlying ethos of what was not so much a plan as a formless and drifting migration of poor Jews into a poor country. In such a process as had been under way since the early 1880s, most of world Jewry would be left behind, and the great majority of them would not care one way or the other, at least until the 1940s, when the Jewish state had at last become a reality.

In Herzl's time there was an unbounded passivity of the Jews to contend with. On the other hand, a determined opposition could be expected from orthodox Jewry, which took a dim view of what was now being characterized as "political Zionism."

For the Orthodox Jew, a return to Eretz Yisrael would fulfill Hebrew prophecy, representing a stopping point on the way to a predestined end: a final resting place with the God-Father, the punishing God who never failed to chastise His chosen people when they strayed too far from His will. After an exile of more than a thousand years their sentence seemed to have been served. Obediently and meekly, this "stiff-necked" people would go home.

Such other-worldliness, indeed such abject resignation, had no meaning for Labor Zionists. Social justice, i.e., deliverance in this world, was their goal. Between orthodoxy and political Zionists there could never be a meeting of the minds. None was a stronger critic of Orthodox Jewry than Max Nordau. A German Jew trained in medicine but with a marked literary taste, he had experienced the same intellectual evolution as Herzl. Assimilated, effectively removed from Judaism, Nordau knew the alienation all educated Jews felt. He was a German, but he was not; he was a Jew, but he was not. Like Herzl, but in more stringent terms, he rejected assimilation. Rejecting Jewish orthodoxy, he espoused what he called "the new Zionism," which "distinguished itself from the old religious, messianic form in that it disavows all mysticism and no longer identifies itself with messianism. It does not expect the return to Palestine to be brought about by a miracle, but rather seeks to accomplish it by its own efforts." [80]

It seems clear that most of the Jewish immigrants arriving in Palestine were not motivated by such rarefied issues as Jewish identity or the prospective loss of their traditions if assimilated to Gentile society. These obsessive fears belonged to the Jewish middle classes of Western Europe and America. Only a small percentage of this comfortable urban Jewry would choose the onerous, and indeed sometimes perilous, life of a pioneer in Turkish Palestine. The great majority of the Palestinian settlers were poor Jews, either rural in origin or lower class out of the big cities of Europe, yearning to live on the land. Poorly educated, they were unaware of the arcane theories spun by the Jewish intelligentsia. In brief, they were not Zionists in their overwhelming number, but merely seekers; and (without being cynical about the matter) they were necessary instruments for the small cadre of political Zionists who wished to seize and to hold for Jewish posterity Eretz Yisrael.

Those of the First Aliyah found a country almost devoid of Jewry. Such statistics as there are suggest that in 1856 there were about ten or eleven thousand Jews in Palestine, six thousand of whom lived in Jerusalem, constituting about one-third of the city's population. Almost all of the Jews in Jerusalem lived on what was termed *Hulukkah*, i.e., a dole. Charitable donations were collected from world Jewry for the support of Jews living in the four Palestinian cities judged to be holy: Jerusalem, Hebron, Safed, and Tiberius. The indigenous Jews *(Yishuv)* entertained no thoughts about recovering the land of their forefathers. Having lived in the country for generations, they were effectively "Arabicized," partaking of Islamic society in all ways save for the observance of their own religious rites. They spoke Arabic; Hebrew known only to the few learned among them. A mutual toleration existed between Jews and Moslems, friction between the two religions so slight as to go unnoticed. But so closely joined were sacerdotal functions, rituals, customs and mores in the Yishuv that they were as distinctive as a people, and as poorly assimilated to the Arabs, as their brethren anywhere else in the Jewish Diaspora.

By 1903 the number of Jews in Palestine had risen substantially, to about 40,000. They were divided evenly between those from Eastern Europe (Ashkenazim) and those who were termed Sephardim or Oriental, Jews. The Ashkenazim lived as if aliens in a strange land, unable to speak Arabic (the lingua franca of the country). They spoke Yiddish, the language of their origins; almost all were from Russia and Poland. It did not occur to most of them, probably, that they were advance agents for a new force in the world, which would change Palestine fundamentally. That sense of destiny belonged uniquely to the Jewish intelligentsia, which spoke for the next wave of immigrants, the Second Aliyah.

The second descent on Turkish Palestine, beginning in 1905, was brief and not very successful, lasting about five years. Half of the settlers gave up in a short time and moved on to other parts of the world. [81] The terms of existence they set for themselves were difficult, though undeniably idealistic. Poorly informed before their arrival of the hardships of the country, great heat in the summer, the scarcity of water, they suffered. They also endured hard labor, for there was agreement among them that they would not be mere colonizers living off the indigenous population. Refusing to hire Arab laborers, they worked with their own hands, living beside their Arab neighbors as equals. They did not doubt that the Arabs had as much right to Palestine as the Jews (but not a greater right). It would be a matter of competition, therefore, a contest between two claimants to the land. "Between us and the Arabs," wrote an influential settler, A. D. Gordon, "the real difference is based on numbers, not on the character of the claim." [82] In other words, the historic claims to Palestine made by Arabs and Jews were irrelevant. The issue was simply one of demographics. The Arabs could not breed as fast as the Jews would enter and populate the country. However, before 1914 and the fall of the Ottoman Empire, this was a boast without substance.

The leaders of the Second Aliyah, of which the settler-author-ideologue A. D. Gordon was perhaps the archetype, celebrated brains and brawn, mind and body, the intellect and the heart: the whole person; especially the one who is close to the earth, the farmer who works with his hands, beholden to no one, self-sufficient and resourceful. Indeed, individualism was not dampened much, if at all, by the needs of the immigrants to live in collectivist farmsteads *(kibbutzim)*.

The body of ideas and practices that underwrote the Second Aliyah was called *Kibbush Avodah* (Conquest of Labor). Against the rude life of their loutish competitors (ignorant, illiterate, unmotivated Arab peasants), Gordon and his companions offered an elevated cultural ethic rather like the ethos of a rural aristocracy: untitled but not humble. Their slogan was *Avodah*, which means "labor" in Hebrew, and is the same word for worship. "To labor is to pray," an old Benedictine saying, applied to Kibbush Avodah also, affirming the dignity of labor. "All that we wish for in Palestine," Gordon wrote, "is to work with our very own hands at all things which make up life, to labour with our hands at all kinds of works, trades and crafts, from the most skilled to the coarsest and most difficult. Then we can consider ourselves to possess culture for then we shall possess life." [83]

A bucolic society of laboring intellectuals, honoring every form of work, from growing orange trees to blowing glass, was a fanciful image without a future. The Arabs were correct in suspecting that the Jewish immigrants would eventually bring into Palestine the advanced features of capitalist society: modernity, sprawling cities, an urban milieu that was as much in contradiction to Islam's traditional way of life as it was to Gordon's pre-industrial utopia. Nor would most Jews in the Diaspora have cared for Gordon's esoteric philosophy, which rejected much of Western civilization's progress in material comfort, its ever-increasing reliance on the machine; the penchant of those in the lowest ranks of society to escape from both rural life and the stultifying existence of the tradesman, to enter the middle class and rise ever higher on the social scale.

As the workers of the world (eventually organized as the Communist International) dreamed how they might take charge of mankind and perfect it, so did the Zionists under the rubric Kibbush Avodah plan to take over Palestine. They would outwork the Arabs and ultimately outnumber them by bringing in more and more inspired workers. Since New Russia, (the Ukraine) was nothing less than a huge reservoir of discontented Jews, mostly poor villagers, the Zionists could expect the Third Aliyah to become an irresistible torrent of workers (thus the Conquest of Labor). But the expected third assault on Palestine did not materialize. Turkish authorities kept track of Jewish activities. Beginning in 1910, immigration to Palestine was severely restricted. The most prominent of the settlers were deported, among these a radical young Polish immigrant named David Green. So great was his fascination with ancient Hebrew culture, its history and sad fate, Green chose a new name for himself, one more appropriate for his calling as a militant Zionist. He would become David Ben Gurion. However, with the outbreak of the Great War, and especially the anti-Zionist policies of the Turkish government, his role as a social revolutionary did not seem to have a future. Expelled "forever" from the Ottoman Empire by Kemal Pasha in 1915, Green chose exile in New York City, believing his career as a Palestine pioneer was over. [84] But the outbreak of the Great War in 1914 had produced a radical new set of circumstances in the Middle East, Palestine in particular, which would result in the collapse of the Turkish empire and the elevation of Zionism to an eminence that could not have been anticipated.

NOTES

33 Leon Poliakov, *The History of Anti-Semitism*, trans., Richard Howard (New York, 1965), p. 5.

34 Arnold Toynbee, *A Study of History*, ed., D. C. Somerville (Oxford University Press, 1946), I, pp. 8, 22-23.

35 Ephraim E. Urbach, "Center and Periphery in Jewish Historic Consciousness: Contemporary Implications," *World Jewry and the State of Israel*, ed., Moshe Davis, op. cit., p. 226.

36 The earliest estimate is thought to be 722 B.C., after the dispersal of the Ten Tribes of Israel by the Assyrians See *Jews in Old China. Studies by Chinese Scholars*, Trans., ed., Sidney Shapiro (New York, 1984), pp. XIII-XIV.

37 Arnold Toynbee, *A Study of History*, II, pp. 172-173.

38 *Jews in Old China*, p. 117.

39 Denmark, Holland, Bohemia, Austria, Prussia (later absorbed into greater Germany) and many more.

40 Frank H. Epp, *Whose Land is Palestine? The Middle East Problem in Historical Perspective* (Grand Rapids, MI, 1970), p. 99.

41 Yiddish was spoken by millions of Jews in central Europe and Russia, but obviously this did not represent a lingua franca for world Jewry.

42 Gideon Shimoni, *The Zionist Ideology* (Brandeis University Press, 1995), p. 170.

43 "I am driven to the conclusion," wrote the historian Hugh Seton-Watson, "that no 'scientific definition' of a nation can be devised; yet the phenomenon has existed and exists. All I can find to say is that a nation exists when a significant number of people in a community consider themselves to form a nation, or behave as if they formed one." Shimoni, *The Zionist Ideology*, p. 4.

44 Michael A. Meyer, *Ideas of Jewish History* (New York, 1974), pp. 181-191.

45 Zion, a hill in Jerusalem, site of the City of David; a metaphor which was destined to be elevated to ideology as Zionism.

46 Martin Gilbert, *Exile and Return. The Struggle for a Jewish Homeland* (New York, 1978), p. 32.

47 Leon Poliakov, p. 211.

48 International Workingmen's Association, organized so as to use the power and influence of world labor to promote the ideas of communism in the *Communist Manifesto*, published in 1848 by Karl Marx and his collaborator,

Friedrich Engels.

49 Shimoni, *The Zionist Ideology*, p. 59.

50 Ibid., p. 21.

51 The Reform Rabbinical Conference at Frankfort, 1845. *The Jew in the Modern World. A Documentary History*, Second Ed., eds., Paul Mendes-Flohr and Jehunda Reinharz (New York and Oxford, 1995), p. 183.

52 Zionism as a term does not have a date for its origin; it is usually attributed to Nathan Birnbaum, an important figure in a group called Hoveval Zion.

53 Shimoni, p. 401.

54 The Pale of the Settlement was established in 1835, specifying the area in which Jews were obliged to live, and also the conditions under which they should live as Russian subjects.

55 Harold Frederic, *The New Exodus. Israel in Russia* (London, 1892), pp. 79-80.

56 Ibid.

57 The original title was *Autoemazipation: Mahnruf an seiner sammegonossen von einem Russischen Juden.*

58 *Jewish Messenger*, 20 May 1881, cited in Ronald Sanders, *Shores of Refuge. A Hundred Years of Jewish Immigration* (New York, 1988), pp. 35-36.

59 Jonathon Frankel, "The Crisis of 1881-82 as a turning point in Modern Jewish History," *The Legacy of Jewish Immigration: 1881 and Its Impact*, ed., David Berger (Brooklyn College Press, 1983), pp. 14-15.

60 Count Molé, Summons for Convening the Parisian Sanhedrin, 18 September 1806. Cited in *The Jews in the Modern World. A Documentary History*. Second Edition, p. 133.

61 *The Legacy of Jewish Migration*, p. 15.

62 Ibid.,, p. 16.

63 Shimoni, p. 36.

64 Ibid., p. 89.

65 Ibid, p. 88.

66 Steven Beller, Herzl (London, 1991), p. 3.

67 Peter Y. Medding, "Patterns of Jewish Identification," *World Jewry and the State of Israel*, p. 122.

68 Theodore Herzl, *Old New Land*, p. 79, 284.

69 _____, *Der Judenstaat*. I have consulted an English edition, *The Jewish State*, trans., Harry Zohn (New York, 1970), pp. 92-94.

70 Ibid.

71 Harold Wilson, *The Chariot of Israel. Britain, America and the State of Israel.* (New York and London, 1981), p. 22-23.

72 "In his grand design, the State would arise powerful from birth and in a brief period neighboring states would so benefit from its creation that they would give it their support." See Frank E. Manuel, *The Realities of American-Palestine Relations*, (Washington, D.C., 1949), p. 82.

73 Herzl also considered Mesopotamia (the future Iraq), at the turn of the century "inhabited by only nomadic Arab tribes." Ibid., pp. 85-86.

74 Desmond Stewart, *Theodore Herzl* (New York, 1974), p. 192.

75 Ibid., p. 192.

76 Resolution of Fourth Conference of the Allgemeine Yiddisch Arbeiter Bund in Russland und Lita, May 1901.

77 Shimoni, pp. 170-71.

78 Ibid., p. 173.

79 Ibid., p. 175.

80 Ibid., p. 170.

81 Howard Sachar, *A History of Israel* (New York, 1976), p. 73. How little Palestine attracted Jewish immigrants may be seen in the fact that Argentina in this same period (circa 1890-1914) received 113,000 of them.

82 Bernard Ashavar, *The Tragedy of Zionism. Revolution and Democracy in the Land of Israel* (New York, 1985), p. 92.

CHAPTER THREE

The Return

ꙏ THE GREAT WAR AND PALESTINE

The question of what was Palestine, who lived there, who possessed it, most importantly, who could rightfully claim to have sovereignty over it, became a matter of dispute after World War One. Once a Roman province (the Romans gave it a name), [85] Palestine came under Arab rule in the seventh century C.E., a time when Islam began to spread over the Middle East to become the dominant religion. Over the centuries after the Arab conquest, Christianity shrank to little or nothing in these regions, while Judaism, for all practical purposes, disappeared. At the beginning of the Roman Imperium an estimated one million Jews had lived in Palestine. [86] Toward the close of the Roman period there would remain only a few thousand.

Beginning in the sixteenth century the Ottoman Turks conquered the Arab regions. Thereafter they ruled easily, but indifferently, over a people who displayed every tendency to accept Turkish domination without complaint, only aroused by the spirit of nationalism late in the nineteenth century. Arab historians have called this period the "long sleep," a slumber that lasted more than 500 years.

In 1862 a reform movement in the Turkish Empire resulted in a far-reaching reorganization of the Sultan's dominions. Provinces

71

(vlayet) were laid out; these were divided into districts *(sandjak)*, and the districts into sub-districts *(kadha)*. The sandjak of Jerusalem, because of its uniqueness as the revered center of three religions, was placed directly under the authority of the Supreme Porte.

The administrative lines drawn on a Turkish map had scarcely any reality on the ground. Without natural boundaries except for the Mediterranean coastline, Palestine disappeared vaguely in the desert wastes beyond the Jordan River. To the north Palestine merged insensibly with another equally uncertain area, Syria. To the south, Palestine became part of the great Negev desert, which merely became another desert area, the Sinai Peninsula.

As Palestine was vaguely defined, so were its inhabitants vaguely called "Arabs." In fact they were a very mixed breed of people. If they thought of themselves as Palestinians they did not say so. If they were a distinctive nationality they were not aware of it. By the same token, if the few Jews living in Palestine for ages (the *Yishuv*) thought of Palestine as their lost patrimony, to which they had a right and an obligation to reclaim, they did not speak of it. Until the mid-nineteenth century, therefore, Palestine was largely a state of mind, a code word for Christians and Jews, some of whom journeyed there, the Holy Land their destination. In their devotion they visited the shrines precious to their faith. The most devoted of the pilgrims (very few in number) elected to live there full-time, to build churches and synagogues and to establish schools.

Periodically over the centuries, devout Jews had entered Palestine with the indulgence of the Arab, then the Turkish, authorities; sometimes by the hundreds, on one occasion at least by the thousands. Admitted from time to time, they were just as frequently expelled. [87]

From the time the Ottoman Turks took control of Palestine in 1517, Jews were permitted to enter the country on a regular basis. There began a thin trickle of immigrants, more or less constant over the next three centuries. A number of Sephardic Jews, led by Don Joseph Massic, established an agricultural colony on the

72

shores of Lake Tiberius (anciently the Sea of Galilee), the nucleus of a population that became known eventually as Yishuv, i.e., indigenous Jews in Palestine.

The Yishuv lived a degraded life vis-à-vis the dominant majority, which was Arab and almost entirely of the Moslem faith. They could neither speak nor read Hebrew, the language of their ancestors, which was dead in the sense that Latin, after the fall of the Roman Empire, became a dead language, known only to the Roman Catholic clergy and serving a tiny intelligentsia as the necessary medium for learning. Such was the case with Hebrew in Palestine also: a dead language that was the exclusive possession of the rabbis and a few Jewish scholars.

Beginning in the 1880s, Jewish immigration (First Aliyah) was modest: fourteen men and one woman. In the next two decades another 25,000 immigrants arrived. Mostly Russian Jews, they imagined they were entering a bountiful land, the fabled land of milk and honey. Supposing it to be virtually empty, they believed ten to fifteen million Jews might settle there. What they found, however, was a long settled country and an alien population. The climate was new and difficult; great heat in summer, little water, and poor soil. The only land available for purchase was scarcely fit for farming.

The second wave of Jewish immigration at the beginning of the twentieth century, though larger, was no more successful than the first. About the time Zionist hopes were beginning to fade, a war broke out in Europe. Becoming a Great War involving most of the world, the exigencies of the conflict produced unexpected opportunities for the Zionists. Well before 1914 their cause had seemed lost, the Beuil Program, calling for a heroic colonization of the land, nipped in the bud by the watchful Turkish government.

The Jewish flight from Palestine in 1914–15 was remarkable, due in part to a voluntary departure of disenchanted pioneers, but also, once Turkey joined the Central Powers, the Jewish identification with the several allied countries made them suspect; many were deported. In 1914 there were about 100,000 Jews in Palestine. A year later the number had shrunk to around 60,000.

Zionist influences during the Great War resulted from multifarious activities hardly to be understood and scarcely to be described. World Jewry possessed a peculiar character that no other ethnic group could claim, being both multinational and international at the same time. Citizens of almost every country on earth, relatives in any conflict would often find themselves on opposite sides. They were "combatants in all armies fighting everywhere and being nowhere recognized," complained Chaim Weizmann, a prominent British Jew, a chemist by profession, whose importance in the Zionist movement would become incalculable. [88]

Citizens of the world, Zionists maintained offices in the major capitals from London to Berlin, to Constantinople, to Washington. A group of twenty-five notable Jews, calling themselves the Zionist Action Committee, began meeting at Copenhagen on 17 December 1914. The war was not yet six months old when the Zionist policy of neutrality, established in 1897, was reaffirmed. From the Zionist point of view, Jewish loyalty did not belong to any country. Theirs was devotion to the cause, constant since Herzl had pronounced the goal: Palestine for the Jews.

On 27 April 1918, the debates among the Zionists over questions of strategy reached a conclusion. The Labor Zionist position was accepted. Hebrew-speaking, collectivist-oriented farmers would colonize Palestine. Organized Jewish labor *(Histadrut)* would be in its urban setting what communal farms were already to the countryside: a network of Jewish influences that over time would control the whole country. This institutional framework would amount to a human grid capable of absorbing however many Jews eventually might go to Palestine.

The policy of neutrality was abandoned; Herzl's idea of seeking a powerful patron revived. For the Zionists, Great Britain became the power of choice, this being the result of changing fortunes of war. Almost at the outset of the war, Italy had renounced its obligations to Germany and Austria-Hungary under the terms of the Triple Alliance, joining the Allies thereafter. Ottoman Turkey took Italy's place. Thus, the Triple Alliance, in the nomenclature of the spreading war, became the Central Powers.

Hard-pressed once Turkey entered the war, the British cabinet felt constrained to bargain with both the Arabs and the Jews. To raise the Arabs in revolt against the Sultan of Turkey, their overlord, only made good sense. But the Sultan, spiritual leader of all the Moslems in his domains, had already pronounced the Jihad against the infidel, the Holy War to which every true Moslem should rally at once. Against this religious call to arms, the British touched another emotion, evoking a greater need among the Arabs: freedom from the detested Turks. Without delay, the Sherif of Mecca, Hussein Ibn Ali, a descendant of Mohammed and guardian of Islam's holy places, began negotiations with British agents. In an exchange of letters between the Sherif and Sir Henry MacMahon, British High Commissioner to Egypt, an agreement was worked out, clear in principle, and in terms of factual detail almost without ambiguity. The operating line was simple and would henceforth be characterized by the Arabs as a promise: Britain agreed "to recognize and uphold the independence of the Arabs in all the regions lying within the frontiers proposed by the Sherif of Mecca." [89] In the north the frontier would run from Mersin-Adana to the Persian borders; in the east up to Persian borders and the Persian Gulf; on the south, the Indian Ocean; and on the west, the Red Sea and the Mediterranean Sea. Perhaps the most compelling line in the agreement was as follows: Britain would not "conclude any peace whatsoever of which the freedom of the Arab peoples ... does not form an essential condition." [90]

On 1 January 1916, Hussein, along with his two of his sons, Feisal and Abdulla, agreed to join the infidels, i.e., Great Britain and its allies, against the Sultan of Turkey. [91] It was as though a Catholic monarch had agreed to make war on the Pope, a perilous step for any believer. But the rewards for Hussein and his sons were great: Great Britain was prepared [the agreement read in part] to recognize and support the independence of the Arabs in all the regions within the limits demanded by the Sherif of Mecca.

The rest of the story is well known: the Arab revolt in the desert; the sudden appearance of the quixotic British office, Colonel T. E. Lawrence (fabled Lawrence of Arabia); the conquest of Damascus; then General Allenby's entry into Jerusalem, the spiritual center of the world's three great monotheistic religions. But the Anglo-Arab agreement was violated almost at once by another agreement made between two diplomats, Sir Mark Sykes of Great Britain and Georges Picot of France, *viz.*, control of Palestine and Iraq would go to Britain and control of Syria to France. Thereafter, the British and French cabinets concurred with their diplomats, which is a reminder that imperial policy is often formed in unofficial ways and responds to the needs of the moment. The French could not stand idly by while their historic presence in the Middle East, continuous since the time of Louis XIV, was about to be eliminated by British opportunism and Arab ambition. Russia, apprised of these developments, demanded a share of the Turkish carcass, whereupon the agreements were revised. The final treaty, dated 23 October 1916, recognized, among other things, that an independent Arab state, or a confederation of Arab states, would be established at the conclusion of the war.

Once the Bolsheviks had gained power, they released copies of the agreements (the earliest dating from March 1815). The Allies' intentions became widely known as a consequence. But the Arabs had perhaps already seen the handwriting on the wall, dismayed to learn of British negotiations with the Zionists, whose ambitions were well known. Their ideas had for long been formulated for public consumption, promoted by Jews with international reputations. It was an influence that spanned the oceans, carried by such stellar figures as Chaim Weizmann, a leading figure in the Zionist Organization and a British subject; Baron Lionel Rothschild, president of the English Zionist Federation, also a British subject; and Louis D. Brandeis, Associate Justice of the United States Supreme Court.

Brandeis summed up the Zionist agenda in a single sentence: "Zionism seeks to establish in Palestine for such Jews as choose to go and remain there, and for their descendants, a legally secured home, where they may live together and lead a Jewish life, where they may expect ultimately to constitute a majority of the population, and may look forward to what we should call home rule." [92]

Although in the past British statesmen occasionally had expressed sympathy for the Zionist hopes, it cannot be said that sentiment was a part of their motives. In the first agreements with France and Russia for the partition of the Turkish Empire, the British Cabinet had proposed placing Palestine under an international administration. But a little later, Foreign Secretary A. J. Balfour indicated that by doing something in support of a Jewish homeland in Palestine they might stir the United States away from its determined policy of neutrality. This alone suggests how strong Jewish influence was reckoned to be among Western governments, and how calculating were the British. On 3 March 1916 the British Foreign Office informed its Russian counterpart of its policy toward the Jews: "It is clear that by using the Zionist idea, important political results can be obtained. Inter alia the Jews in the East, the United States and other countries, a great part of whom are now hostile to the Allies, will change their attitude." [93]

Thereafter the collaboration of American and English Zionists resulted in a document entitled "British Declaration of Sympathy of Zionist Aspirations." This was given in a draft copy to Balfour on 2 November 1917. The declaration was revised in letter form, as if being an emanation of the British will, and mailed to Baron Rothschild with the request that it be distributed among Zionist organizations all over the world. It was a brief and carefully worded statement of British policy, henceforth called the Balfour Declaration:

His Majesty's government view with favour the establishment in Palestine of a national home for the Jewish people, and will use their best endeavours to facilitate the achievement of this object, it being clearly understood that nothing shall be done which may prejudice the civil and religious right of non-Jewish communities in Palestine or the rights and political status enjoyed by Jews in any other country.

Cleverly, Weizmann and his colleagues had drawn out a declaration from the British Cabinet, which, if ambiguous at bottom, represented nonetheless another step toward establishing a Jewish state in Palestine. In his next maneuver Weizmann attempted to exploit British prejudice by reminding Balfour that in Palestine they would be dealing with a degraded people who scarcely deserved the land they lived on. "The present state of affairs," he wrote, "would necessarily trend towards the creation of an Arab Palestine, if there were an Arab people in Palestine. It will not, in fact, produce that result because the Fellahin is at least four centuries behind the time, and the effendi (who by the way, is the real gainer from the present system) is dishonest, uneducated, greedy, and as unpatriotic as he is inefficient." [94] And therefore, to paraphrase Weizmann, one did not see people in Palestine worthy of consideration, but only primitive folk (the Fellahin—"four centuries behind the times"), and a few sharp ones (the effendi—"dishonest, uneducated, and greedy"), whose vices and defects would cause them to be easily managed.

Once the Balfour Declaration was published it served as bombastic propaganda for inciting Jewish soldiers to desert the armies of the Central Powers. Leaflets appealing to their pride were dropped from airplanes:

Jerusalem has fallen! The hour of Jewish redemption has arrived! Every day more of the Holy Land is falling into the hands of the great democratic powers but not only for them, but for the Jewish people. Palestine must be the national home of the Jewish people once more. For 1,800 sad years the Jews have sought Zion and longed for it... Stop fighting the Allies, who are fighting for you, for all the small nations. [95]

There was much more of this in the same vein. Ordinary Jews swallowed the excited propaganda, but so did their sophisticated leaders, who with equal gullibility supposed the object of British policy was the formation of a Jewish state in Palestine. However, the ruling line in Balfour's letter to the Zionists needs to be considered: "His Majesty's Government views with favor the establishment in Palestine of a national home for the Jewish people and will use

their best endeavours to facilitate the achievement of that object."
There is no promise to be seen in Balfour's so-called Declaration,
nor does it say that Great Britain would establish a Jewish state
in Palestine. Moreover, the British concession came late in the
war. The French declaration in support of a Jewish homeland in
Palestine had been issued by the Quai d'Orsay on 4 June 1917.
It was reported that the British revision of the original Zionist
document seemed so equivocal that Weizmann despaired and
seriously considered repudiating it.

The Zionists thought only of a Jewish state, but more than that,
a state able to grow and become commensurate with the whole of
Palestine, perhaps larger than that. In their dreams it would embrace
all that had once been ancient Israel, as Weizmann said, from the
brook of Egypt to the banks of the Euphrates, but that was what
King Solomon might have only dreamed about.

President Wilson, privy to Brandeis' work with the English
Zionists in preparing the Balfour Declaration, had already offered
the world his celebrated Fourteen Points, which assured subject
peoples everywhere that self-determination is (reading between
Wilson's lines) an inalienable right. [96]

It was generally agreed by the powers that an international body,
to be called the League of Nations, should be formed; its purpose
to regulate the coming peace and thereafter to preserve peace in
the world for all times. To make the world safe for democracy
was the way President Wilson thought of it. The subject peoples
living in the defunct empires (Turkish, Austrian, German—the
collapsing Russian empire was a special problem), would gain
their independence. [97]

The mature thinking of the statesmen subtly changed their
outlook. Wartime idealism and the euphoria occasioned by victory
quickly gave way to realism. It was recognized that some people
were more advanced than others: Arabs, for example, could claim
to have a more sophisticated lifestyle than headhunters in Borneo;
Jews could (and would) assert that Arabs were still living in the
Middle Ages and had not yet learned about flush toilets or how to

drive an automobile, much less how to govern themselves. The solution for this problem was a device called the Mandate. Article 22 of the League Covenant decreed that the Occupied Territories were inhabited by "peoples not yet able to stand by themselves under the strenuous conditions of the modern world." By a sort of academic method of grading peoples and cultures, the statesmen at Paris recognized that there were self-evident categories: A, B, C. Thus, tribal people living in New Guinea were manifestly "C" people and would not be able to conduct their own affairs for a long time. "B" people were on the way to a civilized state but would need an indefinite period of tutelage before independence could be assigned to them. The Arabs were judged to be "A" people and would catch up with the civilized world in a short time. It followed that the Western world was the paragon of civilized societies and should be emulated by others.

In practice the great powers would continue to hold sway, each taking its mandate from the League of Nations. Thus a disguised form of imperialism forced its way down from the rarefied idealism Woodrow Wilson had brought to the peace conference. Inevitably, Syria would go under the French wing, while Iraq and Palestine would fall under British protection, but this entailed hard bargaining over the space of a year.

However paternalistic, even pretentious, the Mandate System appeared at first glance, it did represent a step beyond the uncontrollable and arbitrary domination of people around the world that had characterized western imperialism up to 1919. The language describing each mandate had to be approved by the League of Nations before the Mandatory Power could assume its control of a given people. For the protection of the mandate subjects, the Mandatory Power had to submit annual reports to the League.

Given the collaboration of the Zionists and the British "non-Jewish Zionists," with the Americans in tow, it was rather pointless for both Jews and Arabs to send delegates to the peace conference in order to speak on behalf of their separate and mutually inimical aspirations.

All that mattered was actually being decided behind closed doors. While the peace conference had the air of a democratic forum, on an international basis, the Allied and Associated Powers, victors in the late war, ruled the proceedings arbitrarily through hearings conducted before the Council of Ten. [98] Among the first to give testimony on the subject was a French Jew, Sylvain Levi. An Orientalist by profession, his knowledge of the Middle East probably surpassed that of the Zionists. The doubts he raised had troubled many political Zionists from the beginning: Would the Arab world ever tolerate a considerable Jewish population in its midst?

Weizmann offered a successful rebuttal to Levi's foreboding. The French delegates decided that they could endorse a Jewish homeland in Palestine under British protection.

Wilson's idealism was at variance with the hard, self-seeking policies of Lloyd George for Britain and Clemenceau for France. The President wanted to ascertain the will of the subject peoples in the Middle East, and insisted upon sending an Inter-Allied Commission to find the facts and make proposals for the delegates at the conference to consider. This was too democratic for Lloyd George and Clemenceau. At length, only the United States would send commissioners: Henry C. King and Charles R. Crane. The King-Crane Commission, as it devolved from the stillborn Inter-Allied Commission, became merely an American committee. Its first reports confirmed the reservations that Jewish anti-Zionists had expressed for years. The resistance of both Moslem and Christian Arabs would make a Jewish state in Palestine untenable. The Zionist idea, declared Henry Morganthau, Sr., was "the most stupendous fallacy in Jewish history, wrong in principle and impossible of realization." Thirty-nine prominent American Jews went on record to state that while a homeland for Jews in Palestine, or anywhere else in the world, was acceptable to them on humanitarian grounds, the idea of a Jewish state was wrong, for it "not only misrepresents the trend of the history of the Jews, who ceased to be a nation 2,000 years ago, but involves the limitation and possible annulment of the larger claims of Jews for full citizenship and human rights in all lands in which those rights are not yet secure." [99]

King and Crane also rejected the Zionist proposition that the Jews had "a right to Palestine based on an occupation of two thousand years ago," citing the opinion of the British military officers in Palestine that a force of 50,000 would be needed to establish such a homeland as envisioned. [100]

By the time the King-Crane Commission made its first report, the Council of Ten had shrunk to become no more than a coterie composed of three men. Lloyd George and Wilson had gotten in the habit of meeting together with Clemenceau in the latter's study after he had been slightly wounded by a would-be assassin. Henceforth this small cabal made all the essential decisions. Wilson had so little interest, or better to say, so little influence, in the Palestinian matter that he willingly left it to Lloyd George and Clemenceau. The President's neutrality probably reflected the opinion of his Secretary of State, Robert Lansing, who thought the Jews asked for too much. "Many Christian sects and individuals," he wrote the president, "would undoubtedly resent turning the Holy Land over to the absolute control of the race credited with the death of Christ." [101] The stigma attached to Jews as being the killers of Christ had not yet fully departed from the Christian vocabulary.

⌒⌒⌒ THE SYRIAN FACTOR

The publication of the Balfour Declaration stunned the Arabs. Upon first hearing of it Hussein asked for a clarification. The British response came at a low level, Commander D. Hogarth of the Foreign Office's Arab Bureau going to Jedda to explain what the document meant. His interpretation was written down in Arabic, one line obviously important to Hussein:

> Jewish settlements may be allowed in so far as consistent with the political and economic freedom of the Arab population.

To some degree Hussein may be charged with carelessness, too much confidence being placed in what could be called a gentlemen's agreement. On the other hand, he had gained a written agreement stating that the Arabs' alliance with the Allies guaranteed them independence. From Turkey only? Sadly, independence from one imperial master did not guarantee independence from another. The rhythm of empire in the Middle East, which is the pattern of its history for thousands of years, has enthralled some people and liberated others (if only briefly); instrumental also in the liquidation of many ethnic groups in the space of seven millennium. (The slow but certain extinction of the wandering Bedouin people is the most recent example.) Like the Kurds, the Armenians, and many other subject peoples, the Arabs might have believed that the dissolution of the Ottoman Empire signified their independence, as a right. But that could not be. Up to 1919 at least, it was the unspoken rule of warfare that territory taken by conquest belongs to the victor. The Arab regions of the defunct Turkish empire now belonged to Great Britain and France, to be disposed of as its statesmen wished—except for a good part of the Arabian peninsula held by Ibn Sa'ud, King of Nejd. Conceding the latter's right of possession to certain coastal territories in December 1915, the British were willing to honor their agreements with him. [102] But the agreements made with the Hashemites Balfour dismissed as irrelevant.

It was generally believed in the Arab world that Palestine was part of Syria and that it would come under the rule of Hussein's son, Feisal. A Jewish minority living in Greater Syria did not appear threatening to the Arabs just then. In a government-controlled newspaper, *Al Qiblah*, Hussein made an appeal to the Arab people, reminding them that the religion of Mohammed required that they treat the Jews with respect and tolerance, as brothers of the Arabs. To his army units Hussein sent a confident message that Jews settling in Palestine would not constitute a threat to Arab independence. But a reading of British imperial history for the past three centuries would have eroded Hussein's confidence considerably. The Arab world in the early twentieth century was in miniature what the subcontinent of India had been in earlier times: a hive of small states and a congeries of peoples in motion; the inevitable upheaval that occurs when an empire has fallen. In India during the eighteenth century, finding the Mogul power to be mostly fiction, a few English adventurers had taken possession of a vast territory. In the Arab world a similar confusion prevailed, presenting the British with new opportunities too great to pass up.

At the invitation of the British authorities, a Jewish Commission headed by Weizmann traveled to Tel Aviv. On 27 April 1918, at a reception for the Zionist Commission in Jerusalem, Weizmann gave a speech insulting both in tone and substance. "Cries of opposition," it was reported, came from the assembled Arab notables. The Mufti, Sheik Kamal al-Husseini, spiritual leader of Jerusalem's Moslems, walked out of the reception in protest. Palestinian songs were sung and slogans affixed to the stage. One of these expressed Arab fears exactly: "Will they remove us from our beloved country in order to put others in our place?"

The Palestinians might have viewed the incoming Jews in much the way American Indians had watched the arrival of the first European settlers. In the beginning there weren't many and they seemed not so much dangerous as troublesome. Then there were more and still more, and finally it seemed there might be a torrent of newcomers. But by then it was too late. By 1919 the average Arab who thought about it would have believed that it was not too late, but the eleventh hour had arrived without a doubt. On 28 January 1919 a great rally was held in Jerusalem; both Christian and Moslem Arabs, united not only to prevent further Jewish immigration, but to oppose the new imperialism being fastened upon the country. Again there were slogans and shouts, among these recorded: "Palestine is part of Syria, and the Arabs of Palestine are part of it." [103]

It is noteworthy that one did not see nor hear slogans to the effect: "Palestine is our country," or "Palestinians are a nation," or "Palestinians demand independence." Those ideas, as a vital thing in the consciousness of the average Palestinian, were more than half a century away from revealing themselves. Yet, the sense of an imperiled community was very much alive. Palestine was a country of Arabs, whether Christian or Moslem. Jews were not wanted and did not belong.

Afterward, Weizmann expressed surprise at the extreme hostility he had encountered. The Sherif of Mecca and his sons, he noted, and the other effendi, had been courteous, even sympathetic, to the Zionists, but the ordinary Palestinian Arabs were intransigent, taking "a stand," complained Weizmann, "that made any negotiations impossible."

In Weizmann's speech one sees nothing other than intransigence. His misunderstanding and indifference to the sensibilities of the Palestinians seems remarkable, certainly politically inept. He was perhaps enlightened by one who knew the Arabs better than he, Major Ormsby-Gore, who told him that Arab resentment was not directed against Zionism in particular, but aimed more generally at all foreign powers, their immediate target being Great Britain, whose ambitions in the Middle East were transparent. [105]

Certainly, imperial interests took first place in the minds of British statesmen. Two were of overriding importance: oil resources in Iraq and security for the Suez Canal in the future, that distant time when they would have to leave Egypt as overlords. In the view of the pro-Zionists in the British cabinet, Palestine might become the client they could count upon, were it dominated by pro-British Jews. [106] None were more outspoken in that regard than Richard Meinertzhagen, a pro-Zionist career diplomat. In his conversations with Weizmann he envisioned a rosy future for the British Empire should the Zionists be able to establish a sovereign state in Palestine. In that case, "Great Britain would be granted air, naval, and military bases in Palestine in perpetuity. With British bases in Palestine our position in the Middle East is secure forever." [107]

It was in keeping with the British imperial mentality to think that if they should arrange a face-to-face meeting between Feisal and Weizmann, a personal understanding between them would obviate future Jewish-Arab friction. Accordingly, from Jerusalem the Zionist Commission went across the Jordan to Amman to meet with Hussein. These were cordial interviews.

In June 1918, Weizmann journeyed to Aqaba to meet Emir Feisal, who was serving as commander of the Sherifian forces. A forty-five-minute conversation convinced him that they could cooperate. Since Feisal and Weizmann had several cordial meetings after that, the latter supposed that Arab-Jewish relations would proceed smoothly. Because they did not, Zionists generally believed thereafter that British machinations destroyed a good working relationship between the Jews and Arabs, as similarly, they later believed that Anglo-Zionist collaboration came to an acrimonious end because of British cupidity and deceit. This feeling would never die out, Benjamin Netanyahu writing, as late as 1993, many purple pages on British treachery. [108]

Aside from the eventually unsatisfactory relationship of Feisal and Weizmann, the inherent antipathy of Jews and Moslems played an important role in the everlasting quarrel between the siblings. Weizmann had scarcely arrived in Tel Aviv on his first visit, before the Arabs were condemning the British for bringing more Jews into the country. A working relationship between Feisal and Weizmann was widely condemned by the Arabs, not only in Palestine but also in Syria.

The contrast between two people, two cultures, seemed incarnate in the personalities of the Feisal and Weizmann. The former, an Eastern naïf, was wholly Semitic in character. Weizmann was a wily politician and diplomat, a Europeanized Jew whose bourgeois values caused him to think in terms that Feisal could not quite imagine. Feisal, it is thought, possessed a gentle temperament, a crippling complement for his large ignorance of international politics. Secretary Lansing was entranced when hearing Feisal speak before the Council of Ten, calling him the "noble Arab," remembering that "his voice seemed to breathe the perfume of frankincense and to suggest the presence of richly colored divans, green turbans and the glitter of gold and jewels." [109]

Generous, chivalric in the ancient Bedouin tradition, genuinely sympathetic to the sorrowful history of Jewish homelessness and age-old persecution, he sincerely believed there was room in Palestine for both Jews and Arabs. (This, as so amply demonstrated, was not Weizmann's view of the future.) Feisal's good will and spirit of fairness (or naiveté if one wishes to say so), is to be compared with the long-range goal of the Zionists, their essential purpose from the beginning: the expulsion of all (or at least most) Arabs from Palestine. The King-Crane Commission left Palestine with that precise conviction. "The fact came out repeatedly," they reported to Wilson, "in the commission's conferences with Jewish representatives, that the Zionists looked forward to a practically complete dispossession of the present non-Jewish inhabitants of Palestine by various forms of purchase." [110]

In the minds of westernized Jews this could hardly be thought of as unjust criticism. In a Western society all is bought and sold. Why not a country? The two corrupting influences experienced by Western Jewry in a thousand years of exile sprang from the ethos of capitalism: anything can be bought, everything is for sale; and second, so closely tied to the first, the colonial spirit moved all westerners over time to think they were superior to those they dominated. To occupy, to exploit, to eliminate those inferior to themselves, became to all westerners, Jews and Gentiles alike, the several essences of their imperialism. And always these predations were justified on the grounds that essential goodness had been achieved, thereby outweighing any incidental evil. Had not the ignorant victims of Western imperialism been taught to read and write? To learn modern science? To appreciate the value of hygiene? To eschew superstition? And finally, most lately, to understand the meaning of democracy and to try to practice it? The list of good things the West commended to those whom they commanded was very long. And therefore, if the Zionists should be able to take Palestine away from the people who lived there, they would compensate them for any fancied wrong they might incur. To wit, where presently one saw poverty on every hand, in the future there would be plenty for everyone, for Arabs as much as for Jews.

⌒⌒⌒ ANGLO-ZIONIST COLLABORATION

In 1919 the British occupation force in Palestine (which at that time included present-day Jordan), acted as a provisional administration until a general pacification of Europe should be accomplished. It was called the Occupied Enemy Territory Administration. General Allenby, the chief administrator, governed through thirteen district military governors (reduced to ten in 1919). Under international law, no changes in local law could be made until the occupation had come to an end. (As for example, under Turkish law Jews could not display their blue and white flag.) [111]

Within the context of the Balfour Declaration, the Jews could claim consulative rights in Palestine. This the British cabinet acknowledged at once, allowing the Zionists to travel in Palestine in order to make a proposal for a homeland. Moreover, the Zionists were allowed representation in the Occupied Enemy Territory Administration. The Arabs, understandably, would conclude that the Jews in this less-than-innocent way had arrived as part of the British occupation force, and, more than this, participated in the governance of the country. Shortly, the Arab Christians and Arab Moslems formed an association, The Moslem-Christian Society, in order to counter Jewish pretensions. Most of the members were upper-class Arabs. Leadership arose out of that sector of society, and consequently Arab Christians led their Moslem compatriots in opposing the ambitions of another minority, the Jews. In a brief time, branches of the Moslem-Christian Society covered Palestine rather like a network. The overt purpose was to influence the Christian power occupying Palestine, i.e., Protestant Britain, in favor of the Arabs. But it is obvious that Protestant Britain had already opted for the Jews in general and the Zionists in particular.

Although Weizmann had a poor opinion of the Arab people, and made no attempt to conceal his contempt for the Palestinian Arabs, he worked assiduously for a cooperative arrangement between the two peoples. An Anglophile, he could not think of a better patron than Great Britain. Until the mandate concept became the effective tool for realizing his aspirations, he favored the establishment of a British protectorate over the country. With the development of a Jewish state, in "the next fifty or sixty years," he predicted, it would be incorporated into the British Empire. [112]

Once the mandate idea came under discussion, the best of two worlds seemed to appear for Weizmann: establishment of a Jewish homeland, protected by the British empire, and a mandate for Palestine to be given to the United States. This fantasy had some substance, but was fatally flawed by the fact of America's traditional isolationism and Woodrow Wilson's political weakness, which only became evident as the peace conference began to meet. Balfour expressed an interest in an American mandate for Palestine, but not without ulterior motives. He believed that Jews, Americans, and Englishmen could cooperate effectively to govern half-civilized Arabs, all the while fortifying British imperial interests in the Middle East. Balfour's opinion of the Arabs was not different from Weizmann's, an indifference bordering on contempt, the restrained hauteur of the English gentleman. Wilson's racial theories were notoriously extreme. The three men believed in the superiority of Anglo-American culture as if an article of faith.

The American mandate idea did not have a future, of course, but neither did Jewish-Arab cooperation, though Weizmann did go to great lengths, even joining the Syrian Welfare Committee in Cairo, a sort of society of patriots made up of Arabs, Armenians, and Zionists.

Negotiations between Zionists, Syrians, and Palestinians were fruitless, the exchanges lasting less than a year. Finally, the Zionist envoy to Damascus, Haim Kalvariski, met with the Syrian Congress in an unofficial capacity, offering them a written proposal that had the appearance of being a constitution for Palestine. It provided for the joint governance of the country by representatives of all religions, races and creeds. In seven articles it contained the germ of political democracy and social justice, and promised the peaceful coexistence of disparate peoples. [113]

Kalvariski's proposal to the Syrians was not borne out of sudden inspiration. He had already presented similar proposals to the Palestinian Jews' Provisional Committee on 31 December 1917. When they read the line, "Palestine is the homeland of all its inhabitants: the Jews, Moslems, and Christians are citizens of equal status," the Jews were offended, calling it "a ridiculous and dangerous plan." Whereupon they drew up their own plan, calling it a Draft Plan for Provisional Rule in Palestine. Among other things, a Jewish national state would be proclaimed at once, "under British protection," and "the Zionist flag will become the official flag of Palestine, together with the flag of the protective government." [114]

Weizmann expressed his disapproval when he learned of the plan. While a Jewish state was ever on his mind, the way to its achievement, he believed, would be long and by hard bargaining and not proclamations.

Kalvariski's proposal was accepted by the Syrian Congress, then by Feisal, who insisted that it be presented to the Palestinian delegates attending the Pan-Syrian Congress. They too accepted the plan, but as already noted, the Zionists had rejected it well before this. "To our regret," Kalvariski wrote later, "the draft was not approved, and for the same reason that it failed the first attempt in 1914: contempt for the Arab national movement and the Arab people, which were dismissed as unimportant, and an exaggerated appraisal of our own strength and the help of Europe and America." [115]

It was not without irony that at the same moment that the Zionists and the several Arab factions were falling into an impasse, Weizmann and Feisal were making progress toward an understanding. Feisal, a poor prince with big ambitions, was seduced by the prospect of receiving Jewish money. Weizmann played on this need with great skill, leaving Feisal to think that if he should cooperate with the Zionists, money would flow into Syria from a grateful world Jewry.

It would be hard to say who was the greater idealist, the one most naive, Woodrow Wilson or Feisal. During the latter stages of the war, the president had circulated his foreign policy principles in several important documents: the Fourteen Points, Five Particulars, Four Ends, and Four Principles. The independence of small, helpless people, subordinated to those more powerful than themselves, had become the touchstone for his foreign policy, with the slogan "national self-determination."

Both Weizmann and Feisal shared the illusion that they were representatives of two national movements that could cooperate. "We Arabs," observed Feisal, "especially the educated among us, look with deepest sympathy on the Zionist movement. The Jewish movement is national and not imperialist. Our movement is national and not imperialist, and there is room in Syria for both of us." (But when Feisal said Syria he meant "Greater Syria," which would include Palestine.)

Feisal was almost alone among prominent Arabs in speaking favorably of the Zionists. One may conclude with the historian Ma'oz that he played the difficult, probably impossible, role of political opportunist, caught as he was between the Arab nationalists (both Syrian and Palestinian) on the one hand, who deplored his relations with Weizmann, and on the other, the two predatory European powers, France and Great Britain. As has been said, probably "to nullify France's claim to control Syria, Feisal conditionally agreed to the creation of a national home in Palestine (as a separate entity or, according to another version, as part of his Syrian dominion)." [116] He felt no animus toward Jews in general, nor that special type, the Zionists. He was in favor of developing Palestine, and Syria as well, on the western model. Given the size of the state he envisioned, a homeland for the Jews seemed almost inconsequential, a "small Palestinian notch," as he put it. Throughout, and particularly in his written agreements with Weizmann, he expressed always the same reservations: if the Arabs should be denied independence, then all agreements between himself and the Zionists would be null and void. [117]

The two men agreed that the British cabinet should be pressed to renounce the Sykes-Picot Agreement, a necessary prelude to forcing the French out of Syria (6,000 French troops occupied the Syrian coast). The general understanding was as follows: a homeland for the Jews would be established in Palestine. [118] Feisal would become King of Syria. Through his connections with world Jewry, Weizmann would foster Jewish investment in Syria. Feisal would allow Jewish settlements in Syria. A draft treaty, prepared by their Anglo surrogates, (Arnold Toynbee of the Foreign Office, and T. E. Lawrence), and the Secretary of the Zionist Commission, Israel Sieff, was signed on 5 January 1919.

The ambiguity of the agreement lay in the inability of Weizmann and Feisal to resolve clearly the meaning of two expressions: "Greater Syria" and "Jewish State." Second, but not less important, the British cabinet had not yet reached a consensus as to whether they would cooperate with the French in exploiting the Middle East or gratify the desire of the several restive nationalities in those regions for independence—the Jews and Arabs merely the most troublesome of them all.

In this same period rumors abounded that Syria would be given to France as a protectorate. Once enthroned at Damascus, Feisal would become in reality no more than a French puppet. One may reasonably believe that the Emir was less than sincere when, on 3 March 1919, he sent a letter to Felix Frankfurter, a prominent American Jew and an outspoken Zionist, in which he endorsed French support for a Jewish homeland in Palestine.

With the establishment of the Syrian and Palestinian mandates, Feisal and Weizmann found themselves in roughly the same situation: clients of European great powers. Feisal was destined to be a puppet subordinated to French authority. Weizmann would remain what he had been thus far: a British collaborator, a moderate Zionist who had worked for the establishment of a Jewish state in Palestine; who, under British direction and some pressure, had attempted to establish a *modus vivendi* for the Yishuv in Palestine and the great Arab majority that surrounded them.

In July 1919, an Assembly of Notables met at Damascus and elected Feisal King of Syria. Once the French mandate was announced, the notables elected Feisal to the throne for a second time. Shortly thereafter Feisal began his brief and ill-starred reign.

In this same time the British government terminated their military occupation, replacing General Allenby with a civil figure, Sir Herbert Samuel (a British Jew and a pronounced Zionist), with the title of High Commissioner. The Jewish Commission, which had been in the country since the beginning of 1918, was reorganized and renamed the Zionist Commission, a small, but important, change in nomenclature. That the Zionists enjoyed close relations with the High Commissioner goes without saying.

Significantly, authority for affairs in Palestine was transferred from the Foreign Office to the Colonial Office, giving mute testimony that the Palestine Mandate was a British colony in the old tradition. The British authorities, also in the old tradition, persevered in their efforts to bring about a *modus vivendi* for the Jews and Arabs who had become in a sense their wards. In this regard they found themselves (in Weizmann's words) "between the hammer and the anvil," and not many years away from facing a bleak future in Palestine. A British military advisor to Weizmann characterized the attempt to establish a Jewish homeland in Palestine as "an adventure" that he viewed with "apprehension." "We have become an alien and detested element into the very core of Islam, and the day may well come when we shall be faced with the alternative of holding it there by the sword or abandoning it to its fate: the Arabs are under-dogs for the moment but they will bide their time and wait." [119]

Sir Samuel arrived at Jerusalem in the aftermath of severe anti-Jewish, anti-British demonstrations. These were caused, besides an evident xenophobia, by events transpiring in Syria. In June 1920, the French authorities deposed Feisal and a few weeks later expelled him from Syria. Thereafter, they reorganized Syria radically; among other changes, Lebanon became a virtually autonomous region. Arab guerrilla warfare broke out as a consequence, battles along the Syrio-Lebanese border affecting Jewish settlements in the upper Galilee. Joseph Trumpeldor, a Jew and former officer in the Russian Army, directed the Jewish defense forces. He, along with several others, was killed on 20 February 1921.

Besides Trumpeldor's guerrillas, another larger and better-trained force was in the field, organized by a radical Zionist, Vladimir Jabotinsky. A Russian Jew with the proverbial checkered past, and an adventurer of the first order, he had managed to establish a quasi-independent legion within the British army during the war. After the peace settlement of 1919, he had kept a part of his legion intact, constituting a nucleus that could be quickly expanded, for Jabotinsky believed that the Jews would have to fight in order to establish a Jewish state in Palestine. Soon he was hunted down and subjected to British justice: fifteen years' imprisonment at hard labor. Evenhanded in dispensing justice, the British authorities treated the Arab offenders with the same rigor. Among the latter was a prominent citizen of Jerusalem, Haz Amin el-Husseini, the scion of an old and venerable family. Haz Amin could be considered the equivalent of Jabotinsky, an exalted patriot who welcomed what he imagined was the inevitable struggle with the incoming Jews. Like Jabotinsky, he saw British arbitration between Jews and Arabs as merely a means to promote their own dominance in Palestine; moreover, successful arbitration would really go to the advantage of the Jews, not the Arabs. In the oldest Arab tradition, a free spirit and a noble character, Haz Amin became a folk hero when he evaded British justice and fled into the desert. The British sentenced him *in absentia* to fifteen years in prison.

As a measure of his magnanimity, and not less a sign of his sagacity, The High Commissioner decreed an amnesty for the Jewish and Arab malefactors. When the Grand Mufti, Kamal al-Hussein, died, Sir Samuel appointed his half-brother Haz Amin to the office, [120] despite the fact that he had no credentials, no spiritual training, and among five candidates had placed last in recent elections for the office. [121] His family's influence was the deciding factor. Since the seventeenth century, with rare exceptions, the office of Mufti had been almost always assigned to the Husseinis. The High Commissioner's reasoning in the matter is not to be wondered at. His political advisors argued that if the British authorities befriended one of their most redoubtable enemies it would show that Samuel's devotion to Zionism was separate from his duties as High Commissioner, and consequently, moderate Moslems would appreciate his fairness. The naiveté in such a well-meaning calculation meant that Samuel took a veritable tiger by the tail. Any concession on his part was viewed by Haz Amin and his followers as a weakness to be exploited, for Samuel was, after all, a Jew (however British) and the enemy. Samuel's futile balancing act may be followed to its final extremity: to establish an equipoise among the rival Moslem families in Jerusalem, Haz Amin's appointment as spiritual leader of the Moslems was countered by the civil power of the Nashashibi family which had won the mayoral office of Jerusalem.

When Kamal al-Husseini died on 21 March 1921, Samuel had assigned to the Husseini family a much larger pension than was allowed by previous Ottoman law. But favors and pecuniary grants, so large as to be considered bribery, could not assuage Arab resentment for the acts of a Jewish High Commissioner who consorted too openly with his co-religionists. The end result was an intensification of the internecine struggles among the great families, which in time would destroy the traditional leadership of the effendi. [122] The daring of the Husseini followers very soon eclipsed the caution of the Nashashibis. This had the effect of stimulating Jewish extremism. In May 1921 two Jewish factions in the Jaffa-Tel Aviv area fell into conflict, the one group composed of communists who had rallied to Lenin's Third International, the other Marxist Socialists who adhered to the philosophy of the moribund Second International. Strangely, a sectarian quarrel among Jewish socialists precipitated Arab demonstrations near an immigration depot in Jaffa. The spreading riots resulted in the deaths of thirteen Jews and the plundering of shops and homes. The fighting spread to nearby Tel Aviv and in another week erupted at Peta Tikva, site of the original Kibbutzim, established during the First Aliyah. Nearly defenseless, the Jews were eventually protected by British cavalry and airplanes.

The riots were directed by Arab terrorists, members of the Black Hand, who had sworn they would die for Haz Amin. Afterward, when an inquest had examined the facts, it was politic for the High Commissioner to draw the conclusion that an accelerating rate of Jewish immigration had been the root cause of the fighting. But here there was a problem of perception, clouded by propaganda and the unguarded remarks of prominent Jews. The American Zionist, Justice Brandeis, had declared that Palestine could accommodate one million Jews, an appalling specter for Moslems to contemplate. Weizmann, in a speech, called for an annual quota of at least 80,000. These numbers did not square with the facts. In the period between the end of the World War and May 1921, not more than 10,000 Jews had stepped ashore in Palestine (legal immigrants, that is). But to the inflamed minds of Moslem militants this was but the first wave of a veritable flood of unwanted Jews.

Sir Samuel played a dangerous game. In his private remarks, in order to win Arab trust, he said that the Jews could never expect to see a sovereign state established in Palestine. To keep the confidence of the Zionists, he confessed that his remarks were meant to deceive the Arabs until calm returned. While officially he would restrict Jewish immigration, he was not opposed to "irregular" (i.e., illegal) immigration.

For centuries such machinations had served the Paramount Power well in India, a plethora of small states, playing off one faction against another. But Palestine was a different matter. In the end, neither Jews nor Arabs could believe the High Commissioner, and eventually would hate him as much as they were coming to hate each other.

Samuel's "peculiar combination of Machiavellian tactics and high flow apostrophes" had their devious counterpart in Syria and Iraq. By the terms of the original agreement between Britain and the Hashemites, Feisal would have become king of Syria, and his older brother Abdulla, king of Iraq. With his ejection from Damascus, Feisal became an unemployed monarch. Since Abdulla had been slow in taking up his reign, the British remedied the situation by having Iraqi notables at Baghdad elect him the king of Iraq. But this had the effect of disinheriting Abdulla, even before he could arrange his coronation.

At the beginning of this crisis Colonial Secretary Winston Churchill had journeyed to Cairo in order to orchestrate these several steps in king making. Thereafter he went to Jerusalem and met with Sir Samuel, Lawrence of Arabia, and Abdulla. Churchill liked to say later that he created Transjordan in an afternoon. Actually, the deal was struck after a thirty-minute conversation. The Palestinian territory east of the Jordan River, an area about the size of the state of Pennsylvania, almost entirely a desert, would be separated from Palestine and Abdulla installed as Emir under British protection. [123] This latest creation, located on the eastern side of the river, was called Transjordan.

A balance of forces had been achieved: Ibn Saud's ambition to absorb Mesopotamia (i.e., Iraq), Kuwait, and the Hedjaz thwarted; the Hashemites awarded the greater part of Palestine ("Eretz Israel" to the Zionists); and the Jews given a promise, if only a tacit one, that the remainder of Palestine would serve them as a homeland. In 1924–25 the Saudis conquered Jedda, Medina, and Yanbo, compelling Sherif Hussein to abdicate in favor of his son, Ali. But the latter was soon driven into exile, taking refuge with his brother Feisal in Iraq, thereby leaving Mecca to the Saudis. On 20 May 1927 the British, by the Treaty of Jedda, recognized Ibn Saud as King of Hedjaz. Abdulla retained the title of Emir, the impotent puppet of the British. He would become king of Jordan in 1948, by treaty agreement with the British, recognized as such by the United Nations the next year.

Up to the mid-thirties the British imperialists could be confident, deceived by the mere appearance of success. From Iraq to Palestine to Arabia, they had managed and/or stabilized the rivalries of a dozen-or-so tribes (Arab and non-Arab), implanting the Ashkenazi Jews (tribal themselves in behavior) in the Arab midst. All that had been done required only an international sanction. By dividing Palestine, giving the bulk of it to the Hashemites, the British had created the possibility for another mandate. On 24 July 1922, the League of Nations endorsed this *fait accompli*, assigning the Mandate of Transjordania to Great Britain. Jews would not be allowed to settle there, the terms of the Balfour Declaration applying only to the small rump of Palestine that the British had kept for themselves and the Jews. [124] Naturally, the powerless Arabs considered this naked piracy and viewed the League of Nations as merely an instrument for facilitating British imperial policy. The Zionists were equally outraged by the partition of Palestine, since it constituted the larger part of the Promised Land that the British had promised them. The fundamental Jewish belief held that Eretz Israel had been given to Abraham and his posterity by God.

The zeal of the British imperialists in pursuit of oil and security for the Suez Canal is not more remarkable than the extravagant ambitions of the Zionists. Determined to possess and to dispose of a poor country with a large, poverty-stricken peasantry, fundamentally Moslem, they dreamed of the future as Herzl had dreamed: cities arising out of the arid landscape, possessing the attributes of modern civilization, railroads, dams and canals; the sterile desert alive with fruit and flowers, consequence of an immense irrigation system; the steep, stony and denuded mountainsides clothed in evergreen forests, as in antiquity; ports and harbors; a network of roadways to replace the ancient footpaths and trails.

The price to be paid for the realization of this vision escaped calculation. Louis Marshall, president of the American Jewish Committee, thought that a million dollars annually would be required. But Weizmann believed that it would be much more than that. Sir Samuel approved of modernizing Palestine, but not at British expense. Weizmann concurred, relying (as he said) on the contributions of American Jewry.

Curiously, while most American Jews, especially the well-to-do, were anti-Zionist and would remain so until World War II, many of them looked favorably upon what could be called a fabulous enterprise. Their deep pockets would become an essential part of a program to modernize the whole of the Mandate—even the daunting Negev desert—and ultimately, all would belong to the Jews and not at all to the Arabs who merely lived there.

The obsessive conviction that a modern Jewish state could be formed in a small impoverished country without natural resources to speak of, handicapped by a chronic water shortage; in the presence of a large and inert but nonetheless resentful Arab population, was not greater than the illusion entertained by those Zionists who believed that Palestine could be modernized without giving it a sovereign Jewish character. After a long material development, a heavy Jewish immigration, and a steady rise in the standard of living for both Arabs and Jews, the Mandate would fade away as self-government and a harmony of the two people, the two religions reconciled, appeared. This became a profound thought, even a doctrine, called bi-nationalism, of which the British generally approved and the Zionists in their majority opposed.

The possession of Eretz Israel had been the Zionist agenda from the beginning, the elimination of the indigenous Arab population the underlying thought. It was a seemingly irresolvable problem, the "hidden question," confessed a Jewish reporter in 1907. One might buy out the Palestinian peasants but, as a result of this, of what value would a landless Arab proletariat be to progressive Jews? [125] "We shall have to spirit the penniless population across the border," wrote the farseeing Herzl, "by procuring employment for it in the transit countries, while denying it any employment in our own country. Both the process of expropriation and the removal of the poor must be carried out discreetly and circumspectly." [126]

Almost a generation after Herzl's time the matter of world opinion still weighed heavily upon the Zionists as they reflected upon their future policy. "The world," predicted Weizmann, "would judge the Jewish State by what it shall do with the Arabs." [127]

In the summer of 1922 Weizmann toured the United States with the twofold purpose of winning converts for his version of Zionism and gaining contributions from American Jewry. He garnered two million dollars on this first visit. Henceforth American Jewry's ambivalence would be constant: ever ready to contribute money, steadfastly loyal to their co-religionists in Palestine, but always doubtful as to the validity of the Zionist idea.

With the establishment of the Palestine Mandate in 1922, Zionist collaboration with the British patron continued uncertainly for the next two years. British policy remained unchanged, though Lord Curzon had succeeded Balfour at the Foreign Office. The preparation of a document for the rule of Palestine, rather like a constitution octroi, developed much in the way that the Balfour Declaration had evolved earlier. An American Jew, Benjamin V. Cohen, requested the inclusion of a phrase in the preamble: "the historic right of the Jews to Palestine." To enshrine the future Jewish possession of Palestine in a single line was not to Curzon's taste. He preferred a more vague language. [128] On the other hand, the language of the Balfour Declaration, which affirmed the rights of non-Jews in Palestine, was repeated almost verbatim. Principles for a controlled Jewish immigration were agreed upon. Jewish self-government would be permitted through the establishment of an organization to be called the Palestine Zionist Executive, specifically empowered to advise and to cooperate with the Mandatory Power. The World Zionist Organization was designated as the Palestine Zionist Executive. And therefore, with the stroke of a pen, what had been heretofore no more than an extraordinarily important Jewish lobby became a Jewish shadow government in Palestine. [129] Affairs of state would be conducted in three languages: English, Arabic, and Hebrew. The Jews were permitted to fly their flag, the Star of David, implicitly their national standard and symbolizing their frequent demand to have a sovereign state in Palestine. The Palestinians were not permitted to have a flag—presumably because they were not a nation. They were merely, Golda Meir remarked later, "South Syrians."

It is of more than passing interest that a Palestinian Arab Executive was not envisioned. In the imperial mind, as much as in the Zionist mentality, backward Arabs were hardly equipped to cooperate with the Mandatory Power. To the contrary, they would be ruled, administered, improved by the care of a paternalistic government; and this was in fact the underlying ethos of the mandate system. In reality, the Mandatory power in Palestine would be for a short time a diarchy, achieved by Anglo-Zionist collaboration. The Zionist Executive, soon to be called the Jewish Agency, was defined as "a political body for the purpose of advising and cooperating with the Administration of Palestine . . . and, subject to the control of the Administration to assist and take part in the development of the country." [130]

Powerless, without friends or allies, the Palestinians found themselves maneuvered into a false position. To agree to some form of participation in the Mandatory Government was to acknowledge the Balfour Declaration, which assured the Jews of a homeland in their country, with the likelihood of a Jewish sovereign state to follow. To choose not to cooperate with the Mandatory Power was tantamount to allowing Palestine to go to the British and their surrogates by default. "Their logic," as has been noted, "excluded the possibility of effective political action." [131] Inevitably, such a vacuum was filled by another kind of action: demonstrations, protests, violence, and rampant civil disobedience culminating in Arab riots. But it was really civil revolt against the unwanted and arbitrary Mandatory Power. An Arab convention was convened in February 1921, calling for the establishment of a legislative assembly. Samuel's dilatory response was one of the several causes for the demonstrations that began in May of that year, turning into a prolonged civil tumult that continued into the autumn. In September, the High Commissioner promulgated a constitution that provided for an executive council (appointive) and a legislative council (partly elective). The Arabs denounced it as a halfway measure, designed to keep the plenitude of power in the hands of the High Commissioner and his coadjutors, the Zionists, who had already gained a high degree of independence through the establishment of the Zionist Executive. Whereupon Samuel chose to govern by decree.

Further efforts by the Palestinians to establish a legislative assembly based upon proportional representation alarmed the

Zionists. Predicting that it would result in a nullification of the Balfour Declaration, Weizmann argued against the idea. A liberal of the old school, he had no use for democratic practices, believing that in most cases it was "a sheer farce." "Whatever Assembly is created," he declared, "its Arab side will merely be a gathering of feudal effendis . . . they are too primitive . . . to understand what we are bringing them." [132] "Believe me, I know the Palestinian Arabs. If we give way now, we might as well pack up." The ". . . present Arab leaders," he characterized as "murders and thieves [who] want but one thing — to drive us into the Mediterranean." Weizmann's contumely was never more pronounced than when he declared, "We wish to spare the Arabs as much as we can of the sufferings which every backward race has gone through on the coming of another, more advanced nation . . . we must not be driven into the position where any Arab complaint is considered sufficient ground for impeding our work . . ." [133]

Futilely, the Palestinians protested, reminding the British government of the promises made in 1915: "Great Britain proposed to recognize and to support the independence of the Arabs." In response, the British cabinet issued a formal statement of policy, a White Paper, on 30 June 1922. Although signed by Colonial Secretary Winston Churchill, it was really Samuel's work, his argument being that the promises made to the Hashemite family applied to Syria and Iraq, not to Palestine. By establishing a mandate for Palestine, the League of Nations did not expect to see "the imposition of a Jewish nationality upon the inhabitants of Palestine as a whole." Rather, a "Jewish National Home" was to be thought of as only a cultural expression, "the further development of the existing Jewish community with the assistance of Jews in other parts of the world, in order that it may become a centre in which the Jewish people as a whole may take, on grounds of religion and race, an interest and pride." In other words, (should one read the lines of the White Paper in a liberal way), international Jewry in their great majority would remain assimilated to their various host countries around the world while spending plenteously on what might be called a cultural hobby, implanted in the midst of an outraged Moslem community. The concluding observation was compelling: "It is essential to know that it [i.e., Jewish immigration] is in Palestine as of right and not on sufferance." [134] Thus spake the imperial authority, which had a mandate from the League of Nations to decide the right and the wrong of any matter in Palestine.

In August an Arab delegation headed by Musa Kazim Pasha traveled to London in order to confront the Colonial Secretary. Churchill received them less than cordially, indicating that he would speak "man to man in a friendly way." There followed a lecture in the Churchillian manner: intimidating and moralizing in its measured tones, but the Arabs heard nothing new. The Jews had a historic right to be in Palestine, observed Churchill. He was puzzled that they could not understand that ever more Jews in Palestine would mean progress, development: electricity; irrigation systems; the denuded hills terraced and productive. The Arabs should look at the Jews' "thriving colonies" and attempt to emulate them. As for representative government, the main demand of the Arabs and the cause for their appearance in his chambers, he refused, pointing out the obvious: that would give them, as the majority, the means to stop Jewish immigration. "We do not intend you to be allowed to stop more from coming in. You must look at the facts." The facts were, of course, that the British had the power and the Palestinians had none.

Balfour's language had been more brutal than Churchill's. With regard to Palestinian opinion, he declared, "we do not propose even to go through the form of consulting the wishes of the present inhabitants of the country. . . . The four great powers are committed to Zionism and Zionism, be it right or wrong, good or bad, is rooted in age-long tradition, in present needs, in future hopes, of far profounder import than the desire and prejudices of the 700,000 Arabs who now inhabit that ancient land." [135]

The next year, however belatedly, as if to make amends, Samuel suggested that the Arabs might form an Arab Agency. The Arabs refused. [136] For what reason did they spurn what might have seemed a fair and reasonable compromise? The answer must be considered that any compromise offered by the Mandatory Power went to the advantage of that power and established still more firmly the proposition that Palestine was to be shared by both Arabs and Jews. Such a compromise really represented defeat for the Palestinians, and generation after generation they would see it this way. [137]

With Palestinian protests brushed aside, Weizmann, fortified by British approval, continued to work the corridors of power in Europe and America, promoting the idea of a Jewish state in Palestine. He sought the support of wealthy American Jews who, for humanitarian and religious reasons, were disposed to give plentifully to poor Jews living in Palestine, while remaining indifferent to the political aspects of the matter.

Large donations were required because, despite the British having formally limited Jewish immigration, increasing numbers of illegal entrants were being detected. By 1924, census figures revealed that there were 94, 945 Jews in Palestine. But they were still a distinct minority, living in the midst of 804,962 Moslems. [138] And while the Arab population in Palestine had risen considerably since the turn of the century, the number of Jews had scarcely returned to the high point reached in 1914 when so many were harried out of the land by the Turks.

NOTES

83 *The Legacy of Jewish Migration*, p. 70.

84 David Ben Gurion, *Israel. A Personal History* (New York and Tel Aviv, 1971), p. 40.

85 Palestine is derived from Herodotus' use of the name falastin, since he believed that the indigenous people living in the ancient land of Canaan were descendants of the Philistines.

86 Leon Poliakov, *The History of Anti-Semitism*, op. cit., p. 5.

87 A useful summary of these migrations is given by Aharon Cohen, *Israel and the Arab World* (New York, 1970), pp. 25-26.

88 Perhaps as many as 700,000 Jewish soldiers saw active service during the War. Cohen, Ibid, p. 129.

89 Fred J. Khouri, *The Arab-Israeli Dilemma*, Second Edition. (Syracuse University Press: New York, 1976), p. 8.

90 Ibid.

91 The oldest son, Ali, would succeed his father as Sherif.

92 Louis D. Brandeis, "The Jewish Problem," *The Curse of Bigness. Miscellaneous Papers of Louis D. Brandeis*, ed., Osmond K. Frankel (Port Washington, New York: 1965), pp. 209-229, passim.

93 Cohen, p. 123.

94 *Palestine Papers*, 1917-1922: *Seeds of Conflict*, Doreen Ingrams, ed. (London: 1972), pp. 31-32.

95 Cohen, p. 124.

96 Despite pressure from important Jewish Zionists such as Jacob Wise and Justice Brandeis, Wilson would not publish an American equivalent of the Balfour Declaration.

97 A revolution in Russia took that country out of the war before it was quite finished. Subsequently a Bolshevik take-over eliminated the possibility for the newly formed League of Nations to have any influence on Russian affairs; thereafter the Bolsheviks (renaming themselves Communists) restored the old Czarist empire, giving it an up-to-date remodeling and calling it a Union of Soviet Socialist Republics. By this title alone they embraced the most radical ideas advanced in the past two centuries: republicanism, socialism, and direct universal democracy through a system of popular councils (i.e. Soviets).

98 These were the Allied and Associated Powers who had fought and defeated

the Central Powers. A total of seventy delegates from 27 countries attended the peace conference.

99 Robert Silverberg. *If I forget Thee O Jerusalem: American Jews and the State of Israel* (New York, 1970), p. 89.

100 Frank E. Manuel, *The Realities of American-Palestine Relations*, op cit., p. 172.

101 Ibid., p. 172.

102 The territories that had been in dispute were Nejd, Quatif, and Jubail.

103 Cohen, p. 147.

104 Ibid., p. 138.

105 Ibid., 139.

106 Richard Meinertzhagen, *Middle East Diary*, 1917-1956 (London, 1959), p. 149.

107 Benjamin Netanyahu. *A Place Among the Nations*, op. cit., p. 56.

108 Netanyahu's chapter, "The Betrayed", is typical of these polemics.

109 Manuel, *The Realities of American-Palestine Relations*, p. 227.

110 Frank H. Epp, *Whose Land is Palestine?*, op. cit., p. 142.

111 Ibid, p. 140.

112 "Palestine will fall within the influence of England ... we could easily move a million Jews into Palestine within the next 50-60 years and England would have a very effective and strong barrier, and we would have a country..." Simha Flapan, *Zionism and the Palestinians* (London and New York, 1977), p. 21.

113 Cohen, pp. 154-55.

114 Ibid., p. 156.

115 Ibid., p. 157.

116 Cited by Moshe Ma'oz, *Syria and Israel: From War to Peacemaking* (Oxford: Clarenden Press, 1995), p. 2.

117 This reservation Feisal wrote in his own hand on the written agreement signed by himself and Weizman.

118 In the final document, Feisal substituted the word "Palestine" for "Jewish state."

119 Flapan, *Zionism and the Palestinians*, pp. 28-29.

120 To cultivate the Husseini faction, Sir Samuel had attached to the title Mufti, the prefix "Grand" and bestowed it on the current Mufti, Kamil-al Husseini, Haz Amin's half-brother.

121 Haz Amin's only claim to spirituality was based upon a pilgrimage to Mecca in 1913, allowing him to adopt the soubriquet Haz (i.e., Pilgrim), and to don a turban and grow a patriarchal beard.

122 Simha Flapan, *The Birth of Israel. Myths and Realities* (New York, 1987), p. 61.

123 Protection from the Arab tribes under Saudi leadership who were preparing to take Medina, Mecca, and the rest of the Hedjaz.

124 This much-reduced "Palestine" was approximately 10,000 square miles, about the size of the state of Maryland.

125 Yitzhak Epstein, "The Hidden Question," *Hashiloah*, 17, no. 97 (August 1907), trans., G. Svirsky, pp. 193-205, *passim, The Jew in the Modern World*, op. cit., p. 358.

126 Theodore Herzl, *Complete Diaries*, ed., Raphael Patai, trans., Harry Zohn (New York, 1960), I, p. 88.

127 Chaim Weizmann, *Trial and Error. The Autobiography of Chaim Weizmann* (New York, 1959), p. 462.

128 Silverberg, p. 118-19.

129 Ibid., p. 466.

130 Ibid.

131 David McDowall, *Palestine and Israel. The Uprising and Beyond* (Berkeley and Los Angeles, 1989), p. 21.

132 Simha Flapan, p. 70.

133 Ibid., p. 70-71.

134 Silverberg, p. 121.

135 Edward W. Said, *The Question of Palestine* (New York, 1979), pp. 16-17.

136 William R. Polk, *The United States and the Arab World*, 3rd ed. (Harvard University Press, 1975), p. 189.

137 If towards the end of the twentieth century the Palestinians would accept "peace" with Israel, which implied a co-existence of Jews and Arabs on the same holy land, it was the unspoken admission that they had failed to expel the unwanted Jews; because world Jewry and its allies were too strong, and the Arabs were too weak and too disunited to resist the Jewish incursion any longer.

138 74,094 Christians, Arab and Occidental, were living in Palestine in 1924.

CHAPTER FOUR

The Mandate

THE END OF ANGLO – ZIONIST COLLABORATION

fter 1919 none of the contenders in the Palestinian question got what they wanted. Feisal's ambition was easily extinguished by the British and French. The Zionists' desire for a Jewish state in Palestine was stillborn. The British imperial design failed to develop.

Unwittingly, the British participated actively in the erosion of their own hegemony, by reason of the mixed motives that had come to invest European imperialism generally at the beginning of the twentieth century: *viz.*, the atavistic impulse of the great powers to dominate others; the need to compete with imperial rivals; the obligation to find markets and resources for an industrial establishment, essential for maintaining Britain's relatively high standard of living; and finally, the moralizing middle-class ethos at the end of the Great War, which required the strong and fortunate to improve the lot of the poor and underprivileged of the world. This paternalism, present in international politics at the end of the nineteenth century ("the White Man's burden"), had played a significant role at the Paris Peace Conference, resulting in the formation of a League of Nations and the evolution thereafter of an experiment: the Mandate.

Behind the idea of the mandate, a paternalistic conception that required a great power to act toward its subject people much as a benevolent father would care for a son, lay a long practice in imperialism called the "protectorate." A number of these had been established in the nineteenth century, each a veiled domination, allowing the world at large to believe these were disinterested administrations; and the subject people encouraged to think that they were virtually free, because, generally speaking, so long as they remained quiet they were not abused but rather ignored by the occupying power. Beneficent neglect would be the best expression for such "protection" as the imperial power afforded its subject people.

Mandate practices reflected this ethic, but with a subtle difference. In the heyday of European imperialism it was presumed that a protectorate would last forever, because the empire would last just as long, providing its policies were progressive and just. By contrast, the mandate, a new protectorate, had an indeterminate life span depending upon the "maturity" of the subject people. Over time, it was supposed, the mandate would fade away as each enthralled people arrived at a point of self-government. [139] Not revolt, but "development," not revolution, but an orderly evolution, would lead in time to a sovereign independence for every people. (Incidentally, the Kurds, the Moluccans, the Palestinians, and a number of others are still waiting for independence.)

The fundamental policy advanced by the British in Palestine was a forcible conciliation of Jews and Arabs, a resolve that successive cabinets pursued up to 1936 before abandoning it. But the Zionists had a different agenda. After the riots of 1922 Weizmann had proposed transporting the approximate half-million Palestinians to Transjordan. (The vicissitudes of Middle East politics would result in this very thing in 1948). To the British imperialists Weizmann's idea had merit. After WWI the irreconcilable differences between Turks and Greeks had provoked great power intervention, finally producing an agreement between the Turkish and Greek governments for a massive and enforced relocation of the two populations along disputed borders. The Jewish-Arab problem was small by comparison. What Weizmann proposed would have cost an estimated one million pounds sterling (about two pounds a Palestinian head). But evidently the British did not care to incur public disapproval by moving people as though they were cattle. They preferred what was now being called "bi-nationalism." Palestinians (more frequently called "Arabs") and Jews could be encouraged to develop their separate cultures, all the while living together on the same territory.

There can be no doubt that most British politicos (both Labor and Conservative) wished to honor the pledge made to the Zionists as expressed in the Balfour Declaration—it was a matter of honor. To that extent, they favored the Jews over the Arabs. As if to give testimony to this, Lord Balfour journeyed to Jerusalem in April 1925 to officiate at the opening of the Hebrew University. In July of the same year, to placate the Arabs, the Zionist High Commissioner, Sir Samuel, was replaced by a more neutral individual, Field Marshall Plumer. But it is to be noted that in this case a military man was chosen to succeed a civilian, just as Sir Samuel had established a civil administration to replace General Allenby's original military establishment.

By 1924 there had been three distinct waves of Jewish immigration, almost all coming from Russia and Poland (the former Pale of the Settlement). These were pioneers (*chalutzim*) in the traditional mold: religiously conservative, ordinary men and women who wanted to make the desert bloom, to win the good life on the land that they believed was their rightful inheritance.

The character of the Fourth Aliyah was fundamentally different. Those immigrants who possessed $2,500 (a substantial amount for the time) would not be subject to the quota established for that year. Ordinary, poor Jews could enter Palestine up to a certain number, but well-to-do Jews beyond that number were given ingress.

The cause for the injection of a petty bourgeois capitalist class of Jews into what heretofore had been an agrarian and working-class migration was largely owed to American immigration policy. In 1924, the American Congress virtually closed the door to East European immigrants. In effect, the Ashkenazic Jews were shunted off to Palestine (not their first choice for a new home, it is to be suspected). And they were welcome, for it had been the Zionist policy to lure investors to Palestine, despite the trepidation expressed by its socialist leaders. These latest newcomers were of the type that had in their great numbers already transformed New York City. Ambitious, able, secular-minded, progressive, they possessed all those traits that would help to make Palestine a modern country in the next couple of generations.

While the earlier Jewish immigrants had spread out over the countryside rather diffusely, establishing small self-sufficient colonies *(kibbutzim)*, the newest arrivals preferred to settle into towns, which soon began to swell enough to deserve to be called cities. Tel Aviv, for example, established on the Mediterranean coast near Jaffa in 1909, counted a hundred people in 1917. In the next two decades it would become a thriving metropolis. By 1925 three-quarters of the Jewish population lived in Palestine's towns and cities. The pronounced secularism of the newest immigrants was noted in the Peel Report of 1936. [140]

As a percentage of the Jewish population the rural settlements constituted an ever-diminishing number. Between 1909 and 1972, two hundred and thirty kibbutz settlements were established in Palestine. They were never large, on average "about 400 in population." [141] They reached a high point in terms of percentage of the population in the 1930s (about 6 percent), then dropped back to 3.6 percent by 1970. Overall, the kibbutz movement became a failed attempt to make small-scale collectivist farms a model for the future. But what the Palestinians, or more exactly, the effendi, watched with apprehension was the development of Jewish urban life: Western culture in all its manifestation. Dislike for a way of life so unlike their own was naturally transferred to the Jews, who were seen as the bearers of this alien culture. There was no doubt that the West they saw emerging in Palestine was due to the collaboration of the Mandatory Power and the World Zionist Organization (in Palestine called the Jewish Agency after 1929).

There were renewed riots in 1929, sparked at what might have seemed to be the most appropriate place: Temple Mount in Jerusalem, where the sacred structures of two religions were mingled. On the foundations of the ruined Second Temple, the Moslems had raised an impressive monument, the Mosque of Omar, commonly called the Dome of the Rock. [142] Adjacent to the mosque was a remnant of the ancient city wall, believed by the Jews to be part of the surviving wall of the Second Temple. Daily, almost hourly, they came to this precious artifact to pray in a peculiar fashion, causing the Moslems to call it with derision the "wailing wall." However, the Arabs considered the wall holy too. They called it *al-Buraq*, this being the name of Mohammed's horse, which had been tethered there during the Prophet's miraculous ascent to Heaven for an overnight stay.

Traditional Judaism is a religion of many exotic, even impenetrable, rituals, mysteries, customs and taboos. Among these was the practice of separating the sexes during worship. For that purpose a linen screen had been erected before the wall to keep female and male worshippers apart. After several disturbances in 1928, the High Commissioner ordered the screen removed; protests from the Jews caused it to be replaced. The Grand Mufti believed that this represented another step by the Jews to take possession of Temple Mount so as to rebuild their temple. The petition of the Arabs to remove the screen again was granted. But then, under pressure from the Jews, the High Commissioner ordered it replaced once more.

The affair of the screen continued into August of 1929. On the fifteenth of that month, the holy day of Tisheh B'av, which memorializes the destruction of the Second Temple, a number of Jews belonging to Jabotinsky's Revisionist Party, placed a Zionist flag on the Wailing Wall. This act, sacrilegious in the eyes of the Moslems, caused thousands of protestors, urged on by the Grand Mufti, to storm Temple Mount and pull down the flag. Surprisingly, there were no deaths on this occasion, but the next day a Jewish youth was stabbed to death. This provoked a Jewish riot. On 23 August a general Arab uprising immeasurably enlarged the riots.

The British force was not large enough to keep order. Jabotinsky's legion, now called *Haganah* (The Defense), established a virtual police authority in the Jewish quarter of the city. A general rampage followed. In not many days, every large city and town in Palestine became swept up in a combination of enthusiasm, rage and hate.

The Arab insurrection of 1929, like the riots of 1921, subsided in a few weeks. In the aftermath of this latest contretemps, the British cabinet ordered an inquest, carried out under the direction of Sir Walter Shaw. The Shaw Commission learned what had been known since at least 1922: the Palestinians wanted the Jews out of the country and they wanted to be independent. Above all, they wanted an end to Jewish immigration.

Evenhanded in its judgments, the Shaw commission concluded that the Arabs had caused the riots, but that the Jews were guilty of provocative acts. Steps were subsequently taken to curtail Jewish immigration to Palestine. Jewish protests and strikes followed. World Jewry professed its sense of outrage, especially American Jewry, whose leaders set up a Palestine Emergency Fund. Over two million dollars was collected in a few months' time.

The report of the League of Nations Mandates Commission, following an investigation of the Palestinian crisis, was exceptionally harsh, condemning the Mandatory Power for failing to provide its subjects with adequate security. In response, the British cabinet ordered another study, directed by Sir John Hope-Simpson. His conclusions were not essentially different from earlier ones. However, this latest report offered some revelations regarding land tenure in Palestine. It was generally known that many of the Palestinian peasants were abjectly poor, and that much of the arable land belonged to a few wealthy Palestinians and/or absentee landlords. The statistics revealed by the Simpson commission were stark indeed. Almost 30 percent of rural farmers owned no land; 40 percent of the holdings were so small that no more than a subsistence level of life was possible.

Obscurely, but nonetheless profoundly, land tenure had a direct bearing on urban development and periodic social disturbances. The exploitation of the peasants by absentee landowners, not to speak of a soaring Arab birth rate, continued to propel the surplus of the desperate part of the population into the towns and cities where it became a proletariat, as easily exploited there as before in the countryside. In 1917 Palestine had been an entirely rural society, without a city or a town of importance. By 1948 more than half the population lived in an urban milieu. "Vast shanty towns" emerged on the outskirts of the bigger towns like Haifa and Jaffa. "Thousands of unskilled workers in Jaffa cannot afford a house to sleep," reported a British investigator. "They sleep in the open. The rent of a decent house in Jaffa amounts to about two thirds of the wages of an unskilled worker. Thousands live in tin huts without the most elementary accommodations and without any water supply except what they can carry in small jars from a far distance." [143]

The explanation for these changing social conditions given by the Arabs was the coming of the Jews with their capital and their Western way of doing things. Especially blamable were the land purchases the Jews made. If this was true, it was only partly true. There also came with the introduction of Western science, technology, and management skills, a certain mystique, which the French historian Alexandre de Tocqueville had called with respect to the French Revolution, "increasing expectations": a revolutionary spirit that animated the masses, heretofore sedentary and passive. It was not that the rural Palestinians were any more used and abused than in earlier times; rather, it was the mood in the air, the belief that a better life was possible in town. Wages in Palestine were three to four times higher than in the neighboring Arab countries, but the cost of living was proportionately higher, also. Competition for work was greater too. The towns, swollen by newcomers, both immigrant Jews and migratory Palestinians, could not accommodate such rapid demographic changes. The failed promise of a better life resulted in sullen outrage and hatred for those who seemed to be responsible for it.

On 21 October 1930 another White Paper issued from the British cabinet. This policy statement was the work of a new colonial secretary, the noted socialist Sidney Webb (now Lord Passfield). To alleviate the plight of the Arab peasants, land purchase by the Jews would be curtailed for the indefinite future. Jewish immigration would be halted also, at least until the worst of Arab unemployment had been eliminated.

The Zionists were incensed by what they considered a breach of the promise made to them in 1919. Under pressure from public opinion, and facing strong opposition from the House of Commons, the cabinet adopted a temporizing attitude, in effect repudiating the White Paper's pro-Arab stance. The Prime Minister, Ramsay MacDonald, sent a letter to the Zionists, assuring them that the restrictions on Jewish immigration and land purchase would be withdrawn. To win public approval for his beleaguered cabinet the Prime Minister had the letter published in *The Times*.

For the Arab, MacDonald's missive was a "Black Letter," another broken promise from perfidious Albion. For the Zionists, who by now required no more from the British government than the posture of neutrality, the MacDonald letter was a victory. The prolonged violence had given the Zionists the occasion, as well as the excuse, to improve their defenses. A militia of sorts, the Haganah, had been created earlier. The search overseas for weapons began. Freer than before, the Zionists pursued with renewed vigor their original goals: fundraising in the west in order to buy land from the destitute peasants in Palestine, and to bring in more Jewish settlers.

The British response to this was predictable. Reluctant to alienate the Arabs any more than they had already, unwilling to irritate the Jews again, the MacDonald cabinet reverted to the failed policy of 1921, *viz.*, giving a little to the Arabs, then taking it away; promising the Jews more, then not delivering on the same promises. To implement this impossible mandate, they replaced Field Marshall Plumber with a new High Commissioner, Sir Arthur Wauchope, on 14 July 1931.

The effendi began to organize politically at this point. Haz Amin convened a world Islamic conference, ostensibly to confront the World Zionist Organization, in practical terms, to rally Moslem opinion in favor of the Palestinians. Beginning in 1932, Palestinian political parties were formed, although the bases for effective political action were absent in a country ruled by the distant government at London. Two parties emerged. One, the National Defense Party under the influence of the Nashashibi family, which had from the beginning advocated a conciliatory policy toward the Mandatory Power, favored an accommodation of some sort with both the British government and the Zionists. In brief, binationalism and a rapprochement of Jews and Arabs, they believed, would be achieved by negotiation.

In March 1935 the Husseini family, ardent naturalists, organized a party called the Palestinian Arab Party. Intransigent, they rejected negotiations of any kind. By this time, the progress and seeming triumph of various national socialist parties in Europe inspired the Husseinis. A "youth troop" was formed, called the "Nazi Scouts." Terror was, if not the order of the day, fast becoming a fact of Palestinian life.

Arab terrorism had commenced as early as 1922, and had been given a rudimentary organization by 1925 with the establishment of what were called Qassimite cells. The inspiration for this was owed to a Syrian zealot, Izz e-Din al-Qassam, a religious sheikh of al-Azhar University. During the guerrilla warfare that accompanied Feisal's ejection from Syria, Qassam had been captured by the French and sentenced to death. He escaped into Palestine and turned his wrath against the British, who in his eyes were as evil as the French.

The Jews, as the clients of the Mandatory Power, could not be immune to the hate and fury of Qassam's followers. In his sermons, inspired and passionate, the sheikh was heard by the poor, the homeless, the rootless, and the restless Arabs who had come out of the poverty of rural Palestine only to discover an even more hopeless existence in the urban slums. [144] The radical tenor of Qassam's teaching and preaching were classically socialist, inveighing against the rich (both Jew and Arab), and condemning the colonial powers (both French and British, the latter now joined, as it appeared, by a new colonial power, the World Zionist Organization).

As the secretary of the Young Men's Moslem Association, Qassam came into close contact with impressionable young people. Their youthful idealism, that sense of justice that smolders in the breasts of those who are innocent and ignorant, was easy for him to ignite. How indeed do the weak, however just and blameless they may be, resist the strength of those who are powerful and, above all, unjust? By terrorizing them, by relying on God's justice when man's justice cannot be had; by hurting their tormentors, killing their wives and children, destroying their property, ruining their businesses and their livelihoods, making them regret that they came to Palestine—and eventually, would not the intruders go away?

In November 1935 the British discovered weapons being smuggled into Palestine and concluded that they were intended for the Jews. To Qassam this meant that time was critical. If the Jews should find the means to arm themselves they would never be driven from the country. Consequently, with a handful of followers he commenced guerrilla activities in the high country of Samaria. The adventure was as brief as it was tragic. They killed a Jewish policeman in Gilboa and thereafter were hunted down by British forces. Five were captured, three killed, among these Qassam himself.

In death Qassam became greater than he had been in life. Transformed into a folk hero, he became a Robin Hood or a Jesse James who had stood up against the rich and powerful. As was the case with the Vietcong, whose strength and durability had depended on the protection and affection of the peasants, the Qassamites relied on the loyalty of the Palestinian country people. Like the many brigands who had rallied to Garibaldi during Italy's national movement for the liberation of the country from the Austrian oppressor, the Qassamites were a mixed cohort, made up of selfless nationalists and the dregs of society, the latter rootless and purposeless men who lived only for action. Criminal elements became inextricably joined with patriotism for no other reason than to drive out the hated foreigners.

The Arab uprising of 1936 had these stygian origins. But the overt cause for a rebellion, which lasted from 1936 until the outbreak of World War II, was socioeconomic in character and operated very largely in an urban atmosphere.

JEWISH LABOR

It is not surprising that a utopian form of Zionism emerged in central Europe at the end of the nineteenth century. Once formed, however, it never seduced world Jewry to any extent. When finally, in the 1940s, emancipated Jews—the majority of these American Jews—evinced an approval of Zionism, they were merely acknowledging a *fait accompli*, i.e., the establishment of a Jewish state, while still doubting its essential validity. [145]

The driving force behind political (or secular) Zionism had been twofold: opposition to the assimilation of Jews in an overwhelming Gentile society; and rejection of the traditional authority of the rabbis who, from time out of mind, had enjoined the Jewish exiles to wait in all purity and patience for redemption when the Messiah would appear and deliver them from the yoke of the Gentiles.

The alternative to this otherworldly message was a secular Zionism, which appealed to Reformed Jews, as they were called in the Western countries. The latter had for long defied their rabbis (by practice more than overt disobedience): choosing sometimes to marry Gentiles, not observing the Sabbath, going to synagogue infrequently, doubting the story of the Messiah, indifferent to kosher dietary rules. Assimilation for them meant their absorption in the host country until finally their Jewishness meant little more than a kindred fellowship. To them the ancient doctrines of Redemption became merely a fantasy.

Paradoxically, political Zionism offered another fantasy, another form of Redemption for the Jewish Diaspora: there could be an escape from persecution, eminently of this world, through a flight to Palestine.

Utopian ideas were very old by the nineteenth century. All the thinkers of this genre, from Plato to Thomas More, to Karl Marx, had offered images of a perfect society. Plato imagined a state ruled by enlightened philosophers. Thomas More wrote a book about a real *Utopia* (literally, "no place"), the title of his work serving thereafter as a rubric for all these ideas about what the good society should be.

Utopian writers in the early nineteenth century conceived of collectivist societies that would control a rampant individualism, abolish private property, create conditions of economic equality; and therefore, it was thought, people in equal possession of goods and services would have nothing to fight over. Karl Marx, building on this long tradition, supposed that after the last class war was over (and there had been many in his opinion), society would become so radically altered that human nature itself would change (for the better). The individual, deprived of the need to compete with others for his livelihood, would become a good citizen, law abiding and content. As a consequence, all forms of social coercion would disappear; even the state apparatus would vanish ("wither away"). In the last stages of this social decomposition, an inspired minority, conscious champions of the degraded underclass, would destroy the last vestiges of capitalism. Establishing themselves as "the dictatorship of the proletariat," they would bring into being a communist society. Under this necessarily ruthless regime, all members of society, though unequal in talents and energies, would become equal in all other ways through the possibility of a universal generosity; thus the famous slogan, "From each according to his abilities, to each according to his needs."

The Marxist vision of a redeemed and purified mankind has been characterized more than once as a secular religion, as persuasive in its teleological dimensions as seventeenth-century Puritanism. [146] Marxist believers, as zealous as fundamentalist Christians, needed only to know how to realize heaven on earth. However, the prophet Marx had never told his followers precisely how all this would take place. After he died there were endless quarrels over this seemingly unanswerable question. One of the chiefs of these "second-generation Marxists," the Russian Social Democrat, Lenin, formed a small revolutionary clique, the Bolshevik Party, which proposed a way to achieve salvation. To his way of thinking, a small, dedicated revolutionary elite would seize power and declare itself the "dictatorship of the proletariat." It was the notion of violent populism in its most extreme form, and most appropriate that it should appear in an oppressive state like Czarist Russia.

The opportunity for the Bolsheviks to put their ideas into practice came toward the close of the First World War when the Czarist regime had collapsed in revolutionary turmoil, at the same time that the Russian army was retreating before the oncoming Germans. Seizing power by force (a categorical imperative for the Bolsheviks), Lenin and his colleagues established a dictatorship in the emergency. Thereafter, the capitalist system, still rudimentary in Russia, was dismantled, the middle class for all practical purposes liquidated. A highly centralized government was established, along with a command economy (the famous *Gosplan*). In 1919 the Bolsheviks changed the name of their party to Communist. As against the bourgeois-dominated Second International, they brought into being a true proletarian Third International, dedicated to unleashing a worldwide revolution. Their goal was to achieve as quickly as possible the communist utopia of which Marx had written; first in Russia, then in the rest of the world, as fast as the proletariat in every country could rise and cast off the bonds of their oppressors.

As it turned out, the effort to realize the proletarian dream in backward Russia required means other than those Marx had imagined. To Marx, guided by what he believed were the natural laws of history, the industrial revolution had facilitated the growth of a greedy, exploitative class (bourgeois), and an ever-growing and desperate working class (proletariat). He supposed the latter would eventually rebel and destroy the class that tormented them. But in Russia there had not been an industrial revolution, nor was there a middle class worthy of the name (in Marxist terms, at least). About 80 percent of the population were peasants, an illiterate, conservative, land-hungry mass of people who demanded little and expected less. As for a proletariat, a large and angry working class, which history required as the violent instrument necessary for those changes that Marx had foretold, such a class was not in place, did not in fact exist.

Labor Zionists, many of them having matured in this cauldron of violent actions and radical ideas, brought the Marxist "theology" to Palestine with them. They brought with them also the intestine quarrels that embroiled the several Jewish labor organizations.

Between the first and third Aliyahs the philosophical bases of Jewish labor changed profoundly. The original Jewish settlers had been innocent pioneers in the classic sense of the term, relying on individualism and self-help, believing in an ennobling kind of labor that would only be degraded by accepting a substitute in hired Arab help. They had not thought of modernizing the country, "building it up," as was so often said after 1919, but rather wanting to absorb themselves in the soil, which allowed for an almost mystical identification of themselves with the land, Eretz Israel. Just then, the indigenous Arabs did not seem to them to be an obstacle to this desire (save for those occasions when wandering Bedouins threatened their lives and property).

The Second Aliyah brought a different kind of immigrant to Palestine, imbued with the ideals of the Social Democratic movement in Europe. These migrants looked upon capitalism as evil, colonialism as a blight on mankind, the exploitation of man by man as immoral. Bringing into Palestine these new ideas, they were instrumental in setting aside the old ones. The ethos of a collectivist rural labor became supplanted for the most part by that of collectivist proletarian ideals.

David Ben Gurion typified this ideological transformation in the vicissitudes of his life and career. Destined to be the George Washington of Israel, he came into prominence out of obscurity as a young pioneer before the Great War, thereafter as a labor leader whose dogmatic activism finally eclipsed the measured pragmatism of his rival, Chaim Weizmann. An authoritarian by disposition, impatient idealist, Ben Gurion could not be a democrat in practice. An admirer of Lenin, tied to the Marxist doctrine of class warfare, he believed that only an enlightened elite could realize the Zionist dream. The dream was as fanciful as Karl Marx's vision: A despairing proletariat would arise eventually, sweeping the greedy bourgeois class aside. Like Lenin, also, Ben Gurion believed that historical process is not automatic, operating according to natural laws, but must be pressed forward by people who are rather like social heroes, willing to throw themselves into the breach so as to realize their historic purpose. "We may regard as important," he wrote, "the moral strength inhering in Communism, in the dictatorship of the idea that subjects all life to it."

The extreme socialists (Russian Communists being the most virulent of that species of reformers), envisioned a classless and stateless world society composed of equals. Similarly, Ben Gurion pictured the end for the Jewish Diaspora to be the recovery of Eretz Israel and the establishment of a Jewish state, one embracing a society composed of working people. Science, industry, capital investment, all those progressive features of the modern West to which the Jewish Diaspora had made significant contributions (and taken a profit along the way), held little interest for him until he reached his middle years. His personal view mirrored that of his party, *Ahdut Ha-avoda*, as stated in 1921: "to shape the life of the Hebrew nation in Eretz Israel as a coming of workers, free and equal, that lives by its own toil, controls its possessions and organizes it labor, its economy and its culture as it sees fit." He strove, he declared, for the establishment in Palestine of "a working class nation." [147]

Russian socialism came to Palestine with several faces. *Hitahdu* (short for *Hitadut Ha-Poel Ha-Tzair*) had been organized in Russia originally, representing a union of diverse socialists who embraced a bewildering variety of ideas: liberal democracy, populism, social revolutionarism, etc. Up to 1910, it is thought, ideology was less important to them than purpose. These immigrants wanted merely to find work as wage earners in the approximately twenty

Jewish colonies that had been established in Palestine by that time. Resentful toward Arab workers who took work that they deemed to be rightfully theirs, they added a further draft to that program Ben Gurion had already adopted himself: No Jew should employ an Arab. Every Jew should do all that he could himself, and if hiring was needed, employ a Jew. Hebrew should be the mediating language for all the immigrants, of whatever national extraction. Jewish labor leaders viewed themselves as the vanguard that must prepare the way for the next wave of immigrants.

There were enough elements in Zionism matching those in Bolshevism (communism after 1919) to provoke serious reflection as to what this meant. Winston Churchill may be considered to have been typical of a small coterie in Britain: social conservatives who feared Bolshevism while admiring Zionism. His fascination with Zionism and communism bordered on an obsession. He perceived the two movements as being antithetical: the one noble, the other evil. Zionism was composed of good Jews, constructive builders; Bolshevism was composed of bad Jews, destroyers of institutions and even society itself. The fact that Bolshevism (i.e., communism) had been fathered by a middle-class Russian, Vladimir Ilyanov (better known as Lenin), who was no more a Jew than was Churchill, did not seem to matter. There were enough prominent Jews in leadership positions within the Third International to justify (in Churchill's eyes at least) the conclusion that this was a Jewish conspiracy directed against mankind: "In the Jewish race," he wrote, evil and goodness had reached a higher level than in any other people. The Jews had produced an ethical tradition "incomparably the most precious possession of mankind, worth in fact the fruit of all other wisdom and learning put together." On the other hand, the Jews were responsible for unleashing Bolshevism on the world, a force "as malevolent as Christianity was benevolent . . . it would almost seem," he wrote, "as if the gospel of Christ and the gospel of Antichrist were destined to originate among the same people; and that this mystic and mysterious race had been chosen for the supreme manifestations, both of the divine and the diabolical." International communism, a "sinister confederation," had resulted, he believed, from the lamentable condition of years of persecution and alienation that had been the fate of the Jewish Diaspora. "Most, if not all of them, have forsaken the faith of their forefathers, and divorced from their minds all spiritual hopes of the next world." Lost souls, they engaged in a "world-wide conspiracy for the overthrow of civilization and for the reconstitution of society on the basis of arrested development, of envious malevolence, and impossible equality..." [148]

After the World War, Lenin's notorious twenty-one conditions, imposed upon the members of the Second International, not only had the effect of sundering the unity of international Social Democracy, but driving a number of socialists out of the Marxist fold entirely. In Palestine these defectors were known as "toilers" (*Trudoviki*), tending strongly to embrace Jewish nationalism. In 1920 various "youth groups" *(Tzeire Zion)* joined with Ha-Poel Ha-Tzair to form what was called a "world union," operating within the framework of the World Zionist Organization. Their goal was to take control of the organization and thereby establish policies for General Zionism appropriate for their proletarian agenda.

For those Zionist leaders who presumed to speak for world Jewry, the future form and content of the Jewish homeland could not be clearly discerned. To say, as the most extreme did, that it would become a sovereign state, was merely to utter an abstraction. The socialists among them simply conceived of a collectivist society. Since the Jewish Agency was at most a shadow government; since a specific territory within Palestine was not assigned to them; since self-government was not (and would not be for many years hence) constitutionally organized, the Jewish Labor Federation (Histadrut) gave a semblance of community for a Jewish population that was dispersed over the Mandate. It was more diverse than one might imagine, ranging from Orthodox Jews who still lived, in mental terms, in the Middle Ages, to secular Jews who were as modern in their outlook as tomorrow.

Established formally in December 1920, the Histadrut represented an unspoken union of socialist and nationalist Zionists. In the Zionist context, "worker" became an almost pejorative term. A farmer, a schoolteacher, an artisan, a locomotive engineer, a day laborer, all qualified as workers. Any Jew who could claim worker credentials might join Histadrut. More than merely members, they were shareholders. Histadrut, by its rapid evolution during the 1920s, tended to make itself a substitute for capitalism. It was rather like a joint stock company and a company store at the same time. Under the direction of a few men, Ben Gurion, soon dominant, Histadrut was constituted as *hevrat ovdim* (workers' commonwealth), extending its supervision over much of Jewish life: vocational training, medical care, land sales, a system of missions abroad to gain new immigrants and money from the Diaspora. Not unlike Mussolini's fascist experiment in syndicalism at the same time, a hierarchy of crafts and shop unions gave the appearance of popular participation within the framework of a caring dictatorship. Finally, almost the whole of the Jewish economy in Palestine was to a large degree regulated by Histadrut. In practice, Histadrut was regulated by a few ambitious and willful men (all Zionists). It became, in miniature and in reality, what the Stalinist regime was in much larger proportions, but only theoretically so: a community of workers who served the larger cause of the nation; representing a new experiment in the world, state socialism. Aware of the Histadrut's uniqueness, Ben Gurion called it "a covenant of builders of a homeland, founders of a state, renewers of a nation, builders of an economy, creators of culture, reformers of a society." [149]

Histadrut was really a revolutionary engine, its inner council, the so-called Workers' Commonwealth (*hevrat ovdim*), a permanent revolutionary party, in its character not different from the permanent revolutionary organizations that would appear in the Third World over the succeeding decades; as for example, in Mexico the Permanent Revolutionary Party, the Communist Party in the Soviet Union, Fidel Castro's seemingly indestructible Communist Party in Cuba; later on the Permanent Revolutionary Party in Iraq under Saddam Hussein and his colleagues.

Much has been written about Ben Gurion's praxis, in the sense that he was adept at reconciling his almost daily self-contradictions. But this is only to say he was an above average Machiavellian operator. The essence of the superior politician is the capacity to speak out of both sides of the mouth while maintaining a single-minded view of his ultimate objective. The Jesuit expression, casuistry, also comes to mind. Ben Gurion wished to eliminate capitalism and found the social state; he wanted to live in harmony with the Palestinian Arabs, but he wanted to expel them from Eretz Israel entirely; he believed in democracy, but he preferred to govern through an unfettered and authoritarian elite; he wanted to establish a proletarian commonwealth, in effect a classless society, yet he wanted to introduce into Palestine a modern society based on Western middle-class capitalist practices.

Since some of these contradictions, and sometimes all of them, troubled many Jews, Ben Gurion seemed to be the indispensable leader, daily explaining away the ironies and contradictions in the faith called Zionism. Put more briefly, Ben Gurion struggled with two dialectical forces that circumstances had imposed on him: his early devotion to secular Zionism, which allowed him to believe without qualification that Eretz Israel belonged to world Jewry and to none others, and his uncritical acceptance later in life of the Marxist myth that the working class would inherit the world. The bloodsuckers, privileged and predatory money classes, would go under. In its Zionist context this meant that the good Jews would inherit the land that was rightfully theirs, and had once been promised to their ancient ancestors and their posterity by God.

Of the several labor organizations making up Histadrut, *Ahdut Ha-avohda* was the most influential, chiefly because its leaders, such as David Ben Gurion, were beginning to give up their antipathy toward capitalism and (in their view) its iniquitous byproduct: middle-class individualism and greed. The extreme Marxist doctrine, that nationalism was a spent force in a world giving way to a universal brotherhood, was also being abandoned. "Truth to tell," declared Ben Gurion in 1932, "the workers do not deny that private enterprise can be a factor in Zionism. Eretz Israel must serve as a refuge for all sectors and classes of the nation, capitalists as much as those without means." [150]

Throughout the 1920s the issue that burned at the vitals of the Jewish labor leaders was Arab labor: how to use it while keeping Jewish and Arab cultures separate. The abundance of cheap Arab labor arriving from rural Palestine continually tempted Jewish employers, whether managers of the kibbutzim, Jewish entrepreneurs raising citrus fruit, or building contractors. Of the several labor factions, Hapoel Hatzair was most vociferous in opposing joint trade unions, that is to say, an integration of Jewish and Arab labor institutions. The bi-nationalists, on the other hand, favored labor integration as one of several necessary steps toward achieving the more general social amalgamation of the two cultures.

Whether Ben Gurion would over time have opted for complete segregation of the two people in the Jewish state of his imagination (apartheid, so to speak) cannot be guessed at, because in his own mind he did not know how to resolve the problem that had plagued the Jewish Diaspora: how to keep the purity of their own kind while at the same time accepting integration with the Arab majority. In Eretz Israel Jews would remain for an indefinite period of time a small minority, finding themselves in another host country, still unable to integrate themselves with the Arab stranger for all the reasons that Zionists had rejected assimilation in the West. Ben Gurion took the middle ground. He foresaw, admittedly vaguely, the creation of a sort of joint national trade union organization, made up of two autonomous sections (Arab and Jewish), governed by a Central Committee composed of delegates drawn from the several unions on the basis of proportional representation. This was an idea complex enough, and unworkable as well, to assure its eventual defeat. The debate for all practical purposes came to an end on 27 May 1929 when the two largest of the Jewish unions, Ha-Poel Ha-Tzair and Ahdut Ha-avohda, merged to become a labor party, *Mapai*, its slogan "100 percent Jewish labor."

This denouement occurred in the unsettling atmosphere of riots sweeping over Palestine. While the riots effectively destroyed any tendency toward social integration of the two people on the basis of labor, they were instrumental in creating a de facto social segregation. Jewish minorities in some cities, notably Gaza, Hebron, and Nablus, fled and would not dare to return for many years. In the "mixed towns," such as Haifa, Tiberius, and Safed, the members of the two communities began to establish what might be called a natural segregation, each moving out of the other's neighborhoods. So many Jews moved from Jaffa to nearby Tel Aviv that the former became a completely Arab town.

The failure of the Zionist labor leaders to establish integrated labor unions really reflected the more general pattern of Palestinian society. By 1930 the British policy of merging the two cultures seemed to be a dead letter. However, this was all to the purpose of the Zionists, who dominated the Jewish labor movement as they had dominated the Jewish Agency from the beginning.

However pragmatic in his day-to-day assessment of things, Ben Gurion's outlook was constant: an immutable substructure of faith in the eventual Jewish preeminence in Palestine. It did not matter that Arabs outnumbered Jews three to one, or that the Mandatory Power was many times more powerful than that of the Jews and Arabs combined. To him, as to most Zionists, both the British and the Arabs were interlopers, occupying land that had always been Jewish and always would be. "The present residents of the land [the Arabs]," Ben Gurion wrote in 1929, "alone do not possess the right of ownership and rule over the land." The right of the Jews to Eretz Israel "emanates from the unbroken connection of the Hebrew nation with its historical homeland, from the right of the Jewish people to independence and national revival in equal measure to that enjoyed by all peoples, from the situation of the Jewish in exile as a minority deprived of a territorial base and dependent on the will of others, from the emigration needs of millions of Jews, from the depopulated state of Eretz Israel . . ." [151]

Like anyone else, Ben Gurion's attitudes were formed by his experiences. As a young and idealistic Jewish immigrant, he had seen firsthand the hard life of the Jewish colonist, perceived the immigrant's almost religious devotion to the soil, and recognized the great dangers Jews faced in the Moslem world. The occasional murders hardened him. "Jews being murdered," he wrote bitterly, "just because they were Jews." [152]

His feeling toward the Arabs was not an implacable hatred, probably not hatred at all; rather, it was a fear grounded in his youthful experience. His abundant speeches, and especially his table talk, reveal beyond any doubt that he was aware that the Jewish claims to Palestine on religious grounds were specious. The land belonged to Arabs in fee simple, but the Jews wanted it. With Britain's help, he believed, the Zionists could take it.

To Ben Gurion cohabitation of Jews and Arabs in Palestine was not possible, except that the Jews should became the majority. From the time of the riots in 1921 he was not deceived as to the future. They faced more than terror from the Arabs, he told his colleagues, but war, "a national war . . . an active resistance by the Palestinians to what they regard as a usurpation of their homeland by the Jews—that's why they fight."

By the early thirties Ben Gurion was sure that the Arabs could not eject the Jews from Palestine. In the long run, the Zionists, entrenched in Palestine and supported by Great Britain, would win out. For the Arabs, he declared, it was "a bit late" because "we already constitute a force in this country which it will not be easy to liquidate. For us it is too soon, because we are not yet strong enough to face this struggle alone. To a large extent the continuation of our efforts depends on England." [153]

That the Jews would win in the long run, and the Arabs lose, was understood from the beginning. A French scholar, Sylvain Levi, speaking before the Supreme War Council in 1919, warned that Palestine was "a small and poor land with a population of 600,000 and the Jews, having a higher standard of living, would tend to dispossess them." [154] But there was more to it than this. It was the case of an advanced culture descending upon a less developed one, the sophistication of urban Jews who had been reared in—and, too often forgotten, contributed to the development of—a competitive environment: in a few words, a particular kind of predation as against a certain kind of innocence.

The harrying of the Arabs from Israel could therefore never be accomplished by a blatant confiscation, an overt expulsion of an unwanted people, so long as world opinion, and especially after 1945, the good will of the American citizens, must be retained. Moreover, the Jewish tragedy, almost the kernel of its long history, was persecution, suffered first in the homeland, then in the Diaspora; culminating in the unspeakable Holocaust visited upon them by the savage Nazis. The Jews bore this travail as a badge of their innocence, and indeed their notorious suffering had finally been one of the most important means for recovering their lost homeland. Could they then impose the same disaster, the same fate, upon their relatives, innocent Arabs? Obviously not.

Yet, the subtlety of Herzl's legacy remained for them to exploit, almost hidden in his words: "While denying it any employment in our own country." The key to success lay in a strategy for settling immigrant Jews on the land. "Jews," wrote Amos Elon, "must do everything themselves." They must be self-sufficient, "do all the physical work with their hands, including the most difficult, the least paying, and the most menial." [155] Under such a system no one could say that the Arabs had been exploited by the newcomer Jews; no one would recognize the inherent purpose, which outwardly seemed to be a noble undertaking.

The middle-class Anglophile, Chaim Weizmann, could have scarcely imagined in 1917 what kind of revolutionary zealot would appear in Palestine after the World War. Even less could he have imagined that a small band of inspired proletarians would take control of the Jewish Agency in a few years, leaving him a veritable cipher in Zionist politics. After the riots of 1929 his influence waned rapidly. Between the temporizing measures of the past (Weizmann the most influential spokesman of this tactic), and the violent apostrophes emanating from the Revisionist Party (Jabotinsky most typical of this), there was the praxis of Ben Gurion's party, *viz.*, a grudging cooperation with the Mandatory Power (never to be forgiven for its treachery in attempting to abandon the Balfour Declaration); likewise, toward the Arab opponent: cordial relations but a steady preparation for the day of reckoning. This meant rapid immigration of Jews into Palestine, and a surreptitious building of a military establishment.

THE PALESTINE UPRISING

The advent of the Nazi regime in Germany and the notorious persecution of the Jews set in motion large migrations. Between 1932 and 1935, approximately 145,000 Jews entered Palestine, many of them illegally. The September Law of 1935, which stripped German Jews of their civil liberties, in some cases sequestering their property, provoked a still larger exodus. The United States would not accept many of these refugees, nor would the other Western countries. While sympathizing with the plight of their fellows in Germany, American Jews were in their majority passive. Fully a quarter of them did not favor German Jews immigrating to the United States. Why this was so is explained by the lively anti-Semitism that animated perhaps a majority of American Gentiles. By the 1930s most Jews in the United States were assimilated, and feared Gentile reaction should the Jews of Germany arrive in large numbers. [156] Anti-Semitism in the United States was also racist; a dark, sinister aspect of the irrational fear that gripped those who were "white" and descendants of the original settlers who had made the country what it was: a republican democracy imbued with English institutions and values. During the hard times that came with the Depression, both racism and anti-Semitism became virulent in the United States, in its psychology no different from the fear and hatred one witnessed in Germany.

Up to 1935, anti-Zionist opinion dominated the thinking of American Jews, but the plight of the German Jews rendered a good many of them more politically minded. The old *B'nai B'rith*, a fraternal order of German-American Jews, heretofore apolitical and determinedly bi-national in its attitude toward Palestine, began to collaborate with the Zionist Organization of America in 1936. Yet, it cannot be said this meant approval of the Zionist desire for a Jewish state in Palestine.

Cleverly, the Nazis exploited the historical exclusiveness of German Jewry. The Jews, it was argued, had always been opposed to assimilation, had become German reluctantly, and certainly not faithfully. They had always prayed for a miraculous return to their homeland. The Zionists in their midst only worked for what Jews had always yearned for; and therefore, to use a biblical phrase, "let them go" back to Palestine. The purpose of the Nuremberg Laws in 1935 was not to exterminate the Jews but to harry them out of Germany. The "Final Solution," mass extermination of an unwanted people, would come a few years later. Perversely, as it might seem, a considerable part of American Jewry agreed with the Nazis, *viz.*, let them go to Palestine. In this unexpected way American Jewry in its majority became pro-Palestinian (in favor of a homeland for persecuted Jews), while remaining anti-Zionist (opposed to the idea of a Jewish state in Palestine). It would be a long time before the concept of a Jewish state appealed to most of them. But, as only seems evident, to be pro-Palestinian, (i.e., in favor of a Jewish homeland), was to become in time pro-Zionist. [157] For the transition of that thought to take place there would be required a horrendous experience, the Holocaust, resulting in the death of at least six million Jews in central Europe, this being the fulfilled logic of Hitler's genocidal policies. Then would American Jewish guilt, and Gentile guilt generally, result in an overwhelming (and indeed irrational) belief that "something has to be done for the Jews."

Until 1939 there was an almost tacit understanding in the West that the exodus created by Hitler's policies could only be resolved by making Palestine a dumping ground for Jews who were as unwanted in the so-called peaceful democracies as in the totalitarian countries. To the Palestinians it was simpler than this: they were the victims of a conspiracy of the Western countries to give Palestine to the Jews and uproot the native population. In February 1936 they demanded again that the "Black Letter" be withdrawn, Jewish land purchases forbidden and Jewish immigration restricted.

Years of infighting by the effendi had diluted the authority of that class. Palestinian protest had become democratic in its expression: spontaneous demonstrations in towns and villages that forced the Palestinian notables to form committees and to voice the general discontent. [158] To force compliance, they began a system of boycotting British goods. There followed protests by Jews whose businesses suffered as much as the British. To better organize their actions, the Arabs, both Christian and Moslem, formed a national organization called the Arab Higher Committee.

Peaceful boycott measures soon turned violent, both Jews and British civilians injured in street fighting. In August 1936, for the first time, Arab rulers in countries adjacent to Palestine intervened diplomatically. When these conciliatory efforts failed, the Arab rulers advised the Palestinians to initiate a general strike. The British reaction to this was to send more troops, then a new commission headed by William Peel, who recommended the establishment of a Jewish state (about one-third of the country) taking up the coastal areas from Lebanon to a point south of Jaffa. The British Mandate would shrink to become no more than a narrow corridor embracing the railway line that ran from Jaffa to Jerusalem, both these cities remaining under the Mandatory Power. The rest of Palestine would become an Arab state to be joined in some form of an alliance with Transjordan.

The Mandates Commission of the League of Nations endorsed the Peel plan on 23 August 1936. After long debates within the Jewish Agency and the World Zionist Organization, a majority of the Jews accepted the partition plan also.

While the proposed Jewish state represented the realization of a homeland for the Jews (thus a fulfillment of the British engagement expressed in the Balfour Declaration), it contained about an equal number of Jews and Arabs (300,000 of the former, 290,000 of the latter), with every likelihood that the Arabs would outbreed the Jews faster than immigrants could be brought in to right the balance. In brief, the Jewish state would be Jewish in name only. Moreover, most of the land belonged to Palestinians. Such a tiny enclave could not expect to absorb the thousands of Jews being uprooted in Germany at that moment. It was also very far from being the territory that the Zionists coveted: Eretz Israel. But the fact that Chaim Weizmann and Ben Gurion accepted the partition plan was enough to make it palatable to most of the Zionists. What could not be said openly, however, was that the Jewish homeland would serve them as a base for further efforts to reclaim Eretz Israel. Those Zionists who opposed the partition plan were reminded by Ben Gurion that a Jewish state, however small, would serve as "a powerful instrument for the total fulfillment of Zionism, an instrument for the redemption of all the land of Israel." [159]

Recognizing the incompatibility of Jew and Arab, the Peel Commission's report called for a separation of the two peoples. The approximately 290,000 Arabs in the proposed Jewish state would be transferred to a new Arab state, which would come under the rule of Emir Abdullah. Thereafter, "transfer" (the euphemism of choice) was regularly discussed within the Mapai, one member proposing that they should "harass" the Arabs "until they get out—let them go to Transjordan." [160]

There was a certain syllogism in Zionist politics. Those who ruled the Mapai (the Jewish Labor Party) ruled the Histadrut; those who ruled the Histadrut ruled the Jewish Agency. Those who ruled the Jewish Agency ruled world Jewry (or at least decided on the policies for what the Zionist believed was the national mission of all exiled Jews).

The pretensions of the Labor Zionists were exceeded only by their rhetoric, Ben Gurion their most outstanding tribune. "The Party of the working class," he wrote after the Seventeenth Zionist Congress, "is responsible for the entire nation [i.e., all of world Jewry], and views itself as the nucleus of the future nation. The Labor Movement, which fifteen years ago had hardly existed as a visible entity, has become the cornerstone of Zionism. Qualitatively and quantitatively , we have become the largest faction, directing and deciding Zionism's fate." [161]

Ben Gurion's rise to prominence was as swift as that of his party. In 1935 he was elected chairman of the Jewish Agency. Energetic and articulate, a tireless debater, his personal philosophy reflected the Zionist faith: Eretz Israel belonged to the Jews and would eventually be restored to the Jews. Consequently, bi-nationalism was a false doctrine that must be constantly exposed for the fallacy that it was.

Moshe Sharett, probably the third most important figure in Zionist politics after Weizmann and Ben Gurion, was a determinedly conciliatory politician, but in a strange and ruthless way. He wished to live in peace with the Palestinians (unlike Ben Gurion, who rather savored conflict). Yet (like all Zionists) Sharett believed that Eretz Israel would become Jewish over time. Like Ben Gurion, he also recognized that the Palestinians had rights, but that these were to be necessarily trampled underfoot. "Their suffering as a nation," he remarked, "does not concern us because we are to have the nation and they have other countries." [162]

The intensity of the Palestinian uprising convinced the Zionists that the coexistence of Jews and Arabs was no longer possible. "Ethnic cleansing," to use a current term, was thought to be the solution. The exasperation of the British also worked in favor of the Jews, for the former might well conclude that a forced transportation of the Palestinians was the only viable solution. Ben Gurion's most generous critics think that up to 1936 he believed Jewish-Arab coexistence was possible, even if the Jews should become a majority in Palestine. [163] After 1936 he became convinced that coexistence was neither desirable nor possible. "We must," he wrote his son, Amos, on 5 October 1937, "expel the Arabs and take their place." [164]

This was not different from Sharett's remark that if the Palestinians could not accept the eventual prospect of becoming a minority in their own country, and a disadvantaged one as well, they could migrate to some other country.

"When we demand Palestine for us it is not at the expense of the Arab Nation as a whole, only at the expense of the demand of the Palestinian Arabs to be recognized as an Arab people of Palestine, the only owner of the country . . .". [165]

Sharett was a sort of Arab aficionado. Raised in an Arab neighborhood, he formed lifelong friendships with Arabs, learned their language, and took an almost scholarly interest in the exotic Arab culture. His Arab connections, as well as his knowledge, allowed him to become the chief of the Arab Section of the Jewish Agency's political department. Given the Zionist agenda, it was probably the most sensitive post in the administration.

Far more than most of his colleagues Sharett recognized that while all Palestinians were Arabs, all Arabs were not Palestinians. He perceived, in other words, a Palestinian nationalism being born, and he knew the reasons for it. "There is no Arab in Palestine who is not harmed by Jewish migration," he told his Mapai colleagues on 9 July 1936: "In his eyes Haifa was an Arab town and now it is Jewish. His reaction cannot be but resistance."

Sharett rejected the illusion that entranced Ben Gurion and his colleagues: that Palestinian Arabs could be drawn toward the mass of Arabs outside Palestine in what began to emerge in the mid-thirties as Pan Arabism. This to Sharett was a great fallacy. He thought there were several Arab national movements underway: Syrian, Iraqi and Palestinian. All these movements were anti-colonial in nature. When Ben Gurion and his like-minded colleagues envisioned a federation of Arab states, they misunderstood the nature of the Arab movement.

The Pan-Arab movement had sprung up as a result of the Palestinian rebellion, causing Ben Gurion to reconsider Zionist tactics. The heavy Jewish migration, a consequence of Nazi persecution, made him think that a Jewish majority in Palestine might be achieved in a relatively short time. Britain's brutal suppression of the Palestinians would, he believed, bring the Arabs to a point of despair from which the Jews could profit. "Only after total despair on the part of the Arabs," he told his colleagues, "despair that will come not only from the failure of the disturbances and attempts at rebellion, but as a consequence of our growth in the country, may the Arabs finally acquiesce in a Jewish Eretz Israel." [166]

But the Arabs overwhelmingly rejected the Peel plan, which proposed nothing less than the dismemberment of Palestine, the severance of Transjordan in 1922 still a bitter memory for many Palestinians. A Pan-Arab Congress meeting, held at Bludan in Syria on 8 September, voted almost unanimously against partition. The delegates to the Congress stated the familiar Arab demands: a cessation of Jewish land purchases, an end to Jewish immigration; but further, Great Britain to repudiate the Balfour Declaration, abandon the policy to establish a Jewish homeland; Palestine to become an independent state in alliance with Britain. Finally, the Congress attempted to make the boycott in Palestine Arab-wide by establishing a permanent executive for directing a boycott of both British and Jewish goods and services.

Earlier in the year, 137 Arab notables, most of them serving in the Palestinian Administration, presented the High Commissioner with a memorandum. It was a plea for the justice that had been denied them all these years:

> The Arab population of all classes, creeds and occupations is animated by a profound sense of injustice done to them. They feel that insufficient regard has been paid in the past to their legitimate grievances, even though those grievances had been inquired into by qualified and impartial official investigators, and to a large extent vindicated by those inquiries. As a result, the Arabs have been driven into a state verging on despair; and the present unrest is no more than an expression of that despair. [167]

The British government, which, as the Mandatory Power had the need to answer the disaffected Palestinians as well as the League Council, undertook still another investigation. To that end, a royal commission arrived in Palestine in November 1936. Its findings, requiring more than a year, were published in 1937, and represented an almost bitter acknowledgement of a failed and mistaken policy;

the recognition, moreover, that however well meant the efforts, two alien people could not be encouraged (much less coerced) into living together on the same territory.

An irrepressible conflict has arisen between two national communities within the narrow bounds of one small country. About 1,000,000 Arabs are in strife, open or latent, with some 400,000 Jews. There is no common ground between them. The Arab community is predominantly Asiatic in character, the Jewish community predominantly European. They differ in religion and in language. Their cultural and social life, their ways of thought and conduct, are as incompatible as their national aspirations. These last are the greatest bar to peace ...The War and its sequel have inspired all Arabs with the hope of reviving in a free and united Arab world the traditions of the Arab golden age. The Jews similarly are inspired by their historic past... In the Arab picture the Jews could only occupy the place they occupied in Arab Egypt or Arab Spain. The Arabs would be as much outside the Jewish picture as the Canaanites in the old land of Israel. The National Home... cannot be half-national ... This conflict was inherent in the situation from the outset. The terms of the Mandate tended to confirm it [and] the conflict has grown steadily more bitter... In the earlier period hostility to the Jews was not widespread among the fellaheen. It is now general ... The intensification of the conflict will continue ... it seems probably that the situation, bad as it now is, will grow worse. The conflict will go on, the gulf between Arabs and Jews will widen. [168]

This bleak assessment was darkened the more on 25 September 1936, when the British Commissioner Yelland Andrews was assassinated. In retaliation the High Commissioner arrested the members of the Arab Higher Committee, deporting most of them to the Seychelles. Facing imminent arrest, the Grand Mufti took flight to Syria on 16 October. The French were gone, Syria having become independent in September of this same year. From his refuge Haz Amin directed the resistance against the Mandatory

Power. Meanwhile, the British occupation forces commenced the well-nigh impossible task of disarming the Arab terrorists, while at the same time permitting the Jews to arm themselves (with mixed motives: so that the Jews might protect themselves and at the same time assist the Mandatory Power in subduing the Arab rebels.)

Given the spreading crisis that embraced much of the Arab world by this time, it was pointless that the Jews had accepted the Peel partition plan. The High Commissioner suspended these negotiations and ordered a new study to be carried out by John Woodhead. A new High Commissioner was appointed, Sir Harold MacMichael, with orders to put down the rebellion. By the end of 1936, 30,000 British troops were patrolling Palestine. Anglo-Jewish collaboration was renewed on the basis of extinguishing the Arab national movement, ostensibly so that the Zionist movement might survive. Ironically, in this atmosphere where Arab terrorism was being combated by Jewish terrorists, the latter were becoming more violent, efficient, and ruthless than the Arab variety already in the field.

The Haganah had been established out of need for defense, and it adhered to its policy of self-restraint (*havlagah*), that is, the Jews would fight, and willingly kill, but only in self-defense; they would not take the offensive against the enemy—up to 1937. But in that year, the Haganah leadership split over both tactics and the matter of morality. The founder of the Haganah, Jabotinsky, believed in "an eye for an eye, a tooth for a tooth;" the need to pay the Arabs in their own coin. But he was in the minority in the question of how much violence was acceptable. His chief lieutenant, David Raziel, despised the ways of politics and diplomacy. In 1937 he formed his own organization, *Irgun Zvai Leumi* (National Military Organization).

Further removed from self-restraint than Raziel was another zealot, Abraham Stern: poet, philosopher, linguist; a man of action. The quintessential terrorist, he was able to entertain edifying thoughts while engaged in the most murderous of acts. He based his violence on a regular reading of the Bible, seeking benediction, *viz.*, God approved of all that he did. An arresting figure, he was "slender, strikingly handsome, with jet-black hair; his face narrow and aquiline, the nose and brow forming one straight line, the eyes dark and brooding...". [169] In his dedication and self-destructive nature, futile and vainglorious, he reminds one of the romantic nihilist Gabriele D'Annunzio, who was his contemporary.

Those who followed this charismatic leader were called the Stern Gang. They differed from Raziel and his comrades in a matter of degree. For example, Raziel thought that a brief warning should be given before a building was blown up in order to give the innocents time to leave. Stern thought this was tactically unsound: better to blow up the building without warning; do not think of the innocents at risk since the cause is greater than any individual or, indeed, any number of individuals.

Stern wrote out a program for his followers, calling it "Eighteen Principles for Revival." Most of it was Zionist rhetoric. The borders of Eretz Israel were those found in the Bible. The original Israelis had conquered the Promised Land; their descendants should do the same. The Hebrews, having won Eretz Israel by the sword, believed it belonged ever after to the Jewish people: "This right is absolute; it has not lapsed and cannot ever lapse." Like most of the Zionists, he believed the ultimate goal was the eviction of the Arabs from Eretz Israel: "The problem of foreigners will be solved through population exchange."

Some of the principles Stern advanced were of a contemporary nature, fascist in tone, and owing something no doubt to his fascination with Italy and its charismatic leader, Benito Mussolini. Thus, thought Stern, a revived Israel would become a great power and find its destiny in Africa.

While the Zionists differed over questions of scruples, honor, the cause of Zionism, etc., they were generally agreed that the working partnership with Britain made possible the eventual fulfillment of the Balfour Declaration. One may imagine their dismay, therefore, when the British Foreign Office published another White Paper in May 1939. In this latest policy statement, the British cabinet came down squarely on the side of the Arabs, the very people they were engaged in putting down. The Cabinet's volte-face, seemingly abrupt and puzzling, had its obvious explanation in events transpiring in Europe generally and in the Middle East in particular. War with Hitler's Germany seemed imminent. British hegemony in the Middle East, the *sine qua non* for its imperial situation, which had gone to the advantage of the Zionists and against the Arabs, now required a détente with the Arab leaders. But the Italians under Benito Mussolini and the Germans under Hitler were already courting the Arabs. The Grand Mufti, from his sanctuary in Syria, played upon these international rivalries skillfully. Ostensibly a Nazi sympathizer, one who could not regret the Nazis' policies that harried Jews from Germany, Haz Amin made large demands, which were met by the British. Henceforth, Jews would be prevented almost entirely from buying land in Palestine, in all but 5 percent of the country; Jewish immigration over the next five years would be limited to seventy-five thousand.

Up to 1939 the Haganah had collaborated with the British forces against the Arab insurgents with loyalty, with honor, as Jabotinsky would have been disposed to say. The Irgun had been less responsible, indiscriminate in its acts of violence, as ready to destroy British facilities as to kill Arabs. In 1939, with the publication of the White Paper, the Irgun pronounced itself (as if a sovereign state) to be at war with Great Britain. When the High Commissioner prepared to read the White Paper over the radio in order to explain it to the Mandatory subjects, the Irgun blew up the radio station. The next day, 18 May, Jewish mobs were incited to enter and plunder immigration offices in Jerusalem, Haifa, and Tel Aviv, seeking to destroy all evidence of illegal immigration. In this same time Jabotinsky sent Stern to Poland in order to purchase weapons and smuggle them into Palestine. Stern, without Jabotinsky's knowledge it is believed, made arrangements with Italian agents for an invasion of Palestine. It would proceed in this manner: Forty thousand Jews, drawn from East European countries, would be trained in Poland by Polish military officers. From bases in Italy, with the connivance of the Italian government, forty thousand exalted Jews would descend upon Palestine and drive out thirty thousand British troops. It was another dream, like Zionism itself, which could not be realized, and if one is to give credence to rumors, the plan was only aborted by the quixotic Stern because he had learned of Raziel's capture and imprisonment by the British. Hastening to Palestine, he went on the secret radio operated by the Irgun and gave personal warning to an old adversary, a CID officer named Ralph Cairns. Since, as it seemed to the Stern Gang, Cairns ignored these warnings, he was duly assassinated.

The British were now fighting two kinds of terrorism simultaneously within Palestine, both Arab and Jewish radicals, who were as daring and merciless toward each other as they were toward the British forces.

The British declaration of war on Germany on 3 September 1939 changed everything. Until that date the Jewish Agency, like the Yishuv generally, had been neutral toward the civil war in Palestine. Speaking publicly against Jewish terrorism, and almost certainly not fostering it clandestinely, the Jewish Agency nonetheless took its eventual profit from a kind of violence it could not prevent, much less condone; yet could only gain from in the long run. The same calculating policy applied to the White Paper, expressed best by David Ben Gurion as the head of the Jewish Agency: "We will fight the war as if there were no White Paper; we will fight the White Paper as if there were no war." One may conclude from these cryptic lines that the Stern Gang saw a complete latitude of freedom to continue their assaults on the British.

Contrary to what might have been expected, the Irgun leadership announced that hostilities against the British occupation forces would be suspended for the duration of the war. But afterwards, it was vowed, they would fight on.

In the war with the Axis powers the British asked for no more than neutrality from the Jewish Agency. When the Haganah offered to put 130,000 men in the field at the disposal of the British forces, it was refused. In fact, the British tried and sentenced to ten-year prison terms a number of Haganah officers who had independently started training officers for service against Germany. By this time the entire Irgun leadership had been captured and placed in detention (the Sarafend Detention Camp).

Stern had rejected the Irgun's decision to follow the Jewish Agency's lead and cooperate with the British. He saw no difference between the Germans, who slaughtered Jews, and the British, who would rather see the fleeing Jews perish at sea than allow them to land on Palestinian shores. When Jabotinsky died of a heart attack in 1940, and Raziel succeeded him, Stern went his own way: a solitary extremist, the epitome of the terrorist, with few friends, without money or much in the way of weapons. But this seemed to confirm British sagacity. In releasing both Raziel and Stern from custody, they supposed there would be a falling out, evidently forgetting that terrorist organizations can produce a new leadership almost as fast as the old is liquidated. Ben Gurion put it this way: "If some get tired, others will replace them." Ergo, terrorist organizations are like weeds: the more they are cut down, the more they propagate themselves.

Stern's end was not long in coming. Taken into custody by the British CID in February 1941, he was, as the police report gave it, "shot while attempting to escape." [170] He was succeeded by men as radical and amoral as himself, but probably saner. Three of them constituted themselves as a joint leadership that might be called a triumvirate, operating under pseudonyms: Isaac Yitaernitsky became "Rabbi Shamir"—a future premier of Israel; Friedman Yellin became "Stein;" and Israel Sheib became "Doctor Eldad."

The tragic loss at sea of the refugee ship SS *Struma*, with eight hundred men, women and children in February 1942, galvanized the Jewish terrorists. While the Haganah remained faithful nonetheless to its commitment to support Great Britain against Germany, the Sternists adopted a policy of "direct terror." The High Commissioner, MacMichael (judged to be responsible for the sinking of the *Struma*), was targeted for assassination. Failing in their attempt, the triumvirate of Stein, Eldad, and Shamir reorganized the Stern Gang. Henceforth, unlike the Haganah and the Irgun, their members would not wear uniforms, the better to escape detection by the British CID. Their organization received a new name: *Lohmey Heruth Israel* (Freedom Fighters for Israel), the FFI for short, often called, almost affectionately by their terrorist rivals, *Lehi*.

In 1944, when it became apparent that Germany would lose the war, the Irgun prepared to resume its campaign of direct terror against the Mandatory Power. They had a new leader by now, a Polish Jew named Menachem Begin, who by reason of his philosophy and his temperament, as well as his occasional barbarous acts, might have been a member of Lehi. At the close of the war the stage was set for the conquest of Eretz Israel, of which Ben Gurion and his colleagues had long dreamed, and the Jewish terrorists now determined to make a reality.

NOTES

139 The Transjordan Mandate, for example, without a Jewish minority to complicate things, was elevated to independence (however fictitious in fact) by 1928. The British mandate there came to a formal end on 28 February of that year.

140 *Peel Report*, p. 54. Cited by Harold Walker, *The Chariot of Israel*, op. cit., p. 67.

141 Haim Barkai, "The Kibbutz: An Experiment in Microsocialism," *Israel, the Arabs and the Middle East*, eds., Irvisky Hower and Carl Gershman (Bantam Books: New York, 1972), p. 69.

142 There is nearby a second mosque, al-Aqsa.

143 Simha Flapan, *Zionism and the Palestinians*, op cit., pp. 216-17.

144 The promise of prosperity in Palestine was also drawing in many migrants from the surrounding Arab countries.

145 See the lengthy argument in Bernard Ashavar, *The Tragedy of Zionism*. op. cit.

146 Alfred G. Meyer, *Communism*, 2nd ed. (New York, 1962), pp. 5-8.

147 Shimoni, *The Zionist Ideology*, op cit., p. 203.

148 Ibid., pp. 127-28.

149 Ibid., p. 201.

150 Ibid., p. 204.

151 David Ben Gurion, *Postulates for the Formulation of a Constitutional Regime in Eretz Israel*. 1929.

152 David Ben Gurion, *My Talks with Arab Leaders* (Jerusalem, 1972), p. 140. Cited by Flapan, *Zionism and the Palestinians*, p. 140.

153 Ibid., p. 140.

154 Edward Said, *The Question of Palestine*, op, cit., pp. 19-20.

155 Amos Elon, *The Israelis. Founders and Sons* (New York, 1972), pp. 220-22.

156 Robert Silverberg, *If I Forget Thee O Jerusalem*, op. cit., p. 141.

157 Ibid., pp. 140-41.

158 William R. Polk, *The United States and the Arab World*, op. cit., p. 192.

159 John Quigley, *Palestine and Israel. A Challenge to Justice* (Duke University Presss, 1990), p. 24.

160 Nur Masalha, *Expulsion of the Palestinians. The concept of "Transfer" in Zionist*

Political Thought, 1822-1948 (Washington, D.C., 1992), p. 9.

161 Ashavar, *The Tragedy of Zionism*, p. 132.

162 Flapan, *Zionism and the Palestinians*, p. 153.

163 David McDowall, *Palestine and Israel*, op. cit., pp. 188-89.

164 On Zionist speculations as how to "transfer" Palestinians to other Arab countries, see Flapan, pp. 259, ff.

165 Ibid., p. 153.

166 Flapan, *Zionism and the Palestinians*, p. 143.

167 Polk, pp. 192-93.

168 Ibid., p. 195.

169 Gerald Frank, *The Deed*. (New York: Simon & Schuster, 1963), cited by Edward Hyams, *Terrorists and Terrorism* (New York, 1974), pp. 146-47.

170 Raziel was killed the next year in Iraq while on a secret mission for the British.

CHAPTER FIVE

Founding the Jewish State

THE AMERICAN CONNECTION

he intrusion of political Zionism in Palestine under British aegis was merely a manifestation of the more general nationalist impulse that had begun to erode the supranational authority of the Ottoman Turks early in the nineteenth century. "There were few districts in the Ottoman Empire," observed Arnold Toynbee in his famous *Study of History*, "whose population was even approximately homogenous in linguistic nationality, and also few which possess even the rudiments of statehood."[171] Immense human calamities were the price paid for the imposition of a national pattern on any given diverse group of people within the confines of the empire. The massacre of the Moslem minority in the Morea by Greek Orthodox Christians in 1821, for example; thereafter the slaughter of the same Christians by their Turkish overlords; the "wholesale flight" of Greek Christians from western Anatolia in 1922; the flight of Palestinian Arabs in 1947 in the face of Jewish terrorism; the genocide the Bosnians suffered in the late 1980s; the similar experience of ethnic Albanians in Kossovo at the end of the 1990s. Nowhere was the "exotic modern western Pattern" established within the framework of the Turkish Empire that there was not a colossal cost in human suffering. Zealous nationalists who thought of the nation-state in integral terms (unity in religion, unity in language, unity in customs and mores), stoically accepted the harm they inflicted upon themselves as well as the harm done to others.

The tragedy of Ben Gurion's long career was his passage from a socialist view of an inclusive Jewish state to the intolerant nationalist vision of a purely ethnic Jewish community. The logic of this exclusiveness required either the absorption of the Palestinian Arabs through their own apostasy, or some form of deportation. Well before WW II, the vision of a purely Jewish state had become a blurred nightmare of endless fright both for Jews and Arabs, promising endless war as one generation of radicals after another perpetuated this dilemma.

Throughout the Second World War, the British policy makers supposed their mandate function in Palestine would continue, as they supposed also that the British Empire would emerge intact from the chaos of a world war. In December 1943 still another partition plan issued from the Foreign Office, proposing an independent Jewish state; Jerusalem to become an enclave under a mandate (British of course). The remainder of Palestine, along with Lebanon, would become part of a "Greater Syria." The plan was stillborn, shelved in reaction to the assassination of Lord Moyne, Minister Resident at Cairo, on 6 November 1944, by Jewish terrorists. The murder, which shocked the British public, dampened the ardor of the zealous Zionists considerably, among them Winston Churchill. "If our dreams for Zionism," he said in the Commons, "are to end in the smoke of assassins' pistols, and our labors for its future to produce only a new set of gangsters worthy of Nazi Germany, many like myself would have to reconsider the position we have maintained so consistently and so long in the past." [172]

From this point forward the Zionists realized that any hope for a Jewish state depended upon the attitude (and influence above all) of the United States. This was Churchill's opinion also at the end of the war, but for different reasons. The Palestinian mandate had always been a gauge for British security in the Middle East.

It became clear at the end of the war that a Pax Britannica would be replaced by a Pax Americana. On the day after his defeat at the polls and his party's replacement by the Labor Party, Churchill suggested that the mandate should be assigned to the United States. His Zionist ardor had cooled considerably, it is clear. "I am not aware of the slightest advantage which has ever accrued to Great Britain from this painful and thankless task. Somebody else should have their turn now." [173]

The return to power of the Labor Party had the effect of changing British foreign policy fundamentally. The Conservative Party's stubborn defense of the empire gave way to a new policy, which (unofficially) committed Britain to an eventual abandonment of its imperial interests in almost every place in the world where nationalism had become too strong a force to be effectively resisted. India, for example, would be given its independence. To satisfy Arab nationalism, the quest for a Jewish state in Palestine would be given up. Here was a stunning contradiction. Labor Zionism and the British Trades Union Movement had shared the same socialist ideals for many years. Steadfast (except for Ramsay MacDonald's brief apostasy in 1932), the Labor Party had remained a staunch supporter of the Zionists, sharing their hopes: with establishment of a Jewish homeland, it would grow through Jewish immigration and inevitably evolve into a Jewish state. But, would this be done at the expense of the resident Arabs? Yes, wrote Hugh Dalton, an important Labor member of the Parliament, "Let the Arabs be encouraged to move out as the Jews move in. We should lean much more than hitherto toward the dynamic Jews, less toward the static Arabs." [174]

Suddenly, as it seemed, public opinion in both the United States and the United Kingdom had come to play a large role. The British people, weary from a wasting war, reduced to virtual poverty, outraged by the mistreatment their occupation forces in Palestine received from Jewish extremists, had little sympathy for Zionist aspirations. Moreover, the Jewish community in Britain, while admittedly influential, was small. In the U.S., by contrast, Jewry was large, a wealthy segment of the American society concentrated in big cities and, all at once, enthusiastic supporters of Zionism; they were supported as well by American Gentiles, enthusiastic like themselves.

During WW I the British non-Zionists had served the Jewish Zionists well by agreeing to establish a Jewish homeland in Palestine. Now, the United States, with its large and influential Jewish minority, might agree to the establishment of a Jewish state.

President Roosevelt was skeptical, however, as was his wife. Eleanor admitted to being puzzled by the Zionist idea. "I fear," she wrote, "that Palestine can never support all the Jews, and the Arabs would start a constant war if all of them came. Why can't Jews be members of a religious body but natives of the land in which they live?" [175] FDR echoed his wife's fears. A Jewish state in Palestine, he predicted could be "established and maintained only by force." "The Arabs live there too," wrote Kermit Roosevelt, "The Arabs also have rights in Palestine. Arabs will fight and die in their cause." [176]

Like Wilson during the First World War, FDR was besieged by influential Zionists. He evaded them when he could and refrained from making any public pronouncement on the subject. Like Wilson also in his old-fashioned progressivism (beginning to be called "liberalism" during his several administrations), Roosevelt believed in national self-determination, *viz.*, let the given nation (or nationality) take care of itself. Whether his fabled political finesse would have been sufficient for him to escape from the toils of the Jewish-Arab conflict is only problematic. He did see both sides of the question clearly, however. Following the Teheran Conference in November 1943, he met Ibn Saud aboard an American warship, the decks of the destroyer covered with "rich oriental rugs, while gilded chairs gave added touches of unusual splendor . . ." Of the problems of Arabia," Roosevelt reported to the Congress afterwards, "I learned more about the whole problem, the Moslem problem, the Jewish problem, by talking with Ibn Saud for five minutes than I could have learned in exchange of two or three dozen letters." [177] Actually, the interview lasted for more than five hours, and what Roosevelt learned was the depth of inextinguishable hatred the King harbored for the

Jews. The President discovered, as had the British in their dealings with the Saudis, a medieval mentality, an isolated, somewhat innocent perception of the world beyond the vast desert in which they dwelt. "Our hatred for the Jews," Ibn Saud told a British envoy in 1937, "dates from God's condemnation of them for their persecution and rejection of Isa [Jesus]....It is beyond our understanding how your government, representing the first Christian power in the world today, can wish to assist and reward these very same Jews who maltreated your Isa." [178]

When Roosevelt suggested that the Jewish refugees from war-torn Europe should have access to Palestine, the king suggested that the place to settle the displaced Jews was Germany. "It is the 'Christian' Germans who stole their homes and lives. Let the Germans pay." Why, wondered the king, should little Palestine be forced to take in millions of Jews? "Why not take the rest into the vast and fertile lands of the Allies?" [179] Needless to say, anti-Semitic America would look askance at a president who made such a proposal.

The inflexible resolve of Ibn Saud, who appeared the incarnation of Arab resistance to Jewish immigration to Palestine, left Roosevelt with the opinion that a Jewish state could be established there only by military means. Death in April 1945 delivered him from the coming dilemma, which had bedeviled British foreign policy for more than two decades. To please the Jews, an imperial power in the Middle East would have to alienate the Arabs. To satisfy the Arabs meant incurring the wrath of the Jews. For an American politician, that meant losing the votes of Jews concentrated in crucial swing states such as New York, where American Jewry was often a decisive voting bloc, particularly in national elections. The matter of the Jewish vote would weigh heavily on Roosevelt's successor, Harry S. Truman.

Lofted abruptly to the presidency, Truman was unsure of himself, painfully aware of his limitations, so guilelessly open in confessing his weaknesses as to puzzle those closest to him. What he brought to the executive office was bureaucratic efficiency, the stubbornness of a Missouri politician, a naive patriotism without sophistication, and a parochial view of the world (a definite ignorance). Typical of the Middle West American, shrewd and practical, with a common sense approach to problems, he lacked the ample vision of his predecessor. Admittedly, he was buffeted by contrary opinions. The Zionists urged him to support a Jewish state in Palestine; the State Department, which reflected the opinion of the Secretary of State, George Marshall, that America's strategic interests in the Middle East outweighed any sentimental regard for the Jews.

In the days before the advent of the Cold War, before a black-and-white image appeared for Truman of a world made up of a great good and a great evil (U.S. vs. USSR), both he and Marshall hoped to cooperate with the Soviets—or more exactly, cooperate with Joseph Stalin, unqualified dictator of the USSR. Stalin did not want to see a Jewish state established in Palestine. Neither did the American State Department. Truman, it appears, did not have a fixed opinion on the matter. Marshal feared that American support of the Zionists would alienate the Arabs and force them into the Soviet orbit. Not less important than this, oil supplies would be imperiled at a moment when Marshall meditated on the problem of rebuilding a prostrate Europe. At Yalta both Roosevelt and Stalin had found they looked upon the Zionists in the same way. It did not appear that Truman wanted to shake off this legacy, and therefore cooperation between the U.S. and the USSR seemed possible.

The odd man out in these changing international relationships was Great Britain, now governed by the Labor Party. Churchill's party, like himself, had been ejected from office by an electorate that yearned for social progress and refused to sacrifice any longer for an empire that had outlived its usefulness. Unexpectedly, even strangely, British labor leaders who had once been the undeviating champions of the proletarian Jews in Palestine were fast becoming the warm friends of the Arabs. Although democratic in practice and outlook, they did not hesitate to cozy up to authoritarian and undemocratic chieftains who ruled the Arab world. The

British need for oil, it appeared, had a greater value than the long-term alliance with the Jews in Palestine, their erstwhile clients in imperial politics.

In this same time a virtual civil war in Palestine was wearing down British resolve to continue its responsibility as a mandatory power. The British were all too familiar with guerrilla warfare and nationalist fanaticism. Ireland had served as a testing ground, demonstrating that the power of a state, even a great state, cannot extinguish the passions of men and women who have resolved to become martyrs; proving also that a virtually disarmed people cannot be wholly subdued when the occupying power becomes weary and finally doubts the validity of the force being imposed upon the subject people, and at last must ask the question "How long shall I sacrifice for nothing?" This confession of impotence would come to British lips long before it would come to the mind of any Zionist.

In the background was the memory of the recent Nazi tyranny, the liquidation of millions of Jews. A civilized regime like Great Britain's could scarcely bear the odium that would come to it if excessive force was used in Palestine. Also, there was the insoluble problem of a passive population (the Yishuv) condemning the terrorists in their midst, yet concealing them from the authorities. If the passive elements of a society, observed a British statesman, "who do not go in for violence, is sufficiently active to succor and give refuge to the active minority of the community, no government, however ruthless, can smash the resistance movement or disarm it." [180]

When captured and brought before British courts, the Jewish guerrillas were sometimes eloquent in their defense; with always the same refrain: they had justice on their side and the British had none. They could justify their violence and the British could not. "Your duty," said one to a British judge, "is to do justice, to restore to us our stolen homeland." [181]

The misfortune for the British was to arrive in Palestine in an era that was beginning to dismiss well-meaning imperialists. Having toppled an archaic empire, the Turkish, they had thought to replace that unprogressive and often repressive regime with their own benevolent and modern authority. But they were being defeated because their will to violence was not so great as that of their subjects, as later the Americans would abandon Vietnam; in the same way that the British had left Ireland in 1921; and a century earlier (1783 to be exact) yielded to the will of the rebelling American colonials. It was an old story in history. The ancient Greeks called such surrenders as these "a loss of nerve," an unwillingness finally on the part of the strong to continue to beat the weak and helpless.

In the end, the difference between the violence of the Jewish terrorists and that of the British Mandatory Power was a matter of degree; *viz.*, the level of barbarism to which one will stoop in order to attain one's goal. To maintain the peace and contain the rebels the British were prepared to use summary justice and methods of torture. The terrorists would go further: killing indiscriminately, torturing (hanging in a slow death by strangulation comes under this heading); in the many acts of destroying the country's infrastructure, liquidating the innocents (children, women, and men); because their zeal demanded that they destroy life and property remorselessly, even proudly. The supposed justification that it was by God's will that they behaved thus was not the root cause for their fanaticism, but their lust for the land of Israel, because they believed that it belonged to Jews and to no one else.

The British could not be so savage, though their imperial interests seemed as vital to them as the cause that impelled the Jewish radicals. To disarm the guerrillas would have required not only the seizure of many hidden weapons, but cooperation from the Jewish Agency as well. But the latter benefited from the mystique that flowed from the late Holocaust in Europe. To treat severely the men of the Jewish Agency, however much they might be connected to the illegal army, Irgun, and the renegade terrorists groups, would have produced a profound reaction in the West, where it was believed the Jews had suffered enough. Not a few agreed with the more demoralized members of the British cabinet that the outrageous violence of the Jews was to be explained, perhaps forgiven, on the grounds that the

Holocaust had produced a kind of insanity among them. Forgotten, or perhaps not known by most of the British, was the fact that the Irgun leaders had suspended their terrorist operations at the beginning of the war, believing that Germany was the greater enemy; but they had vowed also to resume their attacks on the Mandatory Power once the war was over. It was easy to forget also that Jewish violence was almost as old as Arab violence, going back to the riots of 1920–21; that the earliest violence had been directed against Jews by Arabs and by Jews against Arabs; that eventually all the terrorists had turned on the occupying power, judged to be the common enemy.

After WW II the British found themselves in the awkward position of defending the Arabs (their redoubtable enemy) from the Jewish terrorists while at the same time fighting to protect themselves. So pronounced had the danger become by 1945 to British citizens and soldiers alike, that safety was assured by establishing closely guarded zones around Jerusalem. But even this did not give adequate security.

Seeking to be just, concerned that any action taken against the terrorists would be perceived as an attack on all Palestinian Jews, the British deceived themselves with the belief that there was no real connection between the Haganah and the Irgun, or between the Jewish Agency and the guerrilla organizations. Scarcely able to take the steps to prove what they did not want to believe, they allowed the fruits of propaganda to slip away from them, going to the advantage of the terrorists and the Yishuv in general: *viz.*, a brave and innocent little people were molested by an uncaring and brutal imperial power. It could be argued, as the Americans were disposed to do, that Jewish terrorism, whether justified in the abstract or not, was the result of British arrogance and its harsh measures. If the British cabinet should simply relent and allow Jewish immigration to proceed, all would resolve itself in Palestine—so thought Truman and his pro-Zionist advisers.

A turning point came on 22 July 1946, when six members of the Irgun entered the basement of the Hotel David in Jerusalem disguised as workers. They carried milk cans containing high explosives. Although they were detected while leaving the hotel, it was too late for the police to find and defuse the bombs. The blast partly demolished the hotel, resulting in the deaths of ninety-one people (forty-one Arabs, seventeen Jews, twenty-eight British, and five other nationals).

This was not the first bombing of considerable proportions, but the Hotel David was the British command center and carried a peculiar psychology that was decisive for both the Jews and the British. The former celebrated a victory and could not doubt that the British vulnerability was proved; in the long run the Mandatory Power would leave Palestine. As for the British cabinet, a lively desire for retribution was tempered by the realization that they were mired in another Ireland from which an honorable withdrawal was not possible; yet, to stay on was just as impossible.

While the Yishuv generally condemned the bombing of the hotel, they persisted in their intransigence against the unwanted Mandatory Power. In a sense they received the benefits of terrorism without being responsible for its acts. Nor was the Jewish Agency entirely innocent, Ben Gurion and his friends having received advance notice of the Irgun's intention to bomb the hotel. Weizmann, informed of the plot also, had opposed it; but he had become a cipher in Zionist politics by then.

The Truman Administration refused to condemn the Jewish terrorists explicitly, thereby outraging the British politicos. In reaction they mounted Operation Shark, a futile effort to locate what they suspected were immense stores of weapons and munitions. Approximately 13,000 men were deployed in a well-planned sweep across Palestine. This entailed street curfews, strategic roadblocks, search and seizure. The Yishuv remained impassive while the guerrilla leaders went into hiding. One of the chiefs of the Irgun, Menachem Begin, concealed himself in an apartment in Tel Aviv until the British patrols were withdrawn. Operation Shark accomplished nothing, he wrote later with obvious contempt, "with all their troops and all their detectives and all their intelligence agents and all their 'terrorists' photographs and all their elaborate identification..." [182]

While the rampant violence of the terrorists could not be contained, the flood of refugees could not be stemmed. The Palestinian borders were as porous as a sieve. To control these areas the British would have had to establish a large border patrol, not only unlikely, but impossible after a depression and war that had left Britain so poor it could hardly maintain its regular military establishment. To control the Mediterranean coastline would have required a coast guard fleet, and again, the costs were prohibitive.

The illegal migration of the Jews was both daring and sophisticated. The future efficient and ruthless Mossad (Israel's equivalent of the American CIA and FBI joined as one) emerged from these adventures. *Mossad le-aliyah bet* (Organization for Illegal Migration) was formed in 1936 to subvert the restrictions on immigration that the British had imposed that year. The activities of the Mossad spanned oceans and continents, wherever Jews were imperiled, wherever any Jewish community was disposed to send some of its members to Palestine. The funds for supporting these operations were provided by the Jewish Agency, which in turn was subsidized by the JOINT, the major contributor, with its headquarters in the U.S. [183]

The colonization of Palestine was given a decided fillip toward the middle of 1943, when Churchill insisted upon a change in Jewish immigration policy. Any Jew who could get to the Mediterranean coast would be permitted to proceed to Palestine, regardless of the quota that had been established. After that an increasing influx of desperate immigrants made control nearly impossible. The innocents fleeing the horrors of war could not be summarily shot. British impotence in this regard was testified to by Yitzhak Rabin, who established his career by bringing illegal immigrants into the country. The British put up roadblocks, he recalled, but these were ignored by swarms of people who could not be halted, even though the British had machine guns in place for that ostensible purpose. Safely past the barricades, the newcomers were embraced by a sea of waiting Jews, while the authorities watched helplessly. Once in the country the immigrants were moved south of Jerusalem, where the Arab population was slight to non-existent. So accomplished had the settler movement become by this time that it was said a Kibbutz could be established in twenty-four hours—including protective fences and a watchtower.

Contributions from American Jewry had been essential for establishing the Jews in Palestine after WW One. After WW Two, Jewish political influence became decisive in shaping American public opinion, and this had its eventual impact on the American Congress. In May 1942, at a conference held by American Zionists at the Biltmore Hotel in New York City, it was resolved that a Jewish state should be formed in Palestine, as well as a Jewish army.

The American connection with Palestine was older than most Americans realized. In 1922, after repeated requests from the Zionists, a joint resolution of Congress had affirmed "that the United States of America favors the establishment in Palestine of a national home for the Jewish people, it being clearly understood that nothing shall be done which may prejudice the civil and religious rights of Christians and all other non-Jewish communities in Palestine . . ." [184] By affixing his signature to the resolution, President Harding gave to the Zionists the American equivalent of the Balfour Declaration. Less than two years later his Administration negotiated the Anglo-American Convention on Palestine, ratified by the Congress the next year. Britain had found Palestine to be a serious problem by then and was willing to have the U.S. as a consultant and a possible partner further down the road. However, subsequent actions by the United States down to 1945 were usually pro-Arab.

After 1945 the plight of European Jews who had survived the war became an imponderable factor. A joint resolution of the American Congress in January 1945 called upon the British government to rescind the White Paper of 1939, and also called for the creation of a Jewish state in Palestine. Embarrassed probably, Roosevelt's immediate response was to tell two prominent Zionists, the Rabbis Wise and Silver, that his administration had never approved of the White Paper.

Truman could not be so independent. New to the office, president by default as it were, he received scant respect from the cabinet he

160

inherited from his predecessor. Secretary of State General Marshall looked on the man from Missouri as a naive politician who had no real understanding of international relations. [185]

One of Truman's first acts was to name Eleanor a delegate to the United Nations. In the beginning, she, like her husband, had considered Zionism detrimental to American interests, but eventually her insights in this regard were overborne by the emotional reaction she experienced while visiting the refugee camps in 1946. Out of an exceptional empathy for the distressed and destitute she reversed herself. This change of heart simply reflected the more general transformation of American public opinion; namely, something had to be done for the many victimized Jews. That the Arabs might become victims as a consequence of a well-meaning American compassion became an almost meaningless proposition.

Over a longer period of time Truman experienced the same evolution as Eleanor. A simple, but not unintelligent, plainspoken man, he detested what he believed was the cynicism of the State Department. That State was not only opposed to him, but subversive in covertly defeating his purposes, was not far short of treason to Truman; a bunch of "pin stripe conspirators," was the way he put it. State saw the large world, abstractly, in terms of U.S. interests. Truman's view of things was small, neat, clear and uncomplicated.

The images that riveted the attention of not only the president but also the American public were the first details describing the Holocaust, statistics revealing more clearly than words what this meant. In 1939 there were an estimated 16,725,000 Jews in the world. By 1946 the figure had dropped to 10,750,000, a reduction of six million in six years. While a fraction of that number had escaped to other countries (some to Palestine), the bulk of the six million were victims of Nazi extermination policies.

The Jews who had survived in Europe were pitiable creatures, almost dehumanized by their suffering; refugees without income, housing, food; wholly destitute, many without a legal nationality any longer. They lived on the charity furnished by the United Nations Relief Agency. The solution for this immense tragedy was to send them to Palestine, a place agreed upon tacitly by those in power in the West since 1936 as the most suitable dumping ground. [186] The original motive for establishing a Jewish homeland in Palestine (i.e., a refuge for persecuted Jews) had possessed this moral foundation: a haven for persecuted Jews, whether their tormentors were Christian or Moslem.

While the atrocities of the Nazis were horrible, wanton murder without parallel, the Zionists did not scruple to exploit the Holocaust, seemingly ready to make Western society as a whole appear guilty for the aberrant behavior of a totalitarian regime. It could be called the Holocaust card, and they played it relentlessly.

A visceral president, Truman gave an increasingly humanitarian emphasis to his evolving Palestine policy, as, similarly, he would a little later adopt an equally high moral stance in his relations with Stalin, in what he fancied was America's coming struggle with international communism. After long and sterile exchanges between Washington and London, with the recognition that the question of Jewish immigration could not be resolved between the two governments, Truman and British Prime Minister Clement Attlee agreed to place the question before the United Nations. Thereafter an Anglo-American Committee of Inquiry was formed, composed of six American and six British commissioners, charged with investigating and making recommendations to the United Nations.

Significantly, in forming his cabinet, Attlee had turned away from the notoriously pro-Zionist John Dalton, giving the Foreign Office to Ernest Bevin. An erstwhile coal miner and trade unionist, Bevin had supported the Zionists often, but equivocally. There began at once a muted argument between Washington and London over Jewish migration to Palestine. The British believed that the United States, with its great spaces and ample resources, should accept a large number of displaced persons. If an agreement on this basis could be achieved between Washington and London, the Arabs, so the British believed, would understand that both the United States and Great Britain were neither pro-Jewish nor pro-Arab.

Truman rejected the idea. Such immigration laws as might satisfy the British, and at the same time accommodate the immediate needs of the refugees, would proceed in the American Congress at a snail's pace. But every pressure, from Zionist importunities to the distress of millions of displaced persons, demanded timely decisions.

On 13 August the World Zionist Organization resolved that Palestine should be opened for the settlement of a million Jews. A couple of weeks later, Truman requested an immediate admission of 100,000 displaced persons from Europe (almost all of these would be Jews, of course). On 20 October, Egypt, Iraq, Syria, and Lebanon warned the United States that the formation of a Jewish state in Palestine would lead to war.

In the meantime the Anglo-American Committee held hearings and took evidence. Its investigations began in London, then went on to Europe, where the members split into several groups in order to interview the refugees. They discovered that the Jewish Agency had already sent agents, instructing the refugees on how to answer questions, spiriting away those who might inadvertently hurt the Zionist cause. [187]

At Cairo the committee listened to the claims of the Arabs presented by the Secretary General of the Arab League, Azzam Pasha, who offered a brief and insightful appraisal of the ancient quarrel of the siblings.

> Our brother has gone to Europe and the West and come back something else. He has come back a Russified Jew, a Polish Jew, a German Jew, an English Jew. He has come back with a totally different conception of things, Western and not Eastern ... the Jew, our old cousin, coming back with imperialistic ideas, ... with reactionary or revolutionary ideas and trying to implement them first by British pressure and then by American pressure, and then by terrorism ... we do not extend to him a very good welcome. [188]

The Pasha's words suggested a certain fatalism. In the world of international politics that had issued from the First World War, the Arabs were ill equipped to compete. The Ashkenazi Jews, by contrast, were, after two millennia, a Europeanized people (or more broadly speaking, Westernized); they were in their element. But the Arabs, through background, prolonged isolation from the most dynamic part of the planet, were unprepared for political strife as it is prosecuted on the Western model. That the West in its arrogance had presumed to thrust an alien people into a world that did not want them and could not adapt to them seemed inexplicable. Conversely, the aliens (Westernized Jews) could not accommodate themselves to an Arab world that did not operate in terms of progress, and valued the past as much as the present. Finally, the germs promising the dissolution of a valued society were carried by the Jewish migrants, a destructive force as deadly as the microbes the Spanish adventurers had carried to the New World, to carry off into oblivion whole civilizations. Such was the fear of the Arabs, who, having been defeated in the arena of international politics, now waited to be defeated in a mortal fashion.

At Jerusalem the Anglo-American Committee consulted the opinion of the British military establishment. Two of the occupation officers believed that Britain's withdrawal from Palestine would precipitate a full-scale civil war. The Jews would "get what they wanted to begin with," observed Air Marshall Medhurst, but if the Arabs "should get together there would be only one result." The committee members wondered what that would mean in the long run. Would the Arabs eventually "exterminate the Jews?"

"Yes," was the reply. [189]

British thinking came down to this: to issue the 100,000 certificates for Jewish immigration would bring about a civil war, and the Jews would become the eventual victims of such a policy. As the committee stretched out its investigations, lost in deep perplexity, the British Cabinet continued to refuse to issue immigration certificates. Out of patience finally, Ben Gurion ordered an intensification of sabotage, "but no personal terror," he warned.

The opinion of the Anglo-American Committee, after long deliberations, was finally delivered to the United Nations on 29 April 1946. Any partition plan that might be proposed for

Palestine, they predicted, would fail. They suggested an independent Palestine with local and provincial autonomies; that is, a form of bi-nationalism that the Mandatory Power had promoted fruitlessly for the past twenty-five years. Both the Arabs and the Jews rejected the Committee's proposals. The Arab League announced that force would be used to prevent the dismemberment of Palestine. After this, the Jewish terrorists intensified their attacks, without regard for Ben Gurion's admonition that terror should not be "personal," merely destructive of property.

Subsequent events spanning a year may be reduced to a few points. At a conference on Palestine convened in London in the fall of 1946, the Arab delegation called for an independent Palestine. The Zionists boycotted the conference. At the Zionist Congress held at Basel thereafter, the demand was renewed for the creation of a Jewish state. Both Jews and Arabs recommended that Britain abandon its function as a mandatory power in Palestine.

In this same time the United Nations had instituted a system of trusts to replace the mandates. On 7 February 1947 the British government proposed that Palestine be divided into two zones, Jewish and Arab, the administration of the country to be assigned to Great Britain as a trust. Both Arabs and Jews rejected this proposal. The delegates to the United Nations, believing a compromise was still possible, organized the United Nations Special Commission on Palestine (UNSCOP), consisting of eleven members. Except for Canada, all were small or poor countries; most were what eventually would be called Third World countries, so that both Jews and Arabs might believe that a spirit of objectivity and fairness entered into UNSCOP's deliberations. [190]

Truman's inclination to support the Zionists became decisive at this point. Marshall had opposed the President's pro-Zionist policy, going so far as to threaten to resign. Under Secretary of State Dean Acheson was still more adamantly opposed. From his dear friends, Justice Brandeis and Felix Frankfurter, he had learned, Acheson wrote, "to understand, but not to share the mystical emotion of the Jews to return to Palestine and end the Diaspora." But "in urging

Zionism as an American government policy they had allowed, so I thought, their emotion to obscure the totality of American interests." The president, he said afterwards, allowed himself to be "sucked in." Indeed, the stubborn man from Missouri could not be deterred. Although his words and actions suggest ambivalence, perhaps bewilderment, in his memoirs Truman took the position that Woodrow Wilson had favored a homeland for the Jews; and that to support Zionism was to affirm the principle of national self-determination, another part of the prized Wilsonian legacy.

The State Department, having abandoned the idea of partition (as had most of the UN delegates), favored a trusteeship for Palestine. There ensued for a brief time an unspoken contest between the president and the State Department for the hearts and souls of the UN delegates. "By direct orders from the White House," wrote Under Secretary of State Sumner Welles, "every form of pressure direct or indirect was brought to bear by American officials upon those countries outside the Moslem world that were known to be either uncertain or opposed to partition. Representatives of intermediaries were employed by the White House to make sure that the necessary majority would at length be secured." The measures used to get votes favorable to the Zionists in the UN, Secretary of Defense James Forrestal noted in his diary, "bordered closely on to scandal." [191]

While in outward appearance Truman's efforts on behalf of the Zionists were benevolent, he recognized also that Jewish votes would be of crucial importance in the approaching presidential elections. [192] On 29 November 1947 the General Assembly voted for the partition of Palestine. As in 1936, the Jews accepted the partition. On 17 December the Arab League announced that force would be used to prevent the partition of Palestine.

Having long predicted that Palestine would be plunged into a civil war to which the Mandatory Power would become a hostage, the British cabinet decided to renounce its obligations. On 14 May 1948 the mandate came to an end. This same day, a Jewish provisional government headed by Ben Gurion proclaimed the independence of the Jewish state. They called it Israel and named Chaim Weizmann its first president. Truman, already advised of the Zionists' intention, gave a de facto recognition almost immediately (eleven minutes after the proclamation became public). The Soviet Union, which had become, inexplicably it seemed, a warm supporter of the Zionists, accorded the new state of Israel its recognition *de jure*. [193]

THE WAR OF INDEPENDENCE

The underlying philosophy of the League Covenant in establishing the mandate system had been twofold: the rights of peoples and states required safeguards and protection; secondly, a graduated system of mandates, from A to C, presumed an ineluctable evolution of the most disadvantaged people toward a greater self-awareness and finally self-government. All mandates were therefore ephemeral. People living in A mandates, such as Palestine or Syria, could expect to be self-governing much sooner than people living in B or C mandates, but all mandates would in time progress enough to be independent and self-governing. All empires would vanish eventually. A world government composed of delegates from democratic self-governing countries would resolve their differences peacefully. The scourge of war would disappear. At San Francisco in 1945, the United Nations (the League of Nations reborn, as it were) reaffirmed this faith, reflecting also the current mystique that there could, and should be, "one world."

It was the will of the United Nations that Palestine be partitioned, and the two hostile communities, Arab and Jewish, be self-governing. It was the will of the major Arab states to resist this decision. The Zionists submitted to the will of the United Nations (now that they had attained an independent state). There were two reasons for this: the long-standing effort to create a sovereign Jewish state and thereafter to establish a Jewish majority within that state, thereby encouraging a constant migration of world Jewry to Palestine;

and second, to use the newly established state as a base for taking possession of the remainder of Eretz Israel.

The Arab delegates to the United Nations had made it clear once they were outvoted (indeed, before the vote was taken) that they would invade, occupy, and dispose of Palestine according to their lights. That in such an event a Great Power might energize the United Nations enough to carry out a "police action" against the Arabs (as President Truman would do a little later against North Korea), did not seem to occur to them.

In the anticipated aggression against Israel, the Arab states did not intend to declare war, for that would raise the imponderable question: against whom? Israel? the United Nations, which was veritably the author of Palestine's dismemberment? From the Arab point of view the issue was local, regional that is to say, a quarrel between Arabs and Jews in which no other party might presume to interfere. It is quite true, as was written, "The Arab states have, each in its own way, made clear their position, that they regard themselves as being at war, in a state of belligerency with Israel. The absence of declarations of war is merely the absence of irrelevant formalities." [194] In this matter-of-fact way, the war began.

Like all wars of liberation, the Jewish struggle for independence was not legal or illegal, merely revolutionary in its actions and its consequences. There are victors and there are the vanquished, and always there are victims. Ben Gurion and his colleagues believed they were engaged in a revolutionary undertaking, and they liked to use that term. But in the historical sense, the Zionists were actually carrying out a counter-revolution, intent upon recovering what their ancestors had lost two thousand years before. In those ancient times, the Romans had been the revolutionaries and the Jews the reactionaries, setting their faces against the new order of things that the Roman Imperium imposed upon them: one language (Latin), universal citizenship (Roman), a single culture (Graeco-Roman); a uniform code of conduct (Roman law); in contemporary parlance, the Romans promised "a new world order" for the many subject peoples who had come under their sway. Deviants and malcontents (Jesus of Nazareth only one of many rebels) were expendable. Ultimately, the entire Jewish population became the victims of Roman ambition to create one world. In 1947 the Zionists were carrying out a counter-revolution, conscious that they were agents of history. That the Palestinian Arabs should become the victims in their turn did not seem important to modern Hebrews engaged in a mission of these historic proportions. Such fanaticism is worth many armies, as the Arabs would soon learn.

On the face of it the odds were overwhelmingly against the Zionists. A small, poorly equipped Jewish force faced five well-armed Arab armies; a few hundred thousand Jews confronted millions of aroused Arabs. From another point of view, which was one of Ben Gurion's favorite perceptions, the Arab population, composed as a regional bloc, confronted world Jewry (another bloc), which, though not united on a territorial basis, was unified in their determination to spend and to fight, whatever the cost. The contest was not as unequal as it appeared. With the end of the mandate, a torrent of Jewish immigrants would flood the country, eager to fight; and in the first days more numerous than could be immediately armed and trained. What one Israeli officer said about the outcome of a single battle, favorable to Israel, could be ascribed to the entire war: "There was one item which the Egyptians were lacking—a clear idea about the purpose of the battle. But that is precisely what we possessed in full measure. Fearless spirit, the knowledge and conviction about the purpose of the battle..." [195]

Israel's victory, imagined later to be as an unheard-of success—a miracle some said—of a beleaguered and helpless Jewish minority, is not mysterious after all. Five armies approached Israel—not to speak of the internal enemy, armed Palestinians within Israel. [196] Against this advancing juggernaut a few heroic Jews acquitted themselves heroically, thereby saving the newly founded State of Israel. Such is the myth. The facts are somewhat different. One begins with the sure knowledge that the seeming Armageddon of 1947–48 had been anticipated by the Zionists since 1918. The

Zionists had always considered armed force to be the final arbiter in the endless quarrel with the Arabs. Their soldiers, well trained if not yet well armed, were stronger than mere numbers might suggest. The tactics chosen for defense were decisive in the first days of fighting. The so-called Dalet Plan envisioned the necessary capture of "strategic Arab heights" as rapidly as the British occupying forces withdrew, thereby opening the way to Jerusalem. [197]

While the Israelis' military success may be explained in terms of long-range strategy and short-term tactics (Jewish heroism merely a given), the real success lay in the virtual depopulation of the countryside. The Palestinian Arabs simply fled from their native land. Into this vacuum Israeli power flowed, as water fills an empty vessel.

This remarkable denouement was unexpected and has not been explained satisfactorily, though the general panic of a population, mass hysteria, is perhaps never understood entirely. In about a year, 1947–48, an estimated 30,000 middle-to-upper-class Arabs had fled from Palestine, mostly in and around Haifa and Jaffa. It was not war or the sense of immediate danger that drove them out at first; merely the implications they saw in the General Assembly's Partition Resolution of 29 November 1947. There had been a similar flight during the upheavals of the 1930s, and when things had quieted down, they returned. This time it was different. The Jews were by now a force to be reckoned with. Moreover, Jewish terrorism was more relentless, more systematically brutal, than that of the Arab terrorists during the thirties. To instill fear in the mass of the Arab population was a tactic long used, publicly discussed, and bragged about by one of the chief practitioners, Menachem Begin. The precipitating episode may have been the mass murders committed by the Irgun at the village of Deir Yasin on 10 April 1948. The entire population, except for the few who escaped, was slaughtered in a few hours. Afterward, the massacre was widely advertised by the Irgun as a warning to other Arabs. They "were seized with limitless panic," Begin recalled later, "and started to flee for their lives—as well they should have." Begin's Irgun and the other equally deadly organization, the Lehi, respected neither life nor property, neither women nor children. It had been a remorseless war between Jewish and Arab zealots during the thirties, but a more all-encompassing term would have to be found to describe the civil war in Palestine after 1947; it was in reality the uprooting of one people by another. The panic on the Arab side was understandable: fear for one's life. On the Jewish side, the fear was of a different order: fear for the life of a new nation; the Arab states had for long threatened to drive every Jew into the sea, quite literally. The recollection of the Holocaust in Europe was the eternal dread entertained by Jews, who could think only of being liquidated if they did not liquidate the enemy first.

So massive was the flight of Palestinian Arabs of all degrees, all classes, as to virtually empty whole regions of the country, leaving towns almost vacant, and many villages entirely deserted. The simplest answer for this was the nameless fear of many. Also, a plausible explanation, many fled in the direction of the oncoming Arab armies, expecting to receive protection—which did not arrive. An alternative explanation, favored by the Jews, is that the Arabs fled from the scene of coming hostilities in order not to encumber those who were marching to save them.

Such rationalizations do not take human behavior into account. After reflection, and living for long in the refugee camps, John H. Davis, Commanding General of UNRUA, observed:

> Voluntary emigrants do not leave their homes with only the clothes they stand in, or in such hurry and confusion that husbands lose sight of wives and parents of their children. Nor does there appear to be one shred of evidence to substantiate the claim that the fleeing refugees were obeying Arab orders. All the evidence is to the contrary, that the Arab authorities continuously exhorted the Palestinian Arabs not to leave the country...Panic and bewilderment played decisive parts in the flight. But the extent to which the refugees were savagely driven out by the Israelis as part of a deliberate master plan has been insufficiently recognized. [198]

Not saved by their Arab brothers, the Palestinians fled into the neighboring countries, most going into Jordan or to Egypt (the Gaza strip). There they took up a wretched life in exile, becoming public charges, relying eventually on charity from the United Nations.

Scholarly opinion holds that the Arab states had started out with a well-planned military campaign, but that it was never implemented. The fault for this is ascribed to the cross-purposes of the countries involved. Overall command was assigned to the Iraqi General Nur ad-Din Mahmoud, given the grandiloquent title "Commander of the Regular and Irregular Forces for the Saving of Palestine." Haifa, the port city where oil arrived by pipeline from the interior, would be the principal target. [199] To this end the Lebanese army would advance along the coast while the Syrians entered central Palestine. The Iraqi army and Jordan's Arab Legion would arrive from the south and the east. The Egyptian army would march on Tel Aviv. [200]

The contemplated movement of five armies (technically six, since Iraq furnished two) would scatter Israel's small, inadequately equipped force, or so it seemed. How Palestine would be reorganized as the British Mandate died and the Israeli forces perished was a practical question that did not find a place in the Arabs' battle plans.

The attitude of the Emir of Jordan had become crucial some weeks before the Mandate came to an end. Refusing to take supreme command of the Arab armies, Abdulla destroyed the integrity of the Arab war plans by inadvertently betraying his personal ambition. The conquest of the whole of Palestine was of no interest to him, while a war *à outrance* against the Jews was not to his taste. Having received Transjordan out of the lottery of WW I (i.e., most of Palestine—but the poorest part), he wanted the remainder. (He was generous enough, however, to think the Jews were entitled to a small part of Palestine; "a small notch," as his brother Feisal had expressed it.) Abdulla intended to annex the West Bank of the Jordan River, which was almost entirely Arab, and he wanted to control Jerusalem. Throwing his allies into confusion, he began to negotiate with the Israelis, but his proposals had the air of blackmail. If the Jews would agree not to establish a Jewish state for one year, they could expect that the Arabs would suspend their military operations. Should the Israelis refuse his offer, Abdulla would have no choice but to join the other Arab states. Thereafter he offered some bait: A Jewish-Arab state could be established with himself as king. The Israelis spurned his offer with what one may suspect were expressions of disbelief and amusement. [201]

Abdulla's double-dealing is deemed the result of his dependent status, his policy being whatever the British wished to make of it. The Emir's army, the Arab Legion, had been created as a tool for pursuing Britain's imperial goals. Financed by the British, it was commanded by a British officer, John Glubb (called respectfully by the Arabs, Glubb Pasha). [202] Forty-five of the Legion's fifty commanders were British officers. And therefore, even as they were abandoning the mandate, the British were attempting still to orchestrate the quarrel of Jew and Arab through their client Abdulla, and attempting also to determine the outcome of the war: viz., Syria and Iraq would get nothing for their efforts; Jordan could expect to receive the West Bank. (The British government believed, as did the majority of the UN delegates, that Jerusalem should be given an international status). The Jews would be secure in the possession of their new state and at last the curse of the Balfour Declaration would be buried in Palestine.

Abdulla's opportunism disrupted the Arab coalition, the Egyptians discovering suddenly that they were not prepared to fight. While the Egyptians realized that they had no stomach for war, the other Arab states hoped to succeed in what they had traditionally called *Jihad*—Holy War. But the principal belligerents showed no great commitment, while the rest of the Moslem world saw little religious significance in a contest between Israel and its Arab enemies for possession of a tiny, valueless land. Lebanon would not put more than a thousand men in the field, Syria and Iraq about 3,000 each, a total (counting Egyptian and Jordanian forces) of about 25,000 soldiers. This was a strange situation, in which Arab leadership feared a debacle, while their newspapers inflamed the Arab populace with predictions of Israeli soldiers about to be massacred; the Jewish state annihilated at the moment of its birth.

The Arabs' intelligence sources told them of Jewish superiority in numbers, the estimates ranging widely, from 65, 000 to 100,000. But in the last analysis the two sides were about equal in strength. The Arabs possessed more armaments, the Jews more soldiers. The Arabs had heavy equipment, especially tanks; Israel had none. The Arabs enjoyed air superiority; Israel had not a single fighter plane. If the Jewish defense force, *Haganah*, was technically no more than a home guard (rather than a regular army), the Arab armies (except for the Jordan Legion) were armies in name only; rather, they were largely untrained, inexperienced soldiers, more like militia. While the Arab soldiers behaved like mercenaries, unmoved by a sense of a cause or mission, the Jewish soldiers were ardent patriots. Many were zealots, recently arrived from Europe, who realized that the fight would be not only for the survival of the state of Israel, but for the preservation of their own lives and those of their families.

Once military action commenced, the engagements were widely scattered. In some cases the Israelis held their positions, in others they were overrun, and in a few places they actually gained ground. In spite of the modern machines of war, the inchoate and uncoordinated actions on both sides left the impression of the oldest and most primitive kind of combat: tribal warfare, pitting small groups of combatants against each other; fighting for the possession of a small town or village, a hilltop there, a crossroads somewhere else. After four weeks the Arabs realized they could not advance and the Israelis could still resist. A stalemate ensued, as the Egyptian leadership had feared, never having shared the Syrians' vision of a conquered Palestine and a captive Jewish population. A truce on 11 June silenced all guns.

The United Nations had, at the beginning of the hostilities, named a mediator, Count Folke Bernadotte of Sweden. He had twenty-eight days to arrange a lasting settlement (which the British had not been able to do under vastly better circumstances in the past twenty years). The belligerents had the same amount of time to regroup, rearm, and renew the struggle.

Bernadotte believed the truce represented a first step towards conciliation of the two sides. But neither the Arabs nor the Israelis thought of conciliation—they never had. The Israelis could hardly believe that, under the circumstances, they had fought the principal states of the Arab world to a draw. More remarkable still, in a few months the Haganah had been transformed into the equivalent of a modern army, called henceforth the *Zahal.* [203]

To enforce the truce, the American government imposed an embargo on all war materiel going to Palestine (Britain, under the terms of its treaties, continued to supply the Arab countries). Czechoslovakia had at the outset furnished the Israelis with military equipment, but when the communists took over the government, becoming a Soviet satellite, this source dried up—Soviet policy began to harden against Israel at the same moment its relations with the U.S. were deteriorating, a sign of the coming Cold War. Against these odds Israeli arms merchants persevered and usually prevailed: becoming global shoppers, they took what they could get from any government. The American embargo was repeatedly violated; supplies from around the world poured into areas now controlled by Israeli forces.

Surprising as it was that the Israeli forces had fought the Arabs to the point of stalemate, it was perhaps more remarkable that the Arabs had been unable to capitalize on their advantages, namely, a huge population with many conscripts available, more supplies, and shorter lines of communication and transport. (The Jews had to go abroad for nearly everything they needed.) In the final analysis the Arabs suffered from self-defeat: the corrosive effects of the unanswerable question "For what do we fight?" Time would show that this malaise could not be overcome. Remarkably also, they could not refit and rearm adequately for the next battle, though it was clear to both sides that the war would be resumed—the truce would not hold, despite Bernadotte's energetic efforts. There is reason to think also that the Arabs were almost half-hearted in their intended conquest of Palestine, not pleased to think that the sacrifices demanded of them were not for themselves, but for the

Palestinians whom they generally held in contempt. Subsequent events would reveal that each Arab participant in the war was more interested in holding the part of Palestine they occupied than in taking the whole of the country away from the Jews. [204] Had Abdulla been perfectly free to choose he would have withdrawn his legion, which had suffered significant losses. Not less important, Palestinian refugees were streaming across the Jordan River, creating serious political difficulties for him. Ultimately, however, he thought only of Jerusalem, still believing he might become King of Palestine, both Jews and Arabs his loyal subjects. [205]

Futilely did Bernadotte enjoin peaceful reason on men whose only thought was a resumption of the war and the realization of their goals. His invitation, that they parley under his chairmanship on the Isle of Rhodes, was ignored. On 8 July the Egyptians initiated hostilities and the war was on again. Hostilities would last only ten days.

While the Israelis had reformed the Haganah, making it into what could be called a modern army, they were also bringing into the country the implements of modern warfare: fighter planes, armored vehicles, tanks, heavy artillery, and munitions. Jewish immigrants continued streaming into the country. They were immediately enrolled as either combatants or workers dedicated to the cause of national liberation. All were organized for an end: the defeat of the Arabs when the truce should come to an end. Ultimately, the Zahal consisted of about 18 percent or more of newly arrived immigrants, many of them older men who brought military experience gained by service during the Second World War.

As the flood of supplies and the torrent of volunteers were fundamental changes, no less important were the changes given to the Israeli High Command. Changes at this high level embroiled Ben Gurion (a civilian—and an egotist above average) with military men as willful as himself. In the end, Ben Gurion was recognized by his political colleagues and military officers as the single figure of authority. Only the Jewish terrorists refused to take orders.

For several years the Irgun had operated rather like a sovereign state within the Mandate, defying both the British power and the Jewish Agency's authority. A law unto itself, it possessed its own ships and sources of revenue (not a few of these assets gained by robbing banks). Although selfless in serving the Zionist cause, on the morrow of victory they might very well establish a dictatorship that would imperil the men of the Jewish Agency who had their own agenda to fulfill. Ben Gurion and his colleagues realized that the time had come to extinguish terrorism as an instrument of policy, bring the renegades into line and take them into the reformed Haganah. After long negotiations, when it became apparent that the Irgun leadership intended to maintain its accustomed independence, the men of the Agency moved decisively. The Irgun's principal ship, the *Atalina*, was trapped in port while unloading cargo. Confused orders and the resolve of the Irgun to resist resulted in heavy fighting during the night and morning of June 21–22. To Ben Gurion's evident chagrin, what was intended to be a brief showdown in the dark turned into a sideshow in broad daylight. To the watching Israeli citizens the conflict seemed to announce the beginning of a civil war.

The cost of disarming the Irgun was not merely the loss of forty lives, but unfortunate publicity at a moment when national unity seemed imperative. However, united militarily, politically also as a result of the events of June 21-22, Ben Gurion could evade Bernadotte's latest proposal for a settlement of the war. The compromise the UN mediator suggested seemed (in the eyes of the Israeli government) not only too favorable to the Arabs but gave the Negev desert to them as well. Ben Gurion's fascination with that vast empty space and its future for Israel is impossible to overstate. Equally unacceptable to the Israelis was the idea of Jerusalem becoming an international city—it was a holy city, but it was above all Jewish and would become eventually the capital of Israel, to be shared with no one.

When ready, Ben Gurion declared the truce to have been broken by the Arabs. (In reality both sides had violated the truce). Learning of Ben Gurion's intention to take the offensive, Bernadotte flew to Jerusalem on 17 September. After lunch in the New City of Jerusalem he ordered his driver to take him to Government House. Driving back through the Kataman he was stopped by a Jeep parked crossways in the road. Three men in khaki uniforms got out and walked up to the car. Suddenly, one thrust a Schmeisser automatic pistol through the window and fired six rounds into the vehicle. Bernadotte was mortally wounded. By shooting out the tires the assassins incapacitated the other cars making up Bernadotte's convoy, then jumped into the Jeep and drove away.

While the Israeli government could not deny that the assassins wore army uniforms, they would not admit that the Zahal had participated in the murder. Since the assassins were not caught immediately, there was no direct evidence to implicate either the Zahal or any of the several Jewish terrorist groups. [206] Even so, it was politic for Ben Gurion to outlaw the Lehi.

In whatever way the assassination of the UN mediator may be explained, it was fortunate for the Israelis. With Bernadotte out of the way, his will and that of the United Nations, could not be imposed immediately. The Israelis moved rapidly. To defeat the Bernadotte plan before the UN could act on it, on 6 October Ben Gurion sent the Zahal into the Negev under the code name "Operation Ten Plagues."

The Negev campaign came at the end of several debates between Ben Gurion and his civil and military advisors. An attempt to take Old Jerusalem, the Holy of Holies to both Jews and Arabs, would require such a commitment in men and supplies that the battle for the Negev might be lost. Another stalemate might occur, another cease-fire, and the ultimate goal of the Jews to recover their patrimony perhaps lost for good. With boldness not far short of a reckless gamble there began a race to seize all of Palestine south of Jerusalem before the UN could impose another truce. Ralph Bunche, an American who succeeded Bernadotte, worked vigorously to halt the fighting. As the UN delegates debated and Bunche talked, the Israelis marched, battled, and soon approached the environs of Jerusalem. By 22 October they controlled the

Negev for all practical purposes. Finding little resistance they entered Galilee.

A new truce, announced on 22 October, was not effectively recognized by all belligerents until late in November. When Bunche called for both sides to accept an armistice as a prelude to peace talks, the Egyptians refused, which was enough to instill the spirit of obduracy in its allies. Once more the Israelis found a sufficient pretext to start the war again. On 10 December Operation Ayin commenced: a campaign to occupy the Gaza Strip and at the same time to seize the tip of the Negev, which would give them access to the Gulf of Aqaba. Again, protracted debates at Lake Success by the UN representatives, and the rapid movement of the Zahal, gave the Israelis time enough to achieve their goals. Still another cease-fire on 29 December terminated the hostilities.

By now the war had evolved into a contest between Israel and Egypt. Abdulla would not move, having, as he believed, achieved his principal objective: possession of the West Bank. (He also maintained control of Old Jerusalem with its holy relics: the Temple Mount and the Wailing Wall.) On 1 December at Jericho, a congress composed of Palestinian delegates (mostly refugees from the West Bank who had fled across the river into Transjordan) proclaimed him King of Jerusalem.

This was assuredly an empty gesture, having no meaning to anyone in the world except Abdulla and a few Palestinians, the majority of them still offended that the Hashemites, willing pawns of the British power, had taken most of Palestine in 1922.

At this stage Syria and Iraq had become merely observers of the war. Only Egypt, supported by Great Britain, fought on, because it had lost territory in the Negev that it considered its own. The Zahal had advanced far into the Sinai, the Egyptians having evacuated the Gaza Strip. All that held the Israelis from advancing on the Suez Canal were warnings from London that they had gone too far, and that if they did not commence a withdrawal, Britain would take up the defense of its ally, Egypt. [207]

News of Egyptian reverses in the Sinai precipitated panic in Cairo.

Long fed on false reports of Arab victories, the public learned now of not merely defeats, but a debacle, leaving Egypt open to invasion. Religious fanaticism, best represented by the Moslem Brotherhood, inspired riots. Egyptian Premier Nokransky demanded the Brotherhood be outlawed. He was duly assassinated on 28 December.

The Israelis now defied the UN, setting in motion still another campaign. Sure that the British would bark but not bite, Ben Gurion ordered the occupation of the Gaza Strip, a small territory already swarming with Palestinian refugees. In a futile attempt to aid the Egyptians, the British sent up five reconnaissance planes. The Israeli High Command, preferring to think that these were more than innocent observers, ordered them shot down. This produced consternation for the ruling circle in London, while general public opinion condemned the British government for interfering in a matter that did not concern them.

Israeli and Egyptian negotiators arrived at Rhodes On 12 February, having accepted the mediation offered by Ralph Bunche. These talks became as unproductive as the several truces that had punctuated the war. Finally, on 24 February, Bunche gained an agreement from both sides. Israel gave up any claim to the Gaza Strip. Henceforth, the hundreds of thousands of refugees became Egypt's problem. They would become, in a short time, unforeseen by anyone, Israel's collective nemesis and a heavy burden for the international community.

A Jordanian delegation arrived at Rhodes on 28 February. The tergiversations of Abdulla's envoys dragged out the talks, giving Ben Gurion another opportunity to prepare a new offensive, this time against Jordan. The root cause for this was a misadventure. Since Egypt could no longer protect Elath, on the Gulf of Aqaba, a small detachment from the Arab Legion took possession of the town. Shortly afterward an Israeli brigade arrived in the vicinity, producing a new crisis. To resolve it, Abdulla invited the Israeli envoys to meet with him at his winter palace, located at Shune near the Dead Sea. Following a cordial dinner and some further conversation, the delegates and the Emir entered into an agreement. This was sent to Bunche without delay, and he accepted it.

Iraq and Lebanon had left the war without posing any conditions. As they had started the war without making a formal declaration, they departed without ceremony—no peace, no war. That left only Syria for Israel to deal with. Once talks began they became protracted. Syria had been the moving spirit behind the Arab coalition. The anticipated conquest of Palestine was to be for Syria, not for the Palestinian Arabs, most of whom had by now fled into neighboring countries. Finally, on 29 July 1949, the representatives of Israel and Syria agreed to an armistice. With that the State of Israel was secure, and it might have been thought that peace would follow. But it did not. Over many years to follow, not a single peace treaty would issue from the several armistices Bunche had been able to put into place. [208]

Like the earlier truce lines, the armistice lines were tentative, only descriptive of where Israel's authority ended and that of another state began; so inflexibly and haphazardly established that in some cases the line ran through a village or small town. It would be called for many years hence "the Green Line."

As a consequence of what might be called the unfinished war, Israel held more territory than the UN partition plan had called for. And, of great significance, they had been able to hold the predominately Jewish sector of Jerusalem (West Jerusalem). East Jerusalem, which was overwhelmingly Arab, remained under Jordan's control. (Gaza and the coastal area [Gaza Strip] were held by Egypt, which did not want to annex it, thereby avoiding responsibility for the hundreds of thousands of refugees who huddled there under the care of the United Nations.) Syria held the small town of Al-Hamma, on the Sea of Galilee.

For the Israelis the war had been a glorious liberation of their ancient homeland, a sentimental and romantic mission that resonated with the Westerners, who viewed the struggle in the Holy Land as a recapitulation of revered Biblical history: little David slaying the terrible Goliath (modern Philistines) with no more than the proverbial slingshot. The Arab assessment was quite different: "a prolonged and tragically successful invasion," intoned one, conducted by "an alien people under Western imperialist auspices, ending in the expulsion of most of the people whose country it was."[209]

Large numbers of refugees had crossed the river into Transjordan, producing acute problems that would worsen with the passing years. Abdulla's solution for this was to unite the West Bank with the east bank, allowing Palestinian Arabs to believe that their nationality had changed to become a Jordanian identity. In this case at least, nationality was not deemed to be a matter of ethnicity so much as a citizen's allegiance to a legitimate authority—a matter of law only.[210]

Israel's first national elections were held in January 1949, bringing Ben Gurion's Mapai Party to power; not a surprising result since that party had dominated the Jewish Agency through the will and ability of its leaders, and enjoyed the renown that comes to those who have done the seemingly impossible. Israel was admitted to the United Nations on 11 May 1949, just a little short of twelve months since the proclamation of its independence.

The conquest of some part of Palestine (Abdulla retaining for himself Transjordan and Cisjordan) gave Israel sovereign authority over a territory about the size of the State of Massachusetts. A solution for Jerusalem's status was difficult, if not impossible to achieve: Jordan retained control over East Jerusalem (the Old City) and Israel held West Jerusalem. An international regime for the city had been promulgated by the Trusteeship Council in April 1948. As proposed, the municipality of Jerusalem, including the hinterland (Bethlehem to the south of the city, Abu Dis to the east, Ein Karim to the west, and Shu'fat to the north), had the appearance of being a city-state; all religious sites, churches, mosques, synagogues, as well as antiquarian structures to be protected by international law. Although self-governing, Jerusalem would not be sovereign, but subject to the Trusteeship Council. Early in December 1949, the General Assembly voted to place Jerusalem under "a permanent international regime." Almost immediately the Knesset declared

West Jerusalem to be the capital of Israel. On 14 December, the Israeli government transferred its offices from Tel Aviv to West Jerusalem, mute testimony to the belief long held by the Zionists that one day it would become the capital of Israel. [211]

NOTES

171 Arnold Toynbee, *A Study of History*, op. cit., II, p. 157.

172 Martin Gilbert, *Israel* (New York and London, 1998), p. 118.

173 Martin Jones, *Failure in Palestine. British and United States Policy after the Second World War* (London and New York, 1986), p. 37.

174 Ibid., pp. 40-41.

175 Joseph P. Lash, Eleanor. *The Years Alone* (New York, 1972), p. 109.

176 Frank Epp, *Whose Land is Palestine?*, op. cit., p. 139.

177 Frank Manuel, *The Realities of American-Palestinian Relations*, op. cit., p. 313.

178 Elie Kedouri, *Islam in the Modern World and Other Studies* (New York, 1980), p. 69.

179 Robert Silverberg, *If I Forget Thee O Jerusalem*, op. cit., p. 260.

180 Dr. Saul Zaaka, *Blood in Zion. How the Jewish Guerillas Drove the British Out of Zion* (London and Washington, 1995), p. 173.

181 Ibid., p. 109.

182 Ibid., p. 98.

183 The acronym for the American Jewish Joint Distribution Committee, founded in 1914 to assist Jewish refugees during WWI.

184 Manuel, p. 282.

185 Silverberg, p. 261.

186 British statesmen could not, of course, accept this, having curtailed Jewish immigration to Palestine since 1936.

187 Jones, p. 75.

188 Ibid., p. 76. This was the second visit the committee made to Cairo.

189 Ibid., pp. 77-78.

190 Australia, Canada, Czechoslovakia, Guatemala, India, Iran, The Netherlands, Peru, Uruguay and Yugoslavia.

191 Epp, p. 180.

192 A year later, the Republican candidate for president from New York, Thomas Dewey, would lose to Truman by the proverbial hair, but not in New York where he won the Jewish vote. In California, Ohio, and Illinois the Jewish vote went for Truman, enough to give him a slim victory over Dewey.

193 The Soviet recognition was perhaps not inexplicable. Stalin believed British

supremacy in the Levant would be eroded by a loss of Palestine; not recognizing perhaps that a new power, the US, would replace Britain in the Middle East.

194 "Underlying legal problems," *The Arab-Israeli Conflict. Readings and Documents.* Abridged and Revised Edition, John Norton Moore, op. cit., p. 672.

195 Gilbert, *Israel*, p. 219.

196 It is generally agreed that this was a phantom threat since British reprisals during the 1930's had effectively reduced Palestinian terrorism to a certain nullity, a weakness that would go to the advantage of the Jews.

197 J. Bowyer Bell, *The Long War. Israel and the Arabs Since 1946* (Englewood Cliffs, NJ, 1969), p. 95.

198 John H. Davis, *The Evasive Peace* (London, 1968), pp. 56-57.

199 The pipeline was opened in 1936.

200 The military historians argue over the possibility of two battle plans and the confusion this produced for the Arab commanders. J. Boyer Bell, *The Long War*. pp. 327-28.

201 Ibid., p. 126.

202 Pasha is transliterated variously as Lord or Sir, a title not of rank but merely dignity.

203 Bell, *The Long War*, p. 163.

204 Except for Lebanon which withdrew from the war entirely.

205 With gratitude for the Emir's past loyalty, and perhaps future service, the British entered into a treaty arrangement with Abdullah, elevating him to King of Jordan.

206 In fact, the provisional Israeli government knew the name of the principal assassin immediately: Yehoshua Cohen, a Sternist who had taken his orders from Yitzhak Yseernitsky, one of the Stern Gang's triumvirate.

207 The British cabinet evoked the terms of the Anglo-Egyptian Treaty of 1936 as a justification for this threat.

208 Iraq would not accept an armistice with Israel.

209 John Quigley, *Palestine and Israel. A Challenge to Justice* (Duke University Press, 1990), p. 86.

210 The Jordanian law on nationality offered citizenship to any Palestinian Arab who wanted it.

211 This was a symbolic act. For many years no government which recognized Israel would establish an embassy at Jerusalem.

CHAPTER SIX

The Palestinian Diaspora

THE ZIONIST REVOLUTION

ardly had Israeli sovereignty been established over a relatively small part of Palestine than the expert opinion of legal scholars and international lawyers was sought by both Jews and Arabs, the one condemning Israeli actions, the other defending them. [212] A scholar, Henry Cattan, wrote a reasoned argument that relied upon historical evidence. Long before Mohammed's time the Palestinian Arabs had been in possession of the land. They could trace their lineage back to the Canaanites of antiquity, to a time when the Hebrew tribes were still wandering in the desert. The Palestinian title, Cattan concluded, "rests upon ownership of the country from time immemorial." [213]

In rebuttal Nathan Feinberg expressed surprise that Cattan expected to find a proof for sovereignty in history alone, arguing that the question was "purely juridical in nature." To reduce Feinberg's critique to the minimum, he rejected the organic conception that the sovereignty *de jure* of a nationality grows out of the historical fact of a people living on a territory over a long period of time. To the contrary, sovereignty is a quality that can be assigned to any state, in the case of Israel its sovereignty gained by the powers vested in the United Nations. [214] It was therefore merely a question of law, or more exactly international comity. Israel had the law on its side and the Palestinian Arabs did not. By an extension of this thought, Israel was innocent in the matter and the Palestinians were not; Israel was law-abiding and the Palestinians were outlaws.

One may outflank the erudite and often arcane arguments of the scholars by observing that in the world of rival peoples and quarreling nations, force alone decides these questions. What had once belonged to the Hebrews passed at some point to the Arabs (by reason of force), and thereafter some part of the same property passed back to the Jews (again by force); so, one may presume that in time, perhaps over centuries, what is now Jewish territory may become Arab again. [215]

If it cannot be ascertained with any certainty whether the Palestinian exodus in 1947–48 was a spontaneous flight or the result of Jewish terrorism, military actions, and the Machiavellian policies of the provisional Israeli government, it is only too apparent that a country left almost vacant by fleeing Arabs offered the Zionists an unexpected opportunity to complete the edifice of the long-desired Jewish state. The program, which Weizmann and many like him had nurtured, might have taken many years to be realized but could now be accomplished in not more than months, a few years at most. Sharett, now foreign minister, admitted to being stunned. It was, he wrote Nahum Goldmann, "the most spectacular event in the contemporary history of Palestine, in a way more spectacular than the creation of the Jewish state ... the wholesale evacuation of its Arab population ... The opportunities opened up by the present reality for a lasting and radical solution of the most vexing problem of the Jewish state are so far-reaching as to take one's breath away. The reversion to the *status quo ante* is unthinkable." [216]

The territory assigned to the Jews by the United Nations under the partition plan of 1947 would have been inherently unstable given the mutual antagonism of Arabs and Jews: 495,000 of the former and 498,000 of the latter living on the same territory. The boundaries established provisionally by the several armistices in 1949 promised an even less favorable situation for the Jews. Without the Palestinian exodus (or to put it another way, with the return of the Palestinians), the State of Israel would have contained 692,000 Arabs and 655,000 Jews. Any of these figures would have been, and always had been, unacceptable to the Zionists, for they still thought of the Jewish state as both a religious and cultural entity—a Jewish state would have to be purely Jewish, or nearly so. To be remembered also, the Arab custom of living under the Sharia had been maintained during the British occupation after 1917 and continued unimpaired under the Mandate; namely, secular law for the Arabs had to be in conformity with revealed truth, found only in their holy book, the Koran.

If one should be cynical in his analysis, as is sometimes said of the Zionist leadership, the only questions to be asked are: How would the Israelis prevent the Palestinians from returning, and how might Israel take possession of the ostensibly abandoned property of the Palestinians without offending world opinion (or patently violating international law apropos refugees and private property)? Two simple questions for which there were no easy answers.

To critical public opinion the Zionists offered an explanation that seemed plausible on the face of it. The Arabs started the war and the Jews won it. What had happened thereafter was a "de facto exchange of populations." If hundreds of thousands of Palestinians had taken flight, hundreds of thousands of Jews had fled into Israel from the neighboring Arab countries. However brutal for many individuals these disruptions might have been, it seemed a necessary solution and did not appear substantially different from the solution that Greeks and Turks had given to their nationality problems in 1922.[217]

This rationalization overlooked the obvious. The so-called de facto exchange of populations was but a single episode in the vast screen of Zionist operations, the program calling for massive infiltration of the country by Jews from around the world. So great was the influx that world Jewry, though generous as always, could not underwrite the costs involved. Soon large "tent cities" sprang up across Israel's arid spaces, neither housing nor land enough available for so many.

The Israelis' contention that they were filling an empty land because the Arab leaders had urged the Palestinians to take flight seems indefensible. To the contrary, "the Arab authorities continuously exhorted the Palestinian Arabs not to leave the country…"[218] The Arab states, poor in resources, were not prepared to receive a large influx of destitute refugees. Eventually this miserable horde would exceed 700,000. UN mediator Count Bernadotte initiated relief actions, but so great was the problem, so intractable as it seemed to him, that he made efforts to repatriate the refugees. His inability to get quick action along these lines compelled the UN to approve an emergency fund of five million dollars and the establishment of a relief agency, UNRPR. So long did the attempt to repatriate the refugees to their homeland last that this temporary agency took on an institutional life of its own, constituting a welfare system on an international scale. Over the coming years it would expend many billions of dollars for the maintenance of dispossessed Arabs, while fruitless negotiations for a definitive peace dragged on.

The deeper tragedy shaping up, but unrecognized for a long time, was the emergence of a phenomenon called "camp culture": people demoralized by poverty, degraded as recipients of a grudging generosity, their progeny born in the squalor of the camps; suffering from malnutrition, deprived of the most elemental living standards; children growing up virtually illiterate, feeding on the grievances of the parents; without a prospect of even elementary employment; angry and restless; all this rage to be turned eventually upon what they imagined (not without justice) to be the author of their misery: Israel. Terrorism as it is known in modern time was inevitably born in such an environment as this.

From the humanitarian point of view, relief and repatriation were essential for re-establishing stability in Israel, in the Arab world as a whole. In his brief tenure as UN mediator, Count Bernadotte had pronounced five principles for peace—among these, conciliation. To that end the UN established a Conciliation Commission. The matter of compensation, so closely connected to conciliation, became part of the negotiations: compensation for those Palestinians who had lost everything and did not intend to return to Israel; compensation for those Arabs who, returning to Israel, would find that their villages had not been merely ruined but in many cases wiped off the face of the earth by bulldozers; those Arabs who returned to find that the family domicile that had sheltered them for generations was now occupied by a Jewish family who could offer proof of title to the property; compensation for those Arabs whose possessions had been plundered, sold on the black market, to end up as something like artifacts for decorating the houses of the more affluent Israelis.

At the outset the Israeli government set a nearly impossible condition to be satisfied before reparations could be paid: the Arab states would have to accept a general peace settlement with Israel; that is to say, accept a *fait accompli*. Subsequent talks came to an impasse, much as action on the battlefield had led to repeated stalemate. The Palestinian refugees became in this process unwilling pawns. For their part, the Arabs demanded that reparations and repatriation take place first, and a peace settlement to follow. The Israelis repulsed this out of hand. And so the hostages languished in the camps and the impasse persisted.

For Ben Gurion and his colleagues time was of the essence. The unspoken policy was to liquidate as much as possible whatever the Palestinians had left behind, while keeping the reparation question in a state of limbo. Another policy, very open, was to bring in Jewish immigrants as fast as possible. Where before, under the British Mandate, Jews had been obliged to beg for admission to Palestine, now the sovereign state of Israel would make its own terms, and these were very lenient indeed. Under a law popularly called The Law of Return, any Jew in the world, regardless of race or national origin, might enter Israel and receive immediate citizenship; only his Jewishness had to be certified. [219]

If history could be reduced to slow motion—one frame slowly dissolving to be replaced by another—one would see two successive migrations: the exodus of hundreds of thousands of Palestinians and the almost simultaneous arrival of hundreds of thousands, and finally millions, of Jews.

The political and diplomatic maneuvers of the Zionists were transparent. Having won the military contest, in control of part of the country, they intended to win the political war, to transform a previously Arab country into a Jewish one. Aware of this the U.S. State Department sent the Israeli government an unfriendly note expressing its "disappointment," warning that the policies Israel had adopted were "dangerous to peace." Finally, a threat: the United States might have to "reconsider its attitude toward Israel." [220]

While the "attitude" toward Israel might be reconsidered, U.S. policy could not be fundamentally altered. Having in effect condoned the Zionists' audacity, the Truman administration could not, in a spirit of honor or at the risk of national pride, abandon Israel to its Arab enemies, who one day might do to a defenseless Israel what Israel was now doing to defenseless Palestinians. In a real sense the United States had become as much Israel's hostage as the Palestinians who fretted away their lives in the refugee camps.

Predictably, given the Arabs' long subordination to a succession of imperial powers, Zionism was condemned by them as being another "colonial phenomenon," a masked intrusion of Western imperialism, "the ally of the capitalist powers." Alternatively, they called it a "beach-head of the capitalist world." [221] The West, an alien culture, had descended upon a virtually defenseless culture, the East. The unspoken motive of the Western interventionists was their desire (indeed, their need) to secure their access to oil, the commodity that fires their industries, makes comfortable the lives of their citizens and, one might even say, preserves their lives.

The spoken motive of the Westerners, one not entirely hypocritical since they believed it, was a variant of the oft-told tale of the White Man's burden. The Jews carried with them the blessings of modern science: a higher standard of living than the Arabs could quite imagine; a lofty code for human conduct (magic words—"human rights"); and, of course, the practice of self-government (magic word—"democracy"). How could the lowly and innocent Arab peasantry in its collective millions stand in the way of a movement such as this, however painful its imposition upon the individual might be? This romance colored Israeli books and films and the opinion of Zionist supporters abroad for many years hence.

Zionism, a movement that had been religious in its earliest and deepest motivation, romantic in its aspirations, valiant in its actions, violent in many of its deeds, would naturally produce heroes who seemed to the next generation of Israelis almost magisterial figures. All these qualities were combined in the person of Ben Gurion, who was more than a revolutionary icon: he was considered the source of all authority, almost the incarnation of the Israeli State. Chaim Weizmann, elder statesman, father of the Jewish homeland by common acknowledgement, received the honorary dignity, President of the new State of Israel; but Ben Gurion was its ruler. Invariably his opinion was final in all important questions. So great was the aura of his personality, it was said, that "some even saw him as the personification of history." [222]

A pragmatist, political operator par excellence, Ben Gurion had realized from the beginning of his career as a labor leader that the settlement of Palestine would require a massive migration of Jews in order to overcome the numerical superiority of the Arabs. From the beginning, the Zionists had recognized that (even at parity with the Arabs) they would be out-bred by them. Once the Jewish state was proclaimed, the original motive seemed more pressing than before. Many Jews would be needed to build up a modern state, to construct a basic infrastructure for supporting the Western manner of living. Housing for the millions of Jews arriving from the Diaspora was perhaps the most daunting task among many that faced the founders of the State of Israel.

After 1936 the military factor had become ever more important to Ben Gurion. Since the newly established state existed under the conditions of an unfinished war, with indeterminate boundaries and still confronted by a host of vengeful Arabs, the need for security was far above the ordinary.

The transformation of the Haganah into a conventional army was accompanied by the creation of state institutions: a legislative body (the Knesset), a cabinet, an executive officer (i.e., a premier); and a president (a powerless figure), presiding over what amounted to a republic. [223]

A sovereign state requires diplomatic recognition from its peers. This recognition was sought at once, even though the outcome of the war could not be predicted. Legitimacy and an inherent right to survival in a jungle of sovereign states also demanded admission to the United Nations—this was also sought immediately. Israel's petition was ratified on 11 May 1949.

The Knesset was modeled on that of the Second Temple period, even to the number of deputies, 250. Not surprisingly, the first Knesset was composed almost entirely of political Zionists, overwhelmingly male (there were eleven women members). Older men for the most part, they were almost all Ashkenazic Jews, the plotters and fighters who had taken on both the British and the Arabs and won. An exclusive caste, to paraphrase Financial Minister David Horowitz, they wished for (and they needed) Jewish immigrants, but they did not want to be associated with the newcomers in personal terms. [224] Repetitious of Jewish migration elsewhere over the previous centuries, they identified sentimentally with their fellows; but as established Jews they distrusted the next wave of immigrants. The motive in this seemingly irrational behavior was always the same: fear that the new ones would change the old ways too much. Ben Gurion seemed much affected by this contradiction, saying, "I cannot stand the conservatism of my revolutionaries." [225]

Ben Gurion's ambition, his vision of the country's future, demanded of him endless work, almost beyond belief. Yet, the evidence is found in his diaries and notebooks. This written record of his daily activities and his expansive ideas alone required several hours' work each day. And he was not young—sixty-two years old in 1949. A small man, five foot three, he was unprepossessing in appearance. Tending to stoutness, with a balding pate, the wild white hair flying out from the sides almost comically, his political stature was obviously not decided by his mediocre figure. Rather, it was the immense reservoir of moral authority that had accrued to him in a career that already spanned three decades. He looked upon the state he was founding in more than merely proprietary terms, but rather like a nurturing parent.

There was something of ancient Sparta in the new State of Israel (the most extreme of the Zionists thinking that the Palestinians who had failed to flee might henceforth play the role of Helots). "It probably would be easier to govern them," remarked Lubrani, one of Ben Gurion's colleagues, "if they continued to work as wood cutters and waiters." [226]

The Zionists' treatment, or better to say mistreatment, of the Arab country people was as determined and as pitiless as that of the Khmer Rouge when their turn came to deal with the hapless victims who stood in the way of their ambition. In absolute terms of justice and morality—the one clearing the countryside and the other emptying the cities—the scale of the two operations does not matter. The wholesale killing of the innocents by the Khmer Rouge horrified those who finally learned of it. In the Israeli case, the wholesale eviction of hundreds of thousands of Palestinians would amount to the silent murder of many individuals and promised the extinction of a people's national identity. Yet this hardly stirred the generation that witnessed it.

The Zionists had no doubt they were engaged in a great enterprise, ruthless and relentless in its operations; "a bloodless revolution," remarked Pinhas Lavon, Minister of Agriculture, "proceeding at a much lower price than any revolution in history." [227] From an early time, certainly by the turn of the century, the Zionists conceived of their mission as revolutionary, an almost fanciful reconstruction of the past that could be deterred by no human force. "We cannot allow the Arabs," declared Israel Zangwil, "to block so valuable a piece of historic reconstruction…". [228]

True revolutionaries are determinists by nature and effectively slaves to the ideology that seduces them. Single-mindedness allows for great accomplishments, whatever the price, and the price for Israeli independence was high. As a witness to the plunder of the empty houses and deserted shops, whole villages being demolished, Bernadotte had been tremendously moved, realizing that Palestinian dispersal and dispossession might be permanent. "No settlement," he remarked in his report to the Third Session of the United Nations, "can be just and complete if recognition is not accorded to the right of the Arab refugee to return to the home from which he has been dislodged by the hazards and strategy of the armed conflict between Arabs and Jews in Palestine. It would be an offense against the principles of elemental justice if these innocent victims of the conflict were denied the right to return to their homes while Jewish immigrants flow into Palestine, and, indeed, at least offer the threat of permanent replacement of the Arab refugees who have been rooted in the land for centuries." [229]

To deal with Israeli excesses on the basis of legality is a futile exercise. In the end it was the case, to employ the metaphor of this book, of one sibling turning out the other without scruple or pity. To underscore the rationale of the struggle, a Jew would have said, "Had the tables been turned they would have treated us as badly as we treated them."

Faced with what must have seemed a heaven-sent opportunity to achieve almost at once a Jewish majority in the new state of Israel (the result of the Palestinian flight), the question for those in power was how to make the exodus permanent. "We should," thought Yosef Weitz, Director of the Land Department of the Jewish National Fund, "do something so as to transform the exodus of the Arabs from the country into a fact, that they return no more. Is it not now the time to be rid of them?" [230]

The "something" to which Weitz referred was already underway in different parts of the country where Jews found many opportunities to take whatever was abandoned by those who were fleeing. The long-standing practice of tearing down an enemy's house (a British practice under the Mandate) was now applied to whole villages. Any village in disarray, any village remote enough to be unable to defend itself or appeal to the outside world, was an inevitable target. Within the confines of a country still primitive, a policy of harrying the Arabs went largely unnoticed by either the Jewish population at large (particularly the urban Jews) or the world beyond.

The brutal and seemingly mindless assault on Arab villagers in 1948 almost surpasses understanding. To the degree that it is to be comprehended at all, one may well reflect upon the impressions of Weitz, who late in this same year went to inspect a village called Mu'ar. He arrived to see "three tractors...completing its destruction." He was surprised, he recalled later, that "nothing in me moved at the sight of the destruction. No regret and no hate, as though this was the way the world goes."

It has been said of Hitler's minions, who beat and tortured their victims, that they performed their tasks methodically, mechanically, without emotion; dehumanized themselves as they stripped the last vestiges of humanity from those they tormented. "So," concluded Weitz, "we want to feel good in this world, and not in some world to come. We simply want to live, and the inhabitants of those mud houses did not want us to exist here. They not only aspired to dominate us, they also want to exterminate us." [231]

Regimes based on force rely upon such servants as Weitz. His recollection, a numbed unfeeling account, makes one think of a soldier standing over the corpse of the fallen enemy: no remorse, only indifference. The war of the siblings after nearly three decades had by now so hardened the heart that death and destruction was as commonplace as bad weather. Grieving relatives, maimed men and women; children abandoned, abused, and starving, did not arouse any feeling of compassion in the Zionists; these were merely trifles that stood or had fallen in the way of a great undertaking: the consolidation of a state rendered Jewish almost overnight.

Much has been written about the frailties of the Palestinian country people. The torpor of the sedentary life and the comfort to be found in the seasonal rhythm of a peasant's existence making them apathetic and easily exploited. Unskilled and uneducated, a traditionally docile population for long under the authority of the

Arab landowners; a landless peasantry to a large extent, with no political tradition and no practical political experience; untouched by the nexus of influences called "progress" in the West, which had created a restless energy among all the social classes. All this is but a reminder that the progressive Jews from the West found it easy to take advantage of the Palestinians, without scruple and seldom with apology; and certainly theft was to be accomplished without thought of compensation.

It cannot be said exactly what were the spurious actions of private Israeli citizens in taking what was not theirs, and the government's resolve to make the despoliation of the Palestinians a matter of public policy. Probably the two operated at the same time, the one reinforcing the other. It was easy for the Jews to believe the fleeing Palestinians would not return, for the hope is forever the father of the deed. The wish for long, through the years of recurring terror during the Mandate period, was for an end to civil strife, leading many Jews to hope that the Arabs might disappear entirely; as though the Arab presence alone explained the conflict between the two.

This ambivalence was especially notable in Ben Gurion's words and actions. The one who knew all and heard all could not conceal his dismay when he learned of these widespread depredations. He was "surprised," he admitted, "bitterly" surprised with "the discovery of such moral failings among us, which I had never suspected." The fact is, however, that Ben Gurion, as head of state, was a participant in the widespread looting that was nothing less than criminal activity. More than this, he was the principal agent who had made many of these crimes possible.

While the bulk of confiscated property consisted of land and real estate, a considerable fraction of it consisted of the entire Palestinian economic infrastructure. This too was transferred into Jewish hands. There are, of course, no reliable figures available for the amount seized, but an estimate of what transpired at Lidda suggests what was going on everywhere in the former Mandate:

1,800 truckloads of property, including a button factory,

a carbonated drinks plant, a sausage factory, an ice plant, a textile plant, a macaroni factory, 7,000 retail shops, 500 workshops, and 1,000 warehouses...An undisclosed number of cabinetmaking shops, locksmith works, turneries, ironworks, and tinworks...[232]

In principle the Jews did not want wholesale theft and a naked confiscation, either as a policy of the government or the unspoken will of the Israeli people. Rather, a certain legality attended what was in fact the illegal expropriation of Arab property. The Eternal Fund Israel, more commonly called the Jewish National Fund (technically, *Ha-Keren Ha-Keymeth Leisrael*), had been less than successful in purchasing land during the Mandate period. By 1947 not much more than 7 percent of the total land of Palestine had passed into Jewish hands. Yet, in terms of numbers, by the end of World War Two the Jews had begun to approach parity with the Palestinian Arabs. There were several reasons for this unbalanced equation. A considerable part of Palestine had been designated by the Mandatory Power as public land, not open to purchase. Arabs had been reluctant to sell land because (a) it was considered unpatriotic to do so, any transaction going to the advantage of the Jews in the long run, and (b) because the effendi frowned upon such transactions and sometimes punished Arabs who yielded to temptation. Finally, after 1936, the Mandatory Power had made it almost impossible for the Jews to buy land in Palestine. The money power of world Jewry, upon which the Zionists had counted in so many ways, availed them little or nothing with regard to land.

The establishment of the Jewish state in 1948 changed all that. While arming the Jewish immigrants for the coming struggle with the Arabs, Ben Gurion, on 13 May 1948, made the director of the Jewish National Fund an offer he could not refuse.[233] As fast as the Haganah occupied territory, it would be sold to the Jewish National Fund—an anticipated conquest amounting to perhaps two million *dunums* (a dunum equal to about a quarter-acre). The price would be one-half pound sterling per dunum. Succeeding far beyond their expectations, the Provisional Government had "liberated" 20.5 million dunums by the end of the war. Thereafter there commenced two separate but closely linked actions, the one tending to negate the other. On the one hand, the Israeli government opened negotiations with the Arab states for a general peace settlement, which included proposals for repatriating the Palestinian refugees, and a method of compensation for what they had lost. At the same time an elaborate program for confiscating Arab land commenced. In July 1948 a Customs Officer for managing Arab property was appointed. Said to be temporary until the peace negotiations were concluded, the office became permanent as the result of further actions taken by the Israeli government and its citizens. In order to settle a continuing stream of immigrants on the land, the Israeli government put into force (by special decree of the Knesset) the Development Authority Law, more usually called the Transfer of Property Law. In the next few years, a succession of laws allowed an immense amount of land and real property to pass to the state and from the state to the Jewish National Fund (the state taking a profit from each transaction); the land then passing to agencies that assigned it to immigrants.

In the end, by a kind of chicanery and opportunism, the totality of the land acquired by the Jewish National Fund constituted about 90 percent of the whole land area of Israel—quite remarkable when it is considered that between 1919 and 1947 something less than 7 percent of the Palestinian land had passed to Jews through normal sales. [234]

After the first six months of chaotic confiscation by both state and private means, the Israeli government attempted some regulation by creating an agency called the Custodians of Abandoned Property. Most of the property taken into custody belonged to people who were now called "absentees." The conditions under which these owners could claim what had been left behind were onerous, if not impossible to meet. Although legally speaking the property of the absentees belonged to them, the Israeli authorities did not hesitate to hand it over piecemeal to the Jewish immigrants. Thus, however poor the newcomers might be, a form of capital awaited them, much of it underdeveloped lands. For the resourceful and the lucky, it was a time to get rich in a hurry and would create, almost overnight, the usual social condition of Western capitalism: an overly rich and mighty layer of fortunate people at the top, and a growing class of those less favored who are forever struggling to keep up.

On the matter of stolen property, the Israeli State and its citizens were immune to investigation. The Byzantine avenues by which the goods of the Palestinians were redistributed would forever preclude any inquest. What was perhaps only a fraction of the value of the property expropriated was eventually reported.

On the Arab side, one could not find justice either. One example may suffice. Under the Law of Return about 100,000 Iraqi Jews elected to immigrate to Israel. With almost poetic irony these Jews saw the Iraqi government confiscate their property. Among the 100,000 immigrants, about 15,000 were not to be considered frightened peasants on the run. Rather, they were professional people, educated and sophisticated, affluent by Middle East standards. The Israeli government's solution for the difficult problem of confiscation and compensation was simple: what the affluent Iraqi Jews left behind was judged to have about the same value as what the Palestinians had abandoned in Israel; therefore one could say a veritable equation existed. The books could be closed. [235] Moreover, since the compensation question had been resolved in this way, nothing more needed to be done about reparations. Under the circumstances repatriation also became an academic question. In a major understatement, one student of this subject observed that while "the Iraqi Jews and Israel may have considered this a fair deal [for] the Palestinians now located mostly in UNRWA refugee camps, justice had by no means been done." They were indeed the forgotten people, except for the UN relief agencies that continued to feed and house them. Conciliation, it goes without saying, one of Bernadotte's prized principles, had by this time become a dead letter.

The imperialist ambitions of France and Great Britain in one generation, abetted by an idealistic and naïve American foreign policy in the next, had laid up a bitter harvest in the form of displaced people who had very little prospect of returning to their native land. In 1949 a former chairman of the Tennessee Valley Authority, Gordon Clapp, proposed a sort of public works program for the Palestinians, more than a little reminiscent of the New Deal experiments of the 1930s. Instead of pouring millions of dollars into the refugee camps with no appreciable results, public works would be started in those countries willing to accept the refugees. Employment of the refugees, it was thought, would rehabilitate them; local economies would flourish as a result of the influx of American dollars; the refugees would become absorbed into the host country, assimilated into a culture not substantially different from the one they had left behind.

The Arab states did not take Clapp's ideas seriously. They still thought in terms of the eventual repatriation of the refugees, not so much out of sympathy for their fellow Arabs but rather with the hope that once they were resettled in Israel they would play a part in the now very old contest between Jew and Arab. One may suspect also that the Arabs' rejection of Clapp's ideas, like their rejection of the Jewish presence, was tantamount to a rejection of the Western way of life, so repugnant to most Moslems. Clapp's beneficent proposals merely promised to be another bridgehead the West was building in the East in order to export an unwanted culture, ranging from fast-food franchises to pornographic films.

While one may be impressed by the reluctance of hundreds of thousands of Palestinians to become absorbed by the Arab states, it must be considered from what segment of the old Palestinian society they had come. After the exodus, reported the director of the UNWRA, John H. Davis, "virtually all able-bodied male refugees who possessed skills needed in Arab countries or, for that matter, elsewhere, found jobs almost immediately and became self-supporting and have never been dependent on international charity." [236]

These successful ones who escaped from the trap that the camps soon became constituted about 20 percent of the refugees. Most came from the urban areas of Palestine, suggesting such things as education, skills, talent, professional credentials, regular work habits: all those attributes that are prized in the West and which, in the traditional critique, are thought to be absent in Arab culture. But the better conclusion to draw in this case is that the greater part of the Palestinian Diaspora (about 80 percent) derived from the rural proletariat, which, under the circumstances, Israel could not have absorbed in its efforts as a fledgling state to modernize and develop on the Western model. The bane of all Third World countries is a massive, almost inert, peasant population, living on the land at a subsistence level; disinclined to leave their villages, and, if moved to do so, to arrive in the urban areas as an almost inassimilable mass of people living on day work, unable to compete with better-trained and educated citizens.

While the Israelis profited in several ways from the Palestinian Diaspora, some of the Arab states and large numbers of the world's states (as members of the United Nations) paid a tremendous price for this upheaval; and the paying is not yet over. By 1960, Jordan, Egypt, Syria, and Lebanon had already spent $100 million in direct aid to the Palestinian refugees. But this was a pittance compared with the largesse of other donors. In the early years, American donations covered 70 percent of the expense of maintaining the refugee camps. The United Kingdom and Canada were the next most generous contributors. The costs were nearly overwhelming. In the enlightened days of the twentieth century, much more was required than food and water. What amounted to a society without a country, denied (or unwilling to accept) citizenship in any host country, required the panoply of services that make up a modern civilized existence. Besides ordinary sustenance, there were provided electricity, gas, water, the maintenance of roads and buildings, security fences (which made the camps appear to be cages), medical care, education, special training, and the teaching of skills (called *rehabilitation*). "Rehabilitation" meant a policy of uplift for the refugees, of such scope and ambition that only a dedicated social worker could imagine.

Lest the amenities listed above lead one to conclude that the camps became a paradise on Earth, consider that even the vast sums expended did little more than keep bodies and souls together. Food was rationed, and not all received full rations. The director of UNWRA was proud to report that despite shortages of food, water, and medicine, the death rate was kept lower than the average in the Arab world as a whole. Nonetheless, the birthrate in the camps became a figure to conjure with. Census figures kept by UNRWA show that about 700,000 refugees arrived at the camps eventually. By 1969 the population had reached almost one and a half million. [237] A society effectively incarcerated, kept healthy but always a little hungry, without meaningful work, without possessions of any significance, without entertainment or means of leisure, did in this confinement what peasant societies always do in freer circumstances: breed and breed again. In brief, a poverty that UNRWA could not eradicate resulted in enlarging a captive population, one ever poorer by the accumulation of mouths to feed and bodies to tend.

While the seizure of Arab lands and property was accomplished in a matter of months, the redistribution lasted for years. Demolition of Arab villages continued until 1967, justified on the grounds that they had been abandoned or, in not a few instances, stood in the way of Israeli development plans. An estimated 807 towns and villages peopled by Arabs existed in 1947. In 1967 there were 433, and 328 of these were in the Gaza Strip (thus outside Israel). In summary, about one-half of the Arab habitations had disappeared; about 90 percent of Arab land had gone to the State of Israel or to the newly arrived immigrants. More than 90 percent of the Palestinian population had been driven out of their country and prevented thereafter from returning.

The enormous land grab was naturally connected to massive Jewish immigration, commencing with the formation of the Jewish state; a flood of humanity so great that Jews became the majority of the population almost at once. While hundreds of thousands of Arabs had fled from Palestine, millions of Jews began pouring into it.

The tactics by which the Israeli government took property that did not belong to it are not more interesting than the methods by which Jewish immigrants, the Israeli army, and the *Keren Keymouth* (Jewish National Fund) collaborated in forcing off their land those Arabs who had not fled. Typically, once a kibbutz was established in the vicinity of an Arab village, friction would occur between the indigenous landholders and the newcomers. The latter would, in a given dispute, fence in what they claimed, then patrol the perimeter under arms. If the Arabs yielded, new encroachments would take place. Should the Arabs attempt to seek redress, they found that no recourse to justice was available. Should severe strife occur finally between the Arab village and the encroaching kibbutz, the Israeli army intervened. The usual result was the expulsion of the villagers. After that, prolonged litigation took place, so protracted that the kibbutz might finally come into possession lawfully of what was deemed a deserted village and abandoned land.

Besides this species of theft, instigated by the Jewish settlers, Arab villagers suffered if it even appeared that they meant to collaborate with Israel's enemies. The males of the village, judged to be most likely to serve as spies, would be expelled. The families, reduced to a body of women and children, would after awhile follow their sons and husbands. These depredations occurred most frequently in the Galilee region, where the Arab population was densely settled, the sheer number of Arabs presumed by the Israelis to be a risk to the Jewish state.

So serious had the refugee problem become as an international issue that a conference was held at Lausanne in 1949. The U.S. government pressed the Israelis to receive at once half the Palestinians languishing in the camps. The Israelis refused, fearing that this would give Arab terrorists the means to come into Israel. [238] A compromise proposal for admitting 100,000 Palestinians was also rejected, the Israelis reasoning being that if 100,000 were accepted the world community would soon insist upon another 100,000 and then another. This was not unlike the Arab fear earlier that to accept 100,000 Jews would mean immediate pressure for accepting another 100,000, etc., etc. The fact is, the Israelis no more wanted to see the Palestinians return than the Arabs had wanted to see Jews come into Palestine in the first place.

As negotiations for a return of the dispossessed Palestinians continued, the Israeli government also dealt with the problem of land belonging to absentee owners. A series of decrees (from 12 December 1948 to 14 March 1950) regulated the matter in precise language: "Every Arab in Palestine who had left his town or village after 29 November 1947, was liable to be classified as an absentee under the directives." Arabs within Israel who had changed residences, going from one property to another, were defined as absentee owners also. All land deemed to be "absentee land" was subject to transfer to the Customs of Absentee Property. Once more, land passed to the state and again without any provisions for compensation. Thereafter the prolonged negotiations with the Arab states (the Palestinians having no voice in these matters—save through the impotent United Nations) became meaningless. There was nothing left for the refugees to return to.

Land transfers by law, which gave them a legal face, were also accompanied by the practice of establishing "closed areas." Once more the Israeli government drew upon the Mandate regulations, so despised under the British occupation but now found useful for their purposes. Resuscitated in 1948, these "defense Regulations" served Israel's security needs. Arab villagers in strategic areas were evicted, not allowed to return, and offered compensation for their lost property. Should the expelled villagers appeal to the Israeli government, the military authority would give evidence that the area had been closed for security reasons. Such cases did not reach an Israeli court, but were resolved by the army chief of staff. If a serious case should arise, the final decision was taken by the minister of defense, always in the name of national security. Those Arabs who dared to return were termed "infiltrators."

To protect the state's frontiers, a military rule was established, based on previous British security practices. Along the borders of Syria and Lebanon, areas termed "security zones" were depopulated because the people living there were Arabs (potentially disloyal to the Jewish state). After that, the land considered abandoned was sold to the Jewish National Fund "in fulfillment of an agreement with the legal advisor to the Israeli government at a meeting near the end of 1948."[239]

Israel's borders, a sieve the British could not plug enough to prevent illegal Jewish migration, were closed with a ruthless efficiency that the Mandatory Power had not possessed. Along the borders a strip eight meters wide was designated as a military zone.[240] Any "outsider"/"infiltrator" was summarily shot when apprehended within this zone. However, this barrier, equivalent to an iron curtain, did not deter those few who were determined to return. Ben Gurion's orders were stern and explicit: those defined as infiltrators were to be expelled without recourse to any court; it was entirely a military matter. But such severity was fruitless. "The main problem," recalled one of the Jewish Agency's Arab experts, "was that of the infiltrators. We expelled a few thousand, but we failed to expel tens of thousands. In that sense we failed—the number of Arabs in the country continued to rise steadily."[241]

While it is clear that a significant minority of the Knesset's membership were uneasy with these measures, the majority of Israeli citizens (more than half of the population made up of newly arrived immigrants) were not unhappy with the situation. The myth that fortified them was that Eretz Israel belonged to the Jews; Lord Balfour had promised it to them, and God had at last restored it to them.[242] But behind the legal piracy was an overriding necessity: to forestall any action that would bring the dispossessed Palestinians back to their homeland, not only because such an eventuality would vitiate the Zionist ideal of the Jewish state, but because the Israeli government had been hoisted by its own petard. In drawing hundreds of thousands, and finally millions, of immigrants into Palestine, millions of dunums were needed to settle them. Teeming cities, unstable with hordes of unemployed workers, were no part of the Zionist dream; rather, they wanted a happy yoemanry living in collective harmony on the land. In any case, what had been done could not be undone.

Foreign Minister Levi Eshkol admitted this. "The land has been settled in the meantime," he remarked in July 1956, "hundreds of farms and settlements have been built... on which thousands of people live... In my opinion it is unthinkable to suggest the possibility of turning back the clock after what has happened." In other words, to interpret Eshkol freely, a revolution had been carried out in Israel and revolutions never proceed on the basis of due process of law.

Up to 1953, the word "ownership" did not enter the Israeli lexicon with respect to the confiscated property of the refugees, since all seizures had no validity in terms of international law. Accordingly, in 1953, the Land Acquisition Law, number 5713, was enacted, usually called the Validation of Acts and Compensation. It was a law meant to register a *fait accompli*. Arab property, having been expropriated, could not now be restored to its owners, though there should be compensation. But that presented a problem. Land that had been relatively cheap in 1948 had by 1953 become dear. Severe inflation had the effect of hiking land values while debasing the value of the Israeli pound to about one-fifth of its prewar value. Special committees met on and off over the next six years, attempting to balance figures that were always fluctuating. Finally, unable to make an offer to the Palestinian Diaspora, the committee turned the matter over to the government, which announced officially that it was ready to settle the matter. With whom precisely? Had a people so dispersed as the Palestinians possessed a single voice, or even a spokesman, any Israeli offer would probably have been rejected. To accept ten cents on the dollar, so to speak, could only be considered obscene, but more importantly, to accept compensation would be to admit tacitly that they might never return. Moreover, by1959, the leaders of the various Palestine liberation movements thought only of redeeming their lost land.

The manner in which the bulk of Palestinian lands had passed to the Jews presented a problem that had not been anticipated. The original Jewish colonies had in almost all cases been communal, the land held in common, little islands of Jewry set down in what might have seemed a sea of Arabs. But the new immigrants flooding the country after the Second World War were of a different type. Rather than communal ownership of the land (heretofore a sort of rural communism), a system of shares developed quickly. The solidarity of pioneers living a close-knit collective life in the presence of hostile strangers gave way to individualism, rivalries and competition. Some immigrants soon sold their shares, moved to town and took jobs. They became absentee owners in some cases, renting their share of the land to other Jews, and not infrequently to Arabs. Ironically, those who had founded the Jewish state, despoiling the native people in the doing, now saw their work undermined by a new kind of Jew, an absentee landowner who was restoring an earlier time "when the landowning effendi lived in the cities while the peasants did the farming on the land." It would not be difficult, wrote an Israeli journalist, "to describe the Jews as a negative element turning back the social clock several decades…". [243] So completely had the original concept, Conquest of Labor, been lost.

In truth, the polyglot nationalities of the Jewish Diaspora flowing into Israel did not correspond to the relative homogeneity of the Ashkenazi Jews. "Although we were an Oriental people," wrote Ben Gurion, "we had been Europeanized and wished to return to Palestine in the geographical sense only. We intended to establish a European culture here, and we were linked to the greatest cultural force in the world." [244] He and his fellow Zionists could not conceal their contempt for the Jews they were saving, half of them coming from the neighboring Arab countries, dark and primitive. They called them scornfully *Avak Adam* (human debris), supposing this human rubbish would die out in a generation or so: the Jew of the Diaspora, the pathetic Yid: "ugly," "sickly," "submissive," "easily frightened," and "despised by all." These contemptuous words were written by Jabotinsky, Ben Gurion's cordial political rival, but both men agreed on one thing: the New Jerusalem they were building would be populated by a new breed, better to be called Hebrew. The old Jew, the Jew of the Diaspora, "our miserable step-brother," as Ben Gurion put it, would be replaced by a "new human type." "It is necessary," he said in an interview "to create a Hebrew character and style, which did not exist, which could not have existed in the Diaspora..."[245] This was not unlike the Russian communist belief that out of the mélange of nationalities that comprised the former Czarist empire would emerge a new type: Soviet Man.

As it was imagined that humankind would be transfigured by the policies of the Zionists, so would the landscape become transformed. For most of his adult life, Ben Gurion had speculated on the possibilities of a well-watered Negev, in actuality a vast desert, home to Bedouin tribesmen. To tame this wilderness the Israelis attempted to make farmers out of them. Otherwise, how could a garden be established in the midst of marauding tribesmen? In 1949 there was enacted the Emergency Regulation Ordinance, 5709, called by its authors the Law on the Cultivation of Waste Lands.

During the war with the Arabs, the Israeli government, in order to protect the south flank of its military operations, had entered into an agreement with the Bedouin sheiks. In exchange for their neutrality, the Israelis agreed to "recognize their rights and their ownership of the land they lived on." It might be thought, therefore, that after the war the Israeli government would want to honor its agreements. But the law on "absentee land" was too useful to be ignored. Should a given tribe move, as was its wont, the government could affirm that the land had been vacated (not different from the flight of the Palestinian peasants and townspeople). Shortly, the land would be seized, to become a possession of the Jewish National Fund.

The oldest conflict in history is between nomadic people, whose sense of possession is transitory, and settled agricultural people who define land ownership with mathematical certitude. For ten years, 1949–59, the attempt was made to move the Bedouins into "designated areas," the object being to civilize them. In the words of an Israeli official, "anyone adopting this form of living would become a good citizen and those unwilling to do so would have to move to Sinai or Transjordan."[246]

If the Israelis were disposed to harry the Palestinian peasants off the land, it follows that they would be less than tender toward the nomads. Seizing upon pretexts, they expelled large numbers of them, but the latter, being wanderers, would eventually return to what they supposed was theirs in the first place. These efforts went on for years with inconclusive results. The nomadic people were nearly immune to Israeli authority. Also, even if Jewish immigrants were to be established in the Negev, working capital would have to be furnished by a government perpetually in debt and forever begging for aid outside the country.

Western reporters watched and approved as science and technology in the hands of the industrious Jews began to redeem a sterile landscape. The Zionists had always recognized that Palestine was far from being the fabled land of milk and honey. Arid to semi-arid, it was forever being encroached upon by a creeping desert from all sides except the sea. There was scarcely any soil of quality save the low-lying plains and valleys; desiccated each season by a fierce summer heat, degraded by winter rains that carried away what little soil had been reduced to dust during the long dry spell. The hills were stony, scarcely able to support more than weeds and tenacious grasses. Under these circumstances, a traditional subsistence agriculture could not support such a large population as the Zionists expected to bring into the country. Irrigation on a large scale would become imperative. Yet, little water was available. Only a single river of modest proportions, rather more like a stream, the Jordan flowed through the country, its head of water dependent upon an unpredictable snow pack on the slopes of distant Mount Hermon. In his novel, *Altennewland*, Herzl had pictured a mighty canal drawing water from the Jordan, copious enough to irrigate the whole of Eretz Israel. But the river soon disappears in an immense sinkhole, the Dead Sea, long before it might otherwise reach the Negev. Time would reveal that only underground reservoirs, the aquifers, could furnish enough water, providing the Israeli population did not grow too much; yet even these subterranean chambers are being drained faster than nature can replenish them.

211

⌇ THE PALESTINE LIBERATION MOVEMENT

The Diaspora, which the Jews had experienced for nearly two millennia, is the fate of their brothers and sisters, the Palestinian Arabs. Scattered, they live as expatriates in a dozen or more countries. The numbers are not ascertained with any precision: perhaps three and a half to four million without a legal national identity. About a million live on the West Bank and the Gaza Strip. More than 700,000 live effectively as captives within the Jewish state. Another half-million live in Lebanon.

The Jewish Diaspora occurred over time, indeed, time out of mind. What had happened to the Jews had been natural, as it were, so great the numbers of migrants, spread out over such an immense space of time and area that none could have borne conscious witness to it or remember the cause for it. And, therefore, the conscience of the world could not have been moved by a human phenomenon that had been essentially invisible. By contrast, the Palestine Diaspora was (and is) of relatively brief duration, largely concentrated in two zones, the Gaza Strip and the West Bank. In an age of instantaneous communication, world opinion and the world-conscience are repeatedly struck by the phenomenon. An uprooting of millions of people occurring in the space of two generations seems rather like theatre on the world stage, watched by people everywhere, the eye of the television camera recording the innumerable details.

While the dispossessed Palestinians had few allies at any time, and most of the time none at all, the Jews (then the Israelis) could count upon the aid and sufferance of Great Powers, first the patron Great Britain and thereafter the indulgent United States; the latter having done so much to make the Jewish state possible that it could not, out of mixed motives of pride, sense of honor, and the need to dominate the Middle East in its own interest, abandon the creature to which it had attached itself. In this environment millions of Palestinians were lost to sight, almost forgotten, except occasionally in times of crisis, as a nuisance people. As has been truly written, "many played a role in this great crime, beginning with the British imperialists and their Zionist proteges, who first stunted the economic and social development of the Arab community, and then collaborated to crush its uprising in 1936–39, leaving it disorganized, disarmed, and helpless to resist in 1948." [247]

Like the wandering Jews of the Diaspora, the Palestinians did not forget their roots or cease to think of return. As with the Jews in other times, assimilation within a given host country meant to the Palestinians a loss of identity, a tacit recognition that they had lost their homeland. Cynically, it was in the interest of the Arab states to keep this mentality alive, not necessarily for the benefit of the Palestinians, but because the feeling of a nascent Palestinian nationalism served as a useful lever in the struggle between the Arabs as a whole and their enemy, the Jewish state.

The formation of the *Fedayeen* (commando), inspired and financed by the Arab states, had perhaps the unexpected consequence of stimulating Palestinian nationalism. From a great distance, scarcely involved, the Western mind perceived of the Fedayeen as disturbers of the peace, murderous creatures addicted to killing and maiming innocents. To the Arab mind these were young heroes who risked their lives and were willing to sacrifice themselves for their country. Nathan Hale regretted that he had but one life to lose for his country, but his countrymen over time would appear to have forgotten that noble utterance.

While it seems clear that not one Arab country wished to absorb the Palestinian refugees, it seems equally clear that assimilation of this kind was not wanted by most Palestinians. Weak, without organization or leadership, the Palestinian populace was nonetheless united: by literary and poetic bonds. The poetic gift, often attributed to Semitic genius, served to unite them as a people. Not less important, a profound religious devotion gave them the capacity to endure a hard fate, and to have faith in a common destiny, as similarly religion had served the Jews in their long exile.

Moslem fundamentalism was rooted in Palestine from an early time, another index for revealing how widespread was the phenomenon called Islamic Revival. Most typical of this phenomenon was the Moslem Brotherhood, organized at Cairo in 1928 for the purpose of driving the British out of Egypt. Shortly, the Brotherhood expanded, with the aim of establishing an Islamic society, regulated by the *Shari'a*, the code of law derived from the Moslem holy book and traditions. In 1935 Hassan al-Banna, a brother of the founder of the Moslem Brotherhood, went to Jerusalem to consult with the Grand Mufti Haz Amin al-Husseini. Henceforth, collaboration between the Islamic Council at Jerusalem led by the Mufti, and the Moslem Brotherhood at Cairo, was constant.

In 1948 the Brotherhood furnished the Egyptian government three battalions, an estimated 1500 devoted fighters. Eager to fight, they were equally eager to die in combat, since on the morrow of their death they expected to be in Paradise. It is surprising that the Brotherhood, with a membership of nearly one million, would have sent so few volunteers to fight the Jewish infidels. The most plausible explanation is that the Egyptian government did not want to see an Islamic society such as the Brotherhood envisioned established on its own territory. Consequently, it accepted only a few volunteers, giving them little in the way of arms and money. After the war was lost, the government changed its policy slightly, supporting the Brotherhood to some extent; arming the volunteers for raids into Israel, but limiting support enough so that the Egyptian government would not become a victim itself. To that end, two training camps were established, one at Hakstab, near the Suez Canal, the other at Marsa Matruh, on the Libyan border. These were run by Egyptian military officers.

The defeat of the Arab coalition in 1948 did not mean the defeat of the Brotherhood. Its members continued to operate on a different plane: working among the Palestinian refugees, creating a widespread network of influences. An office had been established in Jerusalem on 25 October 1945. By 1947 twenty-five branches were operating throughout Palestine.

While Abdullah had not hesitated to annex the West Bank, offering Jordanian citizenship to the Arab residents, the Egyptian government would not do the same for the Palestinians in the Gaza Strip, no doubt fearing the ever-growing influence of the Brotherhood. On the West Bank, by contrast, the latter enjoyed a great deal of liberty for pursuing its program, equally inimical to Israel and Egypt, but to Jordan also. Abdullah was either naïve, not recognizing his danger, or merely crafty in promoting a policy of tolerance toward the Brotherhood. The price he paid for this eventually was his life, as did several other notable figures. In the early fifties a series of assassinations swept across the Middle East. The Iranian premier was shot by an Islamic Fundamentalist on 7 march 1951. On 15 July of the same year, a Syrian radical who wanted to see Lebanon incorporated into the Syrian state killed Lebanese Premier Riad Bey e-Sohl. While attending a memorial service for Riad at the Al-Asq Mosque in Jerusalem, Abdullah was assassinated by a Palestinian. Abdullah's seventeen-year-old grandson, Hussein, who witnessed the murder, succeeded him as king of Jordan.

A year later, King Farouk of Egypt was deposed in a military coup led by two men, General Mohammed Naquib and Colonel Gamal Abdul Nasser. A republic was proclaimed; after that, a flood of revolutionary rhetoric swept over the country, calculated to reach the hearts and minds of Egypt's immense depressed class, the *Fellahin*. The ethos of this proposed revolution, originating largely from Nasser's inflamed mind, was an exotic mix of Western progressive ideas (principally, the socialist ideal) and the traditional values of an archaic Egyptian society. The partnership of the general and the colonel soon came to an end when the latter, through his own merit (energy, ambition, and charisma) became dominant in military politics. So complete did Nasser's authority become that one could speak of a dictatorship. It became his policy to promote the Palestinian cause in the Egyptian interest, and in this way he gave a decided impetus to Palestinian nationalism. Like the deposed king of Egypt, Nasser also faced formidable opposition from the Moslem Brotherhood, who viewed his reform ideas as the work of Satan.

The growing influence of the Brotherhood soon produced a profound hiatus in the collective Palestinian mentality; one might even say a schism in the Palestinian soul. Only through the establishment of an Islamic society, argued the Brotherhood, could the Palestinians be redeemed and the Diaspora come to an end. But this ran counter to the tactics employed by the Fedayeen, whose solution for the problem was of this world: valiant and violent war with the hated Jews.

One sees without difficulty that Palestinian redemption was, in its Moslem context, quite like redemption for the Jews in an earlier time. As secular and religious Jews had quarreled (and continued to do so after independence) over means and ends, so did the Palestinian movement become similarly tormented by the antinomies inevitably raised when a supernatural explanation of events is offered in place of a natural one. This dualism of the Palestinian liberation movement would continue up to the present.

On the secular side, the Palestinian liberation movement may be traced in the career of a single individual, Yasser Arafat, whose life reflected the movement to which he became dedicated; and at the same time the movement itself shaped by the vicissitudes of that life.

It is not clear where Arafat was born, possibly Jerusalem, though two of his brothers and a sister believed it was Cairo, and two of his cousins thought he was born in Gaza. [248] The date of his birth seems more certain: 27 August 1929; his name: abd-Rahman Ahd al-Rauf Arafat al-Qudawa al-Husseini.

Arafat's life from childhood on was wreathed in conspiratorial activities. His mother was a cousin of the Jerusalem Mufti, Haz Amin al-Husseini. His father, a wealthy businessman, was one of the first Palestinian members of the Moslem Brotherhood. The family's xenophobia, at first focused on the British, came to include the Jews once the immigration of the latter began to swell. In the eyes of such Arabs as Arafat and his family, the Jews were nothing so much as clients of the British imperialists, faithful puppets who expected for their loyalty to receive a country that was not theirs. Even before this belief had crystallized as a part of his intellectual baggage, it had seeped into the pores of Arafat's being simply by growing up in the environment of the quasi-civil war that consumed Palestine after 1919.

Arafat spent his teen years in Gaza, from 1939 to 1951. Like many Arabs of his class he became involved in the clandestine and often violent struggles between powerful Arab families. In the forties he joined the Putuwwah, a Husseini faction which, in the manner of the blood feud, fought with the Naijadh, a faction of the rival family, the Nashashibis. His formative years prepared him well for the violent and clandestine career he would eventually choose.

During the war years he had an intimate relationship with one of his schoolteachers, a Lebanese named Majid Hababy. Allegedly, it was a homosexual affair. During the thirties Hababy had been a Qassamite terrorist (to be read "patriot"). When the British captured and executed one of the leaders of the Qassamites, Yasser al-Birah, he became a saint in the eyes of his followers. To memorialize him, Hababy bestowed the name Yasser on his favorite student. Henceforth Arafat bore the name proudly, as if a title. [249]

His primary education completed by 1951, Yasser was sent to King Faud University in Cairo to study civil engineering. He was twenty-two. Four years later he still had not received a degree. During the Suez crisis, when Nasser called for volunteers to fight the invaders (British, French, and Israelis), Yasser enrolled for military training. The crisis was almost as brief as his training and he returned to the university (renamed Cairo University after the coup that brought Naguib and Nasser to power). For a brief time he played a part in student politics, becoming president of a Palestinian student group. He made friends with two Palestinian students, Sahah Khalef and Khalil al-Wazir, who were destined to be his collaborators in future years. In the summer of 1956 the three men attended an international student congress at Prague, held under the auspices of the Soviet Union. Afterward, rather than return to the university, Arafat took employment as a civil engineer in Kuwait, working for the government's water department. Apparently his political activism faded. He went into business for himself as a contractor, made a lot of money and indulged himself as a rich man might. "I was a little bit of a millionaire," he confessed later. [250]

Arafat's transition, from the typical educated expatriate who accepted exile and sought the good life, to selfless patriot whose career became a fanatical devotion to a cause, will not be reconstructed in detail. His experience in any case was not unusual. In the years after the Suez crisis the Cold War intensified. With the Soviet Union's increasing interest in the Middle East, restless young Arabs like Arafat could see many possibilities. Conspiracies of the Palestinian exiles had resulted in the formation of societies and clubs almost without number, most of them evanescent. Yasser became involved with these fluctuating and formless groups, as well as their leaders. One of them, a Palestinian named Khalid al-Hassen, had in his travels become familiar with the FLN (National Liberation Front) in Algeria. Influenced by the nature of the organization and its success, Hassen and Arafat formed what they called the Movement for the Liberation of Palestine, probably in 1959. Within two years, Khalaf recalled, the organization had "flowered." About thirty groups in Kuwait, and other groups coming from Qatar and Saudi-Arabia, joined the Hassen-Arafat organization.

Algeria had by now gained its independence from France, the result of unremitting terror that had finally broken the resolve of the French to keep the country. The new president, Ben Bella, allowed Arafat and his comrades to open an office on Victor Hugo Street in Algiers. They had changed the name of their organization to the Palestine National Liberation Committee. Ben Bella allowed Palestinians to enter Algeria on work permits, providing they agreed to pay a percentage of their wages to Arafat's committee. Yasser opened a bank account in Beirut to receive the funds. Hundreds of Palestinians were recruited to come to Algeria for training in guerilla warfare. Ben Bella furnished the instructors.

All did not go well for Arafat's committee, which by 1965 had shrunk to eight members. This attrition was explained by Bella's duplicity in draining away the contributions of the Palestinian workers for his own purposes, then closing the training camps. Another explanation is equally plausible. In 1964, Nasser had taken control of another organization, the Palestine Liberation Organization. Riding high on the prestige that had come to him by nationalizing the Suez Canal, then facing down Britain and France as well as Israel, he was able to draw converts from the several "movements" that Arafat and many others like him had already formed.

The great sensation in the Middle East just then was Israel's National Water Carrier, a source of pride for the Israelis, but to the Arabs another cause for envy and malice. Prolonged negotiations between Israel and the relevant Arab states (carried out through intermediaries) for a regional plan to exploit the upper reaches of the Jordan river had come to nothing; the Arabs doubtless recognizing the contradiction in cooperating with a state that they (a) declared did not exist, and (b) were resolved to destroy, if by chance it did exist. Whereupon the Israelis built their own pumping system downstream in the Galilee.

Given the rivalry of Syria and Egypt for first honors in destroying the "Jewish Entity," it is not surprising to learn that agents from Damascus contacted Arafat's miniscule "movement," proposing that they blow up Israel's National Water Carrier. Arafat and his colleagues accepted the invitation with alacrity and prepared for the anticipated demolition of Israel's prized waterworks. Sure of themselves, they composed in advance of the raid a notice for public consumption: "Military Communiqué No. 1," which described the success of an enterprise still only on paper. Copies of the communiqué were put in the letterboxes of Beirut's principal newspapers on the eve of the operation, describing the successful execution of the planned raid, carried out not by the Palestine National Liberation Committee, but by a bogus group that Arafat and his friends dubbed *El Fatah* (derived from the initials F-T-H, corresponding to the Arabic words that signify "conquest by means of Jihad.") [251]

The next morning, Beirut newspapers gave an account of an event that never took place. The raid, planned by Syrian military officers, to be carried out on the Lebanese-Israeli border by six poorly trained recruits, was aborted when one of them reported it to the Syrian authorities. The plot being exposed in this way, the six were arrested and thereafter Arafat and his companions as well. They were imprisoned for the next forty days, but this only added luster to the name Yasser Arafat, still a tyro in the world of conspiracy and contrived revolutions.

Although unintended, Fatah, by reason of Arafat's maneuvers, entered the revolutionary lexicon of the Middle East and was about to experience a long history as a slogan for Palestinian terrorism. Success in most enterprises requires publicity; in matters of calculated terror, notoriety is preferred. It may be said that Arafat's career as revolutionary *qua* terrorist commenced with this fiasco. Always thinking of ways to promote his cause (and himself—for were they not one and the same?), he began wearing the *kaffiyeh*, a checkered scarf, voluminous enough to conceal the face when required.

Raids against Israeli targets, sponsored and directed by Syrian military officers, increased after this. Most issued from Lebanon and Jordan's West Bank. Always, the object of the Syrians was to embroil Jordan with Israel, while waiting for the profit that might come from these conflicts. Meantime, Arafat and his committee, once they were released from prison, moved to Damascus, where they resumed training recruits for their organization.

Arafat's rise to prominence came about as a result of the obscure ways in which the Syrian government employed, and cashiered, Palestinian malcontents. In 1966 a coup at Damascus brought another faction of the Ba'ath Party to power, and a new head of state, Hafiz Assad. A new leader of Fatah was appointed, a Palestinian officer named Yusef Urabi, who served in the Syrian army. One of his first acts was to dismiss Arafat. A few days later Yusef was found murdered. Suspected of the crime, Arafat and his friends were arrested, imprisoned, and interrogated by the Syrian authorities.

After "long discussions" with Assad, the men were released. They returned to Beirut. It appeared that Arafat's career as a tool of Syria had ended before it was well started.

NOTES

212 Curiously, the sovereignty of the Hashemite family over Transjordan, the larger part of Palestine (a gift from the British) has never elicited much interest from Western scholars; mainly, one supposes, because the Jews never made an issue of it.

213 Henry Cattan, "Sovereignty over Palestine," *The Arab-Israeli Conflict. Readings and Documents*. Abridged and Revised. John Norton Moore, ed. (Princeton, NJ., 1977), p. 13.

214 Nathan Feinberg, "The Question of Sovereignty over Palestine," *The Arab-Israeli Conflict*, p. 47.

215 Benjamin Netanyahu's book, *A Place Among the Nations*, is based on this particular pessimism.

216 Tom Segev, *1949: The First Israelis* (New York and London, 1986), p. 29.

217 Gilbert, *Israel*, op. cit., p. 267.

218 John H. Davis, *The Evasive Peace*, op. cit., pp. 56-57. After the war the Arabs did indeed make a formal statement that they had urged the Palestinians to flee. But it is known (and was known at the time) that this was a false statement, issued in order to assuage Arab humiliation in being defeated. Nevertheless, the Israelis have ever since used this statement in order to buttress their contention that the Palestinian flight was not the result of unreasoning fear. See Silverberg, p. 397. See also Benjamin Netanyahu's use of the Arab statement in his book, *A Place Among the Nations*, p. 142.

219 The Law of Return was not enacted until July 1950, but it reflected a policy in place from the beginning, viz., unrestricted Jewish migration, virtually without conditions for entry.

220 Fred J. Khouri, *The Arab-Israel Dilemma*, op. cit., p. 127.

221 This thesis is developed by Maxine Rodinson, *Israel: A Colonial-Settler State*, trans., David Thorstad (New York), 1973.

222 Segev, 1949, p. xiii.

223 Since a constitution was never promulgated, a formal means for defining the state did (and does) not exist.

224 Ibid., p. xii.

225 Ibid.

226 Sabra Jiryis, *The Arabs in Israel*, trans. Inea Bushag (New York and London, 1976), p. 253.

227 Gilbert, *Israel*, p. 275.

228 Nur Masalha, *Expulsion of the Palestinians*, op. cit., p. 14.

229 George J. Tomeh, "Legal Status of Arab Refugees," *The Arab-Israeli Conflict*, op. cit., p. 173

230 Josef Weitz, *My Diary*, III, p. 293; Gilbert, Israel, p. 159.

231 Ibid., p. 302.

232 John Quigley, *Palestine and Israel. A Challenge to Justice*, op. cit., p. 111.

233 Sabri Jiryis, p. 77.

234 All land which became the possession of the Jewish National Fund was deemed to be inalienable. It could not be sold, although it could be leased; almost always to Jews, infrequently to Arabs.

235 Frank Epp, *Whose Land is Palestine?*, op. cit., p. 222.

236 Ibid., pp. 223-24.

237 1,395,674 is the exact figure reported.

238 Gilbert, *Israel*, p. 255.

239 Sabri Jiyris, p. 91.

240 Tom Segev, p. 63.

241 Ibid., p. 67.

242 For some insight into how widespread these beliefs were, see Gilbert, *Israel*, p. 129.

243 Amnon Rubinstein, *The Zionist Dream Revisited. From Herzl to Gush Emunim and Back* (New York, 1984), p. 4.

244 Ibid.

245 Tom Segev, p. 292.

246 Sabra Jiyris, p. 122.

247 Rodinson, *Israel. A Colonial-Settler State*, p. 19.

248 Jillian Becker, *The PLO* (New York, 1984), p. 41.

249 Thomas Kiernan, *Yasser Arafat. The Man and the Myth*. (New York, 1976), pp. 79 ff. The spelling of the name varies from book to book, sometimes Yasser, sometimes Yasir.

250 Sandra Mackey, *Passion and Politics, The Turbulent World of the Arabs* (New York, 1992), p. 351.

251 The initials from the words Harakat al-tahrir al-Falastini, when reversed, form Fatah (Polk, The United States and the Arab World, op. cit., p. 272).

CHAPTER SEVEN

A State
Besieged

THE NASSER FACTOR

s Arab power had become dissipated during the ninth and tenth centuries, passing finally into the hands of the Turks, so did the Ottoman hegemony begin to fade in the eighteenth century, passing during the next century into the hands of the British, but for only a few decades (roughly 1881–1948). Power, wealth, knowledge, modern science (vital to understanding and exploiting natural forces), all these technical mysteries were being developed in the West, chiefly for the benefit of the West. As a consequence, Islam fell on evil days. A successor to the Turkish empire, the only guarantee for Islamic unity in the Middle East, did not appear. Indeed, the story of the Middle East in recent times is the attempt to find a chief, a slogan, a single purpose that might provide an over-arching unity for fifty million Arabs. The seductive dream of unity has entranced many, but the few who have accepted the daunting challenge can be counted on the fingers of one hand: Gamal Abdul Nasser, who leaned on a weak reed, Egypt, so as to fashion a modern Arab empire; counting vainly on a foreign patron, first the United States, then the Soviet Union. After Nasser came the Shiite *mullahs* of Iran. Deposing the modernizing Shah, they peered into the past and found the

Middle Ages an ideal period to be recovered in its essentials, to be fixed upon the present. Thereafter came Saddam Hussein, the megalomaniac dictator of Iraq, whose passion for Arab unity was not greater than his hatred for the Jewish state, conceived by most Arabs to be a Western outpost thrust into the Islamic body politic by the designs of the United States; for the satisfaction of the Western countries' needs more generally.

In all psychological ways, Nasser became the successor to Mohammed Ali, the Egyptian reformer of the 1840s: determined to build up a poor country, to modernize it, to bring the Arab states under the Egyptian wing in a revived Arab empire. Like Mohammed Ali in his time also, Nasser needed a strong and loyal patron for the realization of his goals. France had served Mohammed faithfully in this regard, but in the end, futilely. Likewise, the Soviet Union would serve Nasser, perhaps not faithfully, but certainly futilely.

French influence in favor of Mohammed in the 1840s had been really directed against the interests of a rival, Great Britain. In the 1950s, the Soviet Union's support of Egypt (and its Arab allies) was directed against a rival also, the United States. Naturally, Nasser realized that he could play upon these rivalries to his advantage. It can be imagined also that the chimera of a united Arab empire, the liberation of Palestine (from both the Israelis and the Hashemite family in Jordan) was ever before his eyes. If he could not quite believe his own bombast, his Arab listeners certainly did. Typical of his romantic reveries is the following: the role of a hero, looking forlornly for someone to play the part.

> The pages of history are full of heroes who created their own roles and also of roles which found no heroes to perform them. It seems to me that there is one such role waiting for its heroic performer within the Arab world. Now, I cannot say why, but I feel that at last, exhausted by its wanderings, this role has halted near the borders of our country and is beckoning to us to bestir ourselves, study the lines and don the costume, since we alone are qualified to play the part. [252]

For long Israel's possession of Palestine was of little consequence to Nasser. On the eve of the coup that toppled King Farouk from power, he told an American CIA agent of the rage he and others of the Free Officers Group directed against "their own superior officers, then other Arabs, then the English, the Israelis—in that order." [253] But when finally in power, Nasser's rational ordering of Egypt's enemies underwent a change, Israel receiving a higher priority. In his restless adventuring, the "Jewish entity" became a significant part of the imperial puzzle that seemed to obsess him. A successful war against the hated Jews might very well draw the Arabs into the unity they desired but at the same time feared; it would be an accomplishment as difficult, yet as possible, as the way in which the Prussian Count Bismarck had drawn the rival German states together after defeating the French in 1870.

In the beginning, the Western statesmen regarded Nasser's megalomania as scarcely dangerous, an almost amusing posturing. While troubled by his revolutionary rhetoric, they sympathized with his desire to raise the Fellahin's abysmally low standard of living. In its poverty and backwardness, Egypt was typical of the Arab world, and the latter only typical of the Third World: a general destitution of the greater part of the population; unchecked diseases and primitive hygiene standards with the usual consequences: a high infant mortality rate, a short life span (in 1956 the average male in Iraq could not expect to live beyond age twenty-nine, in Egypt, forty-six). More than 80 percent of the Arab population was illiterate in 1956; this same number living a life in which daily hunger was accepted as the norm. [254]

For a solution to these well-nigh insuperable problems, Nasser believed he had discovered a panacea: the construction of a high dam at Aswan on the Fourth Cataract of the Nile, which would provide water for an immense irrigation system, not to speak of hydroelectric power in abundance. Overnight, as it were, Egypt might enter the twentieth century, prosperous, modernized and well fed.

Anthony Eden and his Conservative Party had returned to power in Britain and, highly approving of the idea, promoted it in the international community, counting especially on American generosity; Britain had survived the Second World War at the price of a grinding poverty for many of its people and (most humiliating) had become the economic client of the United States.

Nasser's dream-dam would be a massive earth-filled structure, in volume equal to the pyramid of Cheops. In the late nineteenth century British engineers had built a stone and concrete dam of modest proportions somewhat north of Aswan. The Fourth Cataract was the better place to impound the Nile waters, but such an undertaking called for removing more earth than the technical capacity of that generation had possessed. The great changes to earth-moving equipment during the Second World War finally made the construction of a high dam at Aswan possible. Only the enormous cost of the venture gave pause to both engineers and statesmen, an undertaking so great it was reckoned twenty years would be required for its completion.

There were several sources for funding this mighty project: the World Bank, which agreed to advance Egypt 200 million dollars; private investors in the West, and certain governments (the United States, Great Britain, and the Soviet Union) that took a purely political interest in the project. Eventually, the Eisenhower Administration refused to make a contribution, thereby incurring Nasser's unforgiving wrath. But the American decision was taken only after long negotiations. Secretary of State John Foster Dulles made it clear that American money would be forthcoming on the condition that Egypt accept a peace settlement with Israel, his thinking being that if Egypt should acknowledge the existence of Israel in this way, other Arab states would feel constrained to do the same.

A great system-maker, Dulles had managed to combine the doctrine of containment, which he had once condemned as negative and impractical, with the idea of liberation for the seventeen million Europeans who (he argued) lived the lives of slaves behind the Iron Curtain. He believed also with Eisenhower in the so-called domino theory: *viz.*, if one country should fall, the rest would collapse; i.e., a capitulation to Communism that would give supremacy over the world to the USSR. By 1956, the indefatigable secretary had spun around the globe a web of cooperative pacts that served rather like a worldwide fence to keep Communism in check: ANZUS, SEATO, then the Baghdad Pact, usually called METO by the Americans (Middle East Treaty Organization). [255] This pact, nominally led by Great Britain, at U.S. insistence, was composed of that power plus Syria, Iraq, and Lebanon. In practice, METO was directed, managed, and manipulated by the United States (i.e., Dulles).

When invited to join the Baghdad Pact, Nasser declined, unwilling to become a pawn in the struggle for influence beginning to shape up between the U.S. and the USSR. In any case, he had his own imperial ambitions. Besides, there were other pacts in existence, or just being formed. The Saudis, while reviling Nasser's radical, secular ideas, were moved more deeply still by an inextinguishable hatred for the Hashemite family, which had unworthily taken most of Palestine (i.e., Transjordan), which, in Saudi eyes, was part of historic Arabia, the cradle of Islam, the one and only true religion. For a brief time, reactionary Saudi Arabia and revolutionary Egypt could cooperate against a common Arab rival, King Hussein, and agree also that Israel did not exist; and if existing in fact ought to be destroyed. In April 1956, at the time when Nasser was disappointing Dulles in every way (he would not treat with Israel, nor would he join the Baghdad Pact; yet, perversely as it seemed, demanded money for his dam), the Joint Command against Israel was formed: an alliance of Egypt, Syria, Saudi Arabia, and Yemen. It was a revival of the coalition of 1947–48, which had come to grief, but larger than before and more formidable in appearance (on paper at least). To put teeth in the coalition, Nasser began negotiating the purchase of arms from the Soviet Union. Wishing to keep its skirts clean of this transaction, yet profit from the Egyptian *démarche*, the masters of the Kremlin arranged for the arms to be purchased through a client, Czechoslovakia, the same dealer that had earlier helped arm the Israelis.

Dulles's reaction to Nasser's multiple effronteries was to inform the Egyptian ambassador to Washington that America had no money to contribute to the dam project. (Congress had already expressed its disapproval.) Nasser's reaction to this rebuff was unexpected but nonetheless predictable. On 26 July, "in a three-hour harangue," Eisenhower recalled, Nasser proclaimed "the nationalization of the Suez Canal with all its properties and assets…", [256] which was easy to do, since two years earlier (in collaboration with the United States) he had compelled the British to withdraw their garrison along with the whole of the supporting bureaucracy. Henceforth, Nasser believed, the tolls that had enriched the canal's shareholders would pour into Egypt's coffers, and some part of those revenues would serve to build the high dam.

The British response to Nasser's audacity was one of near-disbelief and dismay. In poor health both physically and psychologically, Eden faced a *fait accompli* that apparently could not be reversed. Yet, like Churchill before him, he was not willing (to use the latter's famous phrase) "to preside over the liquidation of the British Empire." Nasser's nationalization of the canal was, in Eden's opinion, simply "theft," the exact title of the chapter in his memoirs describing the outbreak of the Suez crisis. It was also an embarrassment for which he could not forgive Nasser, and would revenge himself upon the dictator if he could.

To take back by force what Nasser had gained peacefully required diplomatic and political skills that Eden had perhaps never possessed, but certainly lacked in 1956. [257] The plan that evolved in his mind, in simplest and crudest form, was to encourage Israel to attack Egypt, giving Great Britain the pretext for re-occupying the Canal Zone. [258] For a partner in this risky adventure, he counted on France, while believing that the United States under Eisenhower's leadership would give support at the most, but certainly neutrality at the least; since he and Ike had been wartime friends.

The several threads that wove the fabric of an Israeli, French, and British entente derived from a single source: an almost violent anti-Nasser sentiment. It was said that in his diatribes Eden would literally froth at the mouth when Nasser's name arose in discussion. [259] The British were now Nasser's enemy, obviously, because he had nationalized the Suez Canal, seized British property, and in the doing humiliated the Eden government with an unforgivable impudence. The Israelis feared Pan-Arabism, which in its current manifestation meant Nasser's attempt to create an Arab empire under Egyptian leadership; always understood that the destruction of the Jewish Sate was his highest priority. His blockade of Aqaba, though not life-threatening to the Israelis, was a continuing provocation to which they must eventually respond in some military fashion.

The French politicos had long suspected, but could not prove, Nasser's complicity in the Algerian rebellion. Intercepting an Egyptian ship on the way to Algeria with arms for the rebels, they had at last the proof they needed; they too resolved to destroy Nasser, one way or another.

Earlier, Ben Gurion had sent a relatively young man, Shimon Peres, to Paris, charged to cultivate the French and, if possible, to buy arms. Peres' success was greater than he and his government could have anticipated. An arms agreement was reached rather quickly, without a treaty being signed between the two governments; thereby not requiring ratification, which would have invited public scrutiny and revealed a secret and well-planned scheme to topple Nasser from power. It was a gentleman's agreement in the old way: a few talks, some handshakes, and an understanding. [260]

Almost immediately the French government began sending armaments to Israel, including *Mystère* fighter-bombers. By October the Israelis were ready for war; and so were the Arabs, or so it seemed. Early in October, another Joint Command, composed of Egypt, Syria, and Jordan, was formed, promising "a war of destruction against Israel." [261]

The crisis, once it arose, caused the Israeli leadership to ask whether, if they waited to be attacked, they could repulse the force being organized against them. In the end the decision was taken to strike first; or to put it another way, the old saw was still valid: the best defense is a strong offense. On 22 October, Ben Gurion, along with Shimon Peres and Moshe Dayan, traveled secretly to Paris, where they conferred with Selwyn Lloyd (the British Foreign Secretary) and French Premier Guy Mollet. As it evolved in these talks, the plan was as follows: as soon as the American presidential elections were over, early in November, the Israeli army would enter the Sinai desert against Egypt. With this, both France and Britain would have a sufficient pretext to intervene in order to protect the international waterway. Once in control of the Canal Zone the two powers would demand a cease-fire. Israel would comply. Presumably, Nasser and his allies would have no choice but to do the same. Ben Gurion and his colleagues were made to understand that unless a compelling threat to the security of the canal existed, France and Great Britain could not (in view of international opinion) intervene militarily. The Israelis agreed, the *quid pro quo* being that Sharam el-Sheikh, on the Straits of Tiran, would become after the war a part of Israel so as "to enable them to maintain passage for their ships to the port of Aquaba." [262] In brief, by such a contrived war as was anticipated, Nasser's blockade of the Straits of Tiran would come to an end, as would his control of the Suez Canal. Humiliated in this way, he would likely be forced to resign.

The decision of the Israeli cabinet to declare war was taken on 28 October, hostilities to commence the next day at 5 A.M. Privately, Ben Gurion acknowledged that Israel would be universally condemned for its actions, but that could be withstood. The main question was whether the United States would acquiesce or interfere. In fact, Ben Gurion wanted no more from the Eisenhower Administration than a statement of neutrality. American Ambassador Edward Lawson was sounded out with the conventional question: If Israel should find itself at war with the Arab states, what would the American government do? Shortly, Lawson gave Ben Gurion Eisenhower's personal answer, asking that Israel take no aggressive action despite Arab threats. In his reply Ben Gurion was intransigent, declaring that he would be perceived to have failed in his duty if he did not act without delay. On 29 October, faithful to their timetable, the Israeli armed forces entered the Sinai. [263] In a movement so rapid it might be called *blitzkrieg,* they "knifed seventy-five miles into Egypt: in one night, arriving at a point only twenty-five miles east of Suez." [264]

In keeping with the charade, as soon as the Israelis were within striking range of the Canal, the British government gave both Israel and Egypt an ultimatum, demanding that they withdraw their forces "at least 16 kilometers from the Canal." Being ordered in effect to abandon territory that he had only lately nationalized, Nasser refused. Israel did not reply to the ultimatum. Britain and France then felt safe in sending troops into the Canal Zone.

These events transpired in the waning days of the presidential campaign in the U.S., creating a crisis for the incumbent president. Eisenhower had had no inkling of the unfolding plot. Dulles, despite having been supplied with abundant clues, could not quite believe the British, French, and Israelis would be so audacious. But audacity might be called Ben Gurion's middle name. Jubilant, he went before the Knesset to report a stunning victory. "Never," he declared, "would Israel humble herself before the great forces of the world." From a position of strength he announced that his government was ready to negotiate a peace settlement. Nasser, however, called upon the United Nations to punish the aggressors who had invaded his country. Indeed, the situation invited propaganda, Soviet Premier Nikolai Bulganin affecting outrage and accusing the Israeli government of "criminality and toying with the fate of the world and its peoples." Without delay the United Nations rebuked France, Great Britain, and Israel; the United States was manifestly unwilling to approve what had been done.

Eden yielded first, then France. After that, Ben Gurion found that he must humble himself, agreeing to withdraw, but under certain conditions: Egypt to dismantle its military forces in the Sinai, an end to the blockade, a guarantee for Israel's secure navigation of the Tiran Straits.

Under other circumstances, freedom of navigation in the Tiran Straits would have seemed only reasonable to any United States government, but Eisenhower remained in a high dudgeon and inclined to sever relations with the errant Israel. Still Ben Gurion would not yield. On 26 February Eisenhower sent his fifth personal message, alluding to the possibility of imposing sanctions on Israel. Thereafter he went on radio to gain support from the American public.

Disenchanted with Eisenhower, a man Ben Gurion had once judged to be great ("great humanity"), the premier would not budge. Unconsciously, but perhaps with calculation nonetheless, he relied upon the precedent forces and influences that had been instrumental in bringing the state of Israel into existence: a worldwide sympathy for the Jews, which had not yet turned to cold ashes; nor had the horror of the holocaust faded from memory. Not least important was the Jewish lobby that for years had steered U.S. congressmen and senators along the correct path. Therefore Israel could tolerate sanctions for a time, and in time Eisenhower would have to yield.

At the outset, as Ben Gurion had anticipated, the American Congress warmly supported Israel. Senate Majority Leader Lyndon Johnson wrote the president to argue that it would be something like a sin to impose sanctions on Israel; embarrassing as well when it was considered that the behavior of the U.S. was nearly passive toward the Soviet Union, which in this same time had taken advantage of the Suez crisis to invade and occupy one of its satellites, Hungary. [265]

The State Department soon reduced its rhetoric, whereupon the Israeli politicians and diplomats, sensing an apparent weakness, renewed their demands: Israeli control of the Gaza Strip in order to halt the Palestinian raids, and a guarantee for Israel's use of the Tiran Straits (considered by the Israelis an international waterway). [266]

Negotiations through the winter, up to March 1957, resulted in Israel losing two out of the three points. It finally evacuated both the Tiran Straits sector and the Gaza Strip. On the third point, freedom of navigation for the Tiran Straits, the most that could be gained was a military presence there; the UN established a force of over three thousand men, called the United National Emergency Force (UNEF). Eisenhower promised the United States would guarantee Israel's access to Aqaba. But a president's promise is as brief and binding as the life of a presidential administration. A decade later, Lyndon Johnson, successor to Eisenhower as it were (John Kennedy having been assassinated), would face the same crisis again, but on a much more dangerous level. He too would confront the man described as "the incarnation of the Arab drive towards independence and modernization." [267] Nasser also typified the modern, secular-minded Arab in despising the long-established imperialism of the Western powers in the Middle East, while at the same time fearing the imperial ambitions of the Soviet Union. As a logical consequence, he embraced the doctrine of "non-alignment" once the Cold War began to heat up in the 1960s. In practice this meant exploiting the opportunities the rivalries of the two superpowers presented to him. Discovering that the revenues from the Suez Canal would not suffice to build the high dam, he reluctantly turned to the Soviet Union for assistance, receiving help that was both technical and financial. With reluctance also, he entered into an unexpected and unusual arrangement with the Syrian leadership, resulting in the union of the two countries. To be called the United Arab Republic, it would in fact be divided, since the "Jewish entity" (they would not say "the State of Israel") existed as a bloc standing between the Syrian and Egyptian territories.

The cause for this unstable and ultimately abortive union is thought to have been the result of Syrian fears that the communists would take over at Damascus. [268] But of equal importance, no doubt, was Nasser's great prestige in the Arab world following the Suez crisis. Defeated militarily, he had emerged triumphant diplomatically. In the Middle East just then, the appearance of things rather than the reality counted the most. Everywhere in the vast region, a movement called Nasserism, now equated with Pan-Arabism, had sprung up. In Yemen, Nasserites began to plot the overthrow of the Imam Ahmed and the establishment of a socialist republic, on the Egyptian model of course. [269] In Iraq also, Nasserites schemed as how they might depose the Hashemite king, Feisal II.

Like Iraq, Syria was not a nation-state in any meaningful sense, both countries the incidental result of the Ottoman Empire's collapse at the end of World War One. Invented by the British and French, both were (and are) multinational states. Out of the vicissitudes of politics, ethnic antagonisms, religious intolerance, both were fragile societies dominated by elites. In Syria, the Alawi Tribe (a Shiite Sect) had achieved an irresistible military domination, capable of ruling all factions and all peoples within the state. One of the least stable countries in the region, Syria was governed by frequent *coup d'état*. Always Moslem in the majority, always Arabic in language, Syria was what the Alawi Tribe would make of it. The ruling obsession for all the factions was "Greater Syria," a fixation driven not so much by Arab sentiment as by an expansive atavism. Since Transjordan had been the major part of historic Palestine (more than half), the Syrians wanted not only what the Israelis had taken, but Jordan's share as well. [270] They claimed Lebanon also, that territory having been, in their eyes, unjustly severed from Syria by the French.

The future Arab empire of Nasser's imagination was probably adumbrated in the way he treated his hypothetically equal partner, Syria. Once Nasser was elected president of the UAR, Egyptians began pouring into the country: officials, teachers, scholars, businessmen, military advisors, Nasser's own secret police; so that it appeared finally that Syria had become an Egyptian province—a good sign of what would befall any Arab country that entered into Nasser's caring arms.

With the country economically exploited for the benefit of Egypt, politically managed to the detriment of its sovereignty, the Syrian elite finally rebelled against its latest master. But in this connection it should be considered that Nasser's domination (however foreign in Syrian eyes) represented no more than another military junta. In a period of little more than two decades since independence, Syrians had seen a score or more of governments overthrown as the result of military coups. Six times the constitution had been revised or thrown out and a new one put in its place.

In September 1961 thirty-seven officers with a following of obedient soldiers marched on Damascus and announced Syria's independence from Egypt. Doubting that the rebellion reflected the real sentiment of the Syrian people, Nasser didn't take the matter seriously. When finally it became clear to him that power had shifted and changed, not in response to public opinion but the jockeying of factions for power, his chance to quell the rebellion had vanished. Ineptly, almost comically, he attempted to send paratroops to regain a country already lost to him. The next day the dictator went on radio and addressed the Syrian people almost tearfully, telling them they were free to go their own way and that Egyptians and Syrians would remain brothers, always ready to defend each other.

Separated once more, yet joined by the elusive vision of Arab unity, the two countries continued to collaborate on the single matter that consumed them: the liberation of Palestine and the destruction of the State of Israel. The Syrians believed with a mystical certitude, and despite the facts of their disjoined history, that should one Arab state descend upon Israel, the other Arab states, galvanized by this example, would follow. But while the Syrians forever urged him to fight Israel *now*, Nasser always hesitated.

The dictator's failure to create a lasting United Arab Republic and then an Arab federation that would include Yemen shaped the contest between himself and the Syrian leadership. Both parties subscribed to the ideal, Arab unity; both countries belonged to the Arab League, ostensibly the first step toward the Pan Arab unity they desired. [271] Both detested the Hashemite families who ruled Jordan and Iraq. Both professed to be champions of the Palestinian Arabs, though as is evident, for different reasons. Both aspired to lead all the Arabs, and that was the dividing difference. When, in 1964, Nasser began to organize commandos for the liberation of Palestine, the Syrian delegation at a "summit" meeting of the Arab League proposed that Palestinian Arabs should be deemed a national entity, and called upon them "to carry out their role in liberating their homeland and determining their destiny." [272]

This was the first time the Syrians had made a public pronouncement suggesting that the former Palestine might not be part of

Syria, and indeed might belong to the Palestinian people. Later this same year the government of Jordan allowed Palestinian notables to assemble in East Jerusalem, calling themselves a "National Congress." A vote was taken to establish a national organization, the Palestine Liberation Organization, dedicated to the liberation of Palestine. Ahmed Shukairy, a volatile, compulsive individual, was named president of the organization. Afterward a manifesto was circulated, stating that the goal of the PLO was "to attain the objective of liquidating Israel." A philosophy and a program for action were combined in a document called the Palestine National Covenant. The essential points, stated and restated in thirty-three articles, were the liberation of Palestine, the indivisible character of Palestine as it existed under the Mandate, and the destruction of the State of Israel.[273] The formation of a Palestinian Liberation Army was also foreseen.

Farseeing too, Nasser recognized the potential value of the PLO as an instrument for the gratification of his relentless quest to unite the Arab countries under his leadership. Nominally, the PLO was subordinated to the Arab League, but in practice it soon became Nasser's organization, and for a time a good many of the Palestinian leaders were his faithful clients.[274]

The subversion of Jordan, or more precisely, the overthrow of Hussein, became the focus of Nasser's numerous conspiracies, a very possible objective since an estimated 60 percent of the Jordanian population were Palestinian, and a significant part of the officer corps had become devoted Nasserites. It would be hard to overstate the peril Hussein faced. In the end he would be saved, as the Israelis always were, by the cross-purposes of his Arab rivals and Nasser's quixotic, rather Hamlet-like penchant for philosophical ruminations in the midst of action: "To be or not to be?" To act, or not to act, that was the question.

The Chinese Communists supported Nasser and his PLO without reservation and only wondered at his caution. Shukairy reported after a visit to Beijing that Arab lethargy and inaction seemed incomprehensible to the Chinese. "You are one hundred million," said Mao Tse Tung, "and they [the Israelis] are two million. So what are you waiting for?"

When Shukairy suggested the likelihood of a large loss of life in any engagement with the Israelis, his interlocutor expressed surprise. "What is a million sacrifices? After independence the birth rate will increase." [275]

Cautious despite his flamboyance, Nasser did not want to seek success at so astronomical a price. Nevertheless, the Syrian leadership continually pressed him for immediate war with Israel, and he steadily resisted.

Prudence alone did not contain Nasser's natural ardor and adventurous spirit. By 1966 Egypt was bankrupt, the country's foreign loans so immense that the interest could no longer be paid. Finally, a crucial matter, Nasser could not extricate himself from the civil war in Yemen, which had become an imbroglio, similar to the American involvement in Vietnam. Like Lyndon Johnson, the dictator did not know precisely why he was there. Like the American president also, he had tried to manipulate affairs at long distance until finally the concatenation of events drew him in directly, an involvement requiring ever more troops and supplies. As the Americans had felt compelled to intervene in defense of their client, South Vietnam, Nasser felt driven to intervene for the same reason. As the Americans believed they could implant their form of democracy in a backward country, Nasser believed he could install his form of revolutionary socialism in a country still essentially medieval. As in Vietnam, conventional methods of warfare by a regular army contended poorly with the guerrilla tactics of native people who were at once xenophobic and patriotic. As the Vietcong could be defeated but never vanquished, the Yemeni tribesmen, however often they were dispersed, would regroup and return to threaten the regime Nasser had elected to defend. At last the dictator realized that he could not win, yet he could not afford to lose. By the end of 1964 fully one-third of the Egyptian army was bogged down in Yemen. Nasser's policy demanded nonetheless that he openly threaten the Israelis with a force he did not possess.

It was all very complex in detail, yet simple in outline. The Soviets had begun by pouring money and technicians into Egypt in order to build the high dam at Aswan, then sending ever more arms to the principal Arab countries. Syria and Egypt became principal beneficiaries. Naturally, the United States would be compelled to match any Soviet démarche in the Middle East, so that by degrees the most typical aspect of the Cold War emerged. The superpowers contested each other through proxies, Israel the client of the United States, its principal Arab enemies dependent upon the Soviet Union.

Syrian attempts to divert water from Israel by building dams on the upper Jordan brought the issue to a head in early 1966. The solution to the problem, Israeli Chief of Staff General Yitzhak Rabin declared in September of that year, was to begin systematically bombing Syria until that government abandoned its policy of staging raids on Israel. Then they would talk about water. Israeli Premier Eshkol echoed those words.

Energized by what they considered to be an imminent war, the Syrians entered into discussions with Nasser. On 4 November a joint defense agreement was signed between them. Fatally, this would draw Egypt into a confrontation with Israel, which very likely would mean a resumption of the war that had begun in 1948 and seemingly could not be terminated.

Since many of the Fedayeen raids were launched from the West Bank (covertly supported by Syria), and Hussein seemingly incapable of stopping them, Jordan became Israel's target as much as Syria. The king's situation was untenable. By 1966 more than half the population of Jordan was Palestinian Arab. The remainder, Bedouins, did not count in any significant way. Half the seats in the Jordan Assembly were assigned to the West Bank constituency. The Palestinian Arabs had crossed over Jordan into a country that practiced a rudimentary democracy, i.e., universal adult suffrage, though many women in Jordan were not disposed to vote or participate in the country's politics.

Syrian influence on the West Bank was enormous because of its sponsorship of the popular Fedayeen. Across the Jordan (East Bank) the PLO had assumed such importance among Arabs generally, and with the Palestinian Arabs in Jordan especially, that it was a continuous threat to Hussein's authority. Yet it appeared the king could do little or nothing to help himself. The Arab League, to which Jordan belonged, had voted unanimously in support of the Palestine Liberation Organization and its covenant, Hussein giving his affirmative vote along with the others. But he had, in effect, voted against himself. It was no secret that the PLO leadership intended to establish a virtual sovereignty in Jordan, a first step to launching a war against Israel for the liberation of all of Palestine.

Hussein clung to the belief that the Palestinian Arabs could be assimilated into Jordan, saying almost whimsically that they could be "Jordanized." No, responded Shukairy, speaking to the Palestine National Council, which was meeting in Cairo. "Our Jordan brothers are already Palestinians." While the king believed his grandfather had annexed the West Bank, what really happened (according to Shukairy) was "the annexation of the East Bank to the Palestinian homeland." [276]

At an impasse therefore, the PLO demanded what amounted to sovereign power in Jordan. The king was adamant in his refusal. At Nasser's direction, Shukairy began a campaign of propaganda and vilification, broadcasting his vituperative messages from Cairo, carried on PLO stations in Jordan. Much of it was directed against Hussein himself.

Clearly, the king had become a cipher in his own kingdom. When he complained to Nasser, the latter sent Shukairy to Amman. The PLO leader's language was contemptuous. "If I wanted to be prime minister [of Jordan]," he told Hussein, "I would rent a house in Amman and after one week I would become prime minister." He reminded the king that the present Prime Minister, Wasfi al-Tal, was not much more than a clerk in ability, and had been one in fact "under me at the Arab Office in Jerusalem in 1946."

More concessions by the king only emboldened Shukairy, but the time came when Hussein talked tough. Relying upon the loyalty of his legion he said, "Any hand raised against our struggling nation will be cut off, and any eye which looks at us with a look of hatred will be gouged out."

Shukairy was undaunted, believing the Palestinian Arabs were behind him. Both Jordan and Israel, he declared, were essentially the same: both the result and the beneficiaries of western imperialism. Back in Cairo he called for an uprising of the Jordan citizenry against an unjust government, appealing to the Arab world for support, predicting that from Jordan as a base they would sweep across Palestine.

Shukairy's inflamed oratory at Cairo, faithful echo of his master, Gamal Nasser, is a reminder that the PLO was the Egyptian dictator's own instrument, Shukairy a tool also, and Hussein his potential victim. In the world of Arab politics Jordan was isolated and weak because this was the condition of its monarch. The "revolutionary" states, Egypt, Syria, and Iraq, were dedicated to removing him from power, dead or alive. The conservative Arab states, mainly Saudi Arabia and the Emirates, were almost indifferent to the king's fate (no love lost between Hussein and the Saudis). Hussein could expect no more than feeble support from the U.S., which, while sympathetic to the king's plight, reserved its full fellowship for the one real democracy in the Middle East, Israel.

To the degree that Shukairy's rhetoric became more vicious, Hussein became firmer in his reactions. In July 1966 his government dared to sever its relations with the PLO. In withdrawing his recognition, Hussein charged that the leadership of the organization was attempting to overthrow his government, and that its leaders operated like an arm of the Egyptian government (all very true). It may be presumed that the prime minister of Jordan spoke the king's mind when he said that he made a distinction between the PLO as such and its leadership. He was, he avowed, anti-Israeli, and as pro-Palestinian as any Arab. Jordan was loyal to the cause of destroying Israel. If war with Israel should come, Jordan would "face up to every battle forced on us, whether we are ready or not." [277]

Up to this point, unbridled terrorism against Israel, and indirectly against Jordan, had been the almost exclusive practice of the Syrians. The PLO, responsible to Nasser's will, had been unwilling to adopt the violence of the Fedayeen. But once the king of Jordan denounced the PLO, Nasser unleashed Shukairy. Egyptian-sponsored raids into Israel commenced from bases in Lebanon. Syria increased Fedayeen raids from its bases on the West Bank. Israel responded with an assault on Fedayeen camps, provoking more raids, then more reprisals. Nasser evidently felt challenged by this and ordered raids to match those of the Syrians. In the Arab world the question was, which of the two, Syria or Egypt, was boldest in dealing with the hated Israelis?

Escalating tensions, a result of attack, riposte, and counterattack, announced the coming war, long awaited by the Syrians but always deferred by Nasser. To incite Israel while Jordan disintegrated would, in the eyes of the fatalistic Syrians, produce the *Gotterdamerung*, the last stage when Palestine would be redeemed. "He who liberates Palestine," said Syrian Chief of Staff, Major General Ahmad Sweidani, on the eve of the Six-Day War, "will be the one to lead the Arab nation forward to comprehensive unity." [278]

This apocalyptic vision was not Nasser's, though his oratory remained inflammatory. He was prudent, considering the Syrians to be just a little short of crazy. Yet, in the Arab world where symbols were so important, he could not allow himself to be upstaged by his rivals.

Nasser's deposition as president of the UAR had been attended by the fall from power of Syria's Ba'ath Party (Arab Socialist Renaissance Party), which had played a part in establishing the union of Syria and Egypt, then elevating Nasser to the presidency. The Ba'ath Party was as strife-torn as Syria itself. It had its extreme wings, left and right, and a diverse middling representation; almost a mirror image of the fractured country. Reorganized after September 1961, its factional rifts sealed temporarily, the Ba'ath leadership had carried out a coup that brought them back to power. This lasted until February 1966, when still another coup brought them down. The newest clique was perhaps more eclectic than any junta before it. They had come together as a matter of convenience, a small group of fanatically patriotic army officers cooperating with an equally exalted faction from the Ba'ath Party (all civilians). Their titular head was Major General Salah Jedid, a member of Syria's ruling minority, the Alawi Tribe. They were held together, after seizing power by a profligate use of guns, planes and tanks, by the same messianic strands of hope that had united all the previous regimes, a vision constant since 1919: Arab unity and the recovery of Palestine (and of course the destruction of Israel). On this basis they could cooperate with Nasser, since they believed he shared their vision. But their ambivalence is hardly to be comprehended. Scathingly, they deprecated the Egyptian dictator in one breath, it has been observed, and in the next heaped upon him an adulation not far short of sycophancy. Their hypocrisy was well understood. "The aim of successive regimes," observed American correspondent Winston Burdette, "was to stay within his orbit but well outside his power." [279] One might go further and say, cynically, they would use Nasser as he intended to use them.

The UN peacekeeping organization had been established on the Egyptian side of the armistice line (the Israelis refused to have them on their territory). For Nasser, for the Egyptians generally, the "Blue Helmets" stationed on their soil were a humiliating symbol of a severe defeat by a state they would not acknowledge even existed; a perpetual reminder that since 1956 volunteers from half a dozen countries had defended Egypt, which could not defend itself. Moreover, should Nasser yield to the bellicose urging of his Syrian allies and attempt to mount an offensive against the Israelis, he would have to think how he might push aside the protecting cordon that the Blue Helmets represented. On 16 May he ordered his Chief of Staff, General Mohammed Fawzi, to demand that the Indian commander of UNEF withdraw, "in case," said Nasser, "an act of aggression should be committed against an Arab country." [280] Reluctantly, and despite Israeli protests, UN forces were removed, giving Nasser the "window" he needed in case of military action. [281]

To the Israelis the removal of the Blue Helmets was at least provocative, perhaps aggressive. Nasser's next step, still more inexplicable, was to restore the blockade of the Tiran Straits, which had been the fundamental cause for the Israeli invasion of the Sinai ten years earlier. Premier Eshkol called it "an act of aggression against Israel," to be considered a *casus belli*.

Thereafter Nasser's offhand remarks provoked outrage among the Israelis: "Israel wants to fight? Fine." The next day he declared to a delegation from the National Assembly, "Israel shall be destroyed." His careless rhetoric was ever greater than the effective power he could command. His language nonetheless revealed his wish, and that perhaps the passing of time would allow its realization. If the Israelis should give him the opportunity to push them back to the line of 1956, he said on 29 May, he would go on to the line of 1948.

Nasser's boast on 29 May was followed the next day by a diplomatic tour de force that must have surprised him as much as it stunned the Israelis. The king of Jordan flew to Cairo and entered into a mutual defense pact with Nasser who, up to that moment, had been nothing less than his malevolent political enemy.

All had miscalculated. The Israelis had believed that the bad blood between Hussein and Nasser would make an entente between their two governments impossible. Hussein thought that in accepting a mutual defense pact with Nasser he would curry favor with the many Palestinians on his territory who threatened his life. Also, since he subscribed to the doctrine that Israel should be destroyed, he thought that in this way time would be gained for making the preparations needed to liquidate the Jewish state. [282] Nasser had gambled that the US, sometimes lukewarm to Israel, would observe a strict neutrality, not wanting to confront the USSR. "The Soviet Union stands with us in this battle," he declared on 29 May, "and will not allow any country to interfere." [283]

By 31 May the Egyptian forces had been augmented by the arrival of troops from Iraq and Kuwait. Nasser's bragging was no greater than that of the Iraqi president, who said to his commanders,

"Brethren and sons, this is the day of the battle to avenge your martyred brethren who fell in 1948. We shall, God willing, meet in Tel Aviv and Haifa." [284]

If the aim of the Arab leaders seemed plain from the remarks they made, i.e., the liquidation of the State of Israel, Shukairy entertained a much vaster vision of eventual revenge. One of his followers wondered what would happen to the "native born Israelis" should the Arabs win the coming war. "Those who survive will remain in Palestine," replied Shukairy. "I estimate that none of them will survive." [285]

Although Eshkol and others in his cabinet believed the Arabs would not be ready to mount an offensive for at least another two years, they could not accept the risk of being wrong in their estimates of Arab readiness. [286] On 5 June they initiated hostilities, their air force taking the Arabs (as Hussein admitted later) by surprise. The Egyptian aircraft did not get off the ground before being destroyed. The coordination of the Arabs' multinational force became hopelessly confused at the outset, a chaos of orders delivered and withdrawn by commanders who had already lost control of their units.

The two superpowers were content to let their respective clients struggle alone and without help. Vainly, Nasser had sent emissaries to Moscow, only to find indifference. The United States, as in 1948 and again in 1956, adopted a neutral stance; "neutral in thought, word, and deed," averred State Department spokesman Robert McCloskey.

The diplomatic casuistry exercised henceforth by the American government explained the nuance of words. Secretary of State Dean Rusk made a distinction between "neutral" and "indifference." The United States was not indifferent. "Indeed," said Rusk, "indifference is not permitted to us." Indeed it was not, because the U.S. had by this time been faithful to its client, Israel, for almost a generation. The Soviet Union's decision to play a major role in the Middle East by backing the Arabs had elevated (or debased, according to how one thinks of it) Israel to the rank of a U.S. surrogate. Chained to its creature for good or bad, the American statesmen could not be indifferent, and in reality could not be neutral.

In the field the Israelis were once more alone and fighting for survival against (as it seemed to the watching world) overwhelming odds, but were saved, as in earlier times, by their excellent organization, outstanding leadership, the inspired discipline of their troops and fliers (as those threatened to the point of extinction may be), and also by the divisions and doubts of their enemies. Hussein's actions reveal this best. He might have chosen to be as neutral as the United States claimed to be. To the Israelis his neutrality seemed imperative, faced as they were with a threatening coalition of Arab states. At the very outbreak of the war, the king received a message from the Israeli government: "We shall not initiate any action whatsoever against Jordan. However, should Jordan open hostilities, we shall react with all our might and he [King Hussein] will have to bear the full responsibility for all the consequences."

Unfortunately for Hussein, deceived by false messages from Nasser that the Arabs were winning the first stage of the battle, he shrugged off the Israeli warning and decided to send his troops into action. Nasser, for his part, saw his air force destroyed by Israeli planes before it could take to the air.

Caught unprepared, having been struck before striking first (if indeed that was his intent), Nasser could now only lie to his public in order to conceal his miscalculations, but for that he must need cajole and bully the frightened Hussein to join him in his deceit. The dictator called the king on the radio, suggesting the aerial onslaught could be called the work of Israel and its allies. "Will we say the U.S. and England or just the U.S.?" he asked.

"The U.S. and Britain," replied Hussein.

"By God, I will make an announcement and you will make an announcement…that American and British airplanes are taking part against us from aircraft carriers."

"Good," responded the King. "All right."

To compound his lie Nasser told Hussein another: "We are with you with all our heart and we are flying our planes over Israel today, our planes are striking at Israel's airfields since morning." [287]

Nasser's air force was in fact at that moment in flames or in ashes. The war was over almost before it had begun. Hostilities would last only six days more, giving a name to the brief conflict that most historians believe neither side wanted.

When American Secretary of State William Seward spoke of "the irrepressible conflict," which was to say the forces driving rational men and women into the cauldron of the American Civil War, he was expressing a profound truth about human nature, when a mixture of pride, egotism, and revered principle may propel rational people into the insanity of war. "A peculiar combination of internal and external events," wrote Theodore Draper in 1967, "was necessary to set off the third Arab-Israeli war." [288]

Jihad, stimulated by Arab nationalism, not to forget Nasser's megalomania, compelled the dictator toward a confrontation he was not prepared for in 1967. The Israelis too were reluctant to risk all they had gained up to that point by entering into a war of which the outcome was doubtful. Yet, in the final analysis, they and not the Arabs precipitated the hostilities. The usual interpretation of international law will assign the first act of aggression to Israel and not the Arabs. The fact that the Israelis won the war of course severely attenuated the meaning of such guilt as might be assigned to them under international law. [289] The old saying "possession is nine-tenths of the law" seemed especially pertinent when it is considered that the Israelis defeated their enemies in less than a week, overran the Sinai desert, took possession of the Gaza Strip, and wrested the West Bank from Jordan, along with its prized jewel, Old Jerusalem. [290]

⟨~⟩ ARMED STRUGGLE

Nasser's PLO did not survive intact the debacle of the Six-Day War. Inevitably, Shukairy had to play the role of scapegoat. He was removed from the presidency of the PLO, first step toward his oblivion. Thereafter the Executive Committee demanded his resignation from the PLO entirely. He complied, accepted a pension and went to London to live in retirement. Yahya Hammuda, a nonentity from the revolutionary point of view, succeeded him. Obedient to Nasser, as Shukairy had been, Hammuda tried to do what Shukairy had attempted and failed to do: bring the Fedayeen into the PLO.

The failure of Nasser and his adepts to harness the energies and win the loyalty of the Palestinian zealots is explained in two ways. From the beginning, these numerous groups of self-appointed saviors of the Palestinian homeland had not wanted to operate under any other insignia than their own. Thus the significance of the slogan "El Fatah" (Conquest with Jihad). It was a spiritual brotherhood, but also sectarian; exalted and violent patriots who scorned order and authority. Secondly, there was at large in the world of dissent, protest, alienation, and revolutionary ardor, a mystique: "Armed Struggle." In psychological terms it was a more potent force than that possessed by well-armed and regulated states. Everywhere—in the Far East, Africa, and the West—there had appeared disruptive forces: Black Panthers, Red Guards, and Baader-Meinhof, to name a few. Among the subject peoples yearning to break the imperial bonds that enthralled them, there were many violent groups, from South Africa to Algeria to Ireland. And there were already revolutionary icons to behold, even to worship; and above all, to emulate: Mao Tse Tung, Che Guevara, Fidel Castro, perhaps the most representative luminaries in a galaxy of dedicated and ruthless malcontents.

While the 1967 defeats were demoralizing for the Arab states, they meant deliverance for Palestinian nationalists who needed only a leader and better organization. In this way Yasser Arafat experienced a reincarnation.

Until the aftermath of the Six-Day War, PLO was just one acronym among half a dozen. Likewise, the name Arafat did not suggest a greater import than that of George Habbach, leader of the PFLP (Popular Front for the Liberation of Palestine); or Nayif Hawatmah, whose group, The Vengeance Youth, had split off from the ANM (Arab Nationalist Movement); or Wajih al-Madani, leader of the Heroes of the Return, to name only a few of the many notable chiefs of factions who rose into prominence abruptly, then just as quickly fell into oblivion. [291] All were exalted types; some were cerebral, thoughtful, and some merely dumb brutes, taking pleasure in tormenting and killing not only the enemy but also their rivals. All practiced terror, but all found ways to explain it and/or explain it away. Semantic exercises allowed the Palestinian extremists to argue that the Israelis were the terrorists, and they [the Palestinians] were the "anti-terrorists," merely defending themselves. Their reasoning was not different from that of Menachem Begin, who in his memoirs wrote: "The historical and linguistic origins of the political term 'terrorist' prove that it cannot be applied to a revolutionary war of liberation…historically we were not 'terrorists.' We were strictly speaking anti-terrorists [i.e., the British were the terrorists]." [292] How like Arafat's remark before the United Nations: "Whoever stands by a just cause and fights for the freedom and liberation of his land from the invaders, the settlers and the colonialists cannot possibly be called terrorist." [293]

Terror, in practice, depended upon the Syrians. The Ba'ath leadership still possessed the power to call and to send its Palestinian minions, to bestow the aura of leadership, and to take it away. This privilege, or better to say, the honor to lead, was assigned to Arafat when he journeyed to Damascus in September 1967. Fatah, which in the beginning had been no more than a committee of eight comrades, had become by 1967 a large body of guerrillas, well armed, well trained, highly indoctrinated. There were about five hundred of them, it is thought. They were ruthless, selfless, determined, convinced of the justice of their calling. Hard and pitiless after years of intrigues, feuds, and murders, they recognized no restraints, which is the acme of gang violence.

Anointed by the Syrians, Arafat was the unquestioned leader of this still amorphous group, surrounded by a close-knit company of friends and associates, some of whom he had known from his college days. Sophisticated men, they knew how to use the instruments

250

of guerrilla warfare, but also how to publicize their acts, how best to exploit the advantage to be found in the most heinous deed they might perpetrate.

It appeared that the Israelis, through an untoward war with unexpected consequences, had overreached themselves. All at once the land they occupied had become a stage upon which a war of national liberation might be mounted, and more importantly, maintained. Ironically, the people they had driven into exile in 1948 were once more within the framework of their authority, existing now as a threat to Israel's continued existence. The Israelis' problem was as simple as it was profound: they occupied a country (the West Bank and Gaza) that they could not safely keep and could not afford to give up.

The men of Fatah believed that a sullen populace, living under the guns of a halfway-frightened occupant, might well rise and drive them out, and that once this flood tide of humanity had begun, Palestine would be entirely liberated. But the expected rising did not occur, Israeli vigilance greater than the men of Fatah could have imagined.

The Fedayeen had infiltrated the villages long ago, fraternized with the people, but without significant results. They were received hospitably, fed, served in various ways, but the people remained supine, almost indifferent. It was the story of the Narodniki again. The exalted reformers came to educate and to stir into life the inert masses of the Palestinian nation, but alas, were ignored. For long, Israeli agents, spies, and provocateurs had infiltrated the Fedayeen. After the Six-Day War the Fedayeen network in the Occupied Territories was dismantled in a few months. Perhaps a thousand young men were detected; most were arrested, imprisoned or deported. Arafat's hideout at Nablus was discovered. With luck he got away, taking refuge in Jordan.

Interestingly, Arafat did not consider this latest reverse to be the result of dealing with (and depending upon) a passive population. Rather, it was to him another evidence of the internal divisions of the Palestinian movement, *viz.*, too many movements, which was really what El Fatah had always been. Consequently, a meeting

251

was held at Cairo in January 1968. There, Fatah, consisting of at least a dozen Palestinian liberation groups, was fused. Ostensibly, it became a single movement. The PLO leadership was invited, but refused to attend, this being a reminder that the PLO was what Nasser would make of it. To have it absorbed by a rival movement was not in his purview.

If the PLO, under Nasser's guidance, had failed to liberate Palestine, Fatah, with its idea of armed struggle and an elemental uprising of an oppressed people, had not succeeded either. Having retreated across the Jordan to the East Bank, the Fatah returned to the original idea of the PLO leadership: Jordan to become the staging ground (a "confrontation state" as they called it) for a war with Israel. Fedayeen camps were set up, and once more Hussein was powerless to stop it. Fedayeen raids across the Jordan border commenced, inviting reprisals. Israeli air sorties became so constant that the villagers began to leave their homes. The Jordan valley became a no man's land.

Among the several villages that served as command centers for the Fatah, Karamah on the East Bank, about four miles from the Allenby Bridge, was most important. An Israeli air attack on 15 February forced out almost all the inhabitants. When an Israeli school bus blew up as the result of running over a Fedayeen land mine, the Israeli government chose Karamah for destruction by land and air. The assault was launched on 21 March, constituting a breach of the armistice, since Jordan's territory was being invaded. Both the Arab Legion and the Fedayeen battled the invaders all day and well into the night. The Fatah leadership, fearing that they might be captured, ordered the Fedayeen to fight to the death, then fled; Arafat was seen speeding away on a motorbike.

In this inglorious way Fatah appeared to be extinguished, and once more it seemed that Arafat had become an unemployed revolutionary. To assume that, however, was to discount Arab enthusiasm for the cause and to underestimate the power of Fatah's propaganda. A victory of the Fedayeen was reported, and the Arab press took it up eagerly: thus, Karamah had been a battle of major proportions; Israel's casualties were severe, losing much equipment as well. The losses of the Fedayeen, it was said, were surprisingly light in an engagement that pitted 300 of the valiant fighters against 15,000 Israeli troops, compelling the invader to withdraw from Jordan.

The figures reported by Israel were at variance with those publicized by Fatah: 170 terrorists killed and 200 captured; twenty-eight Israeli soldiers killed and ninety wounded, none captured. But Fatah's inflated figures were the important ones in a war that was as much emotion and propaganda as it was actual fighting. The hard-pressed king of Jordan put the best face on it he could, congratulating his people on their courage in resisting the invader. Always a survivor, ever smiling, he seldom lacked for a *bon mot.* "We may reach a stage," he remarked, "where we shall all become Fedayeen."

Fortified by its heroism, enjoying the king's endorsement, the Fedayeen continued to operate on the East Bank. When attacked by Israeli planes at Salt, the most important of their several command centers, they survived, but the punishment from the air was more severe than before. Hussein went to see the damage and to inspect other bases. He was turned away. Annoyed at last, he sent a detachment of troops with orders for the Fedayeen to evacuate the camps. They refused and, after some confused wrangling, the Jordanian commander ordered a withdrawal.

After that, to protect themselves, the Fedayeen moved out of the villages they had commandeered earlier, and established themselves in schools, hospitals, and the refugee camps. Their armaments had grown to the point where they possessed rockets able to reach well into Israel. On the East Bank streets they instituted patrols. Thousands of them, heavily armed, reported to Fatah, ignored the Jordanian police and dared the army to act against them. In their night patrols they brought back to their headquarters Palestinian Arabs accused of collaborating with Israeli agents. These were tried in "revolutionary courts;" summary justice inevitably the result.

The parties that had been outlawed by the Jordan government before the war, charged with sedition (Communist, Ba'ath, Arab Nationalists) revived and collaborated with the Fedayeen. Clashes between the Fedayeen and the Arab Legion became more frequent. At this point Hussein asked Nasser to intervene on his behalf. The latter, less than an honest broker, promised to use his influence with the Fedayeen. Shortly, a compromise was reached that might suggest Hussein had won this deadly game. In reality, by coming to an understanding with the Fedayeen in this way, Hussein merely acknowledged that they were a power in the state with a prestige greater than his. No less important, Egypt, a foreign power and Arab neighbor, was the ally of the Fedayeen, not of the king of Jordan.

Nasser had by this time become a convert, however reluctantly, to the Fatah concept, armed struggle of the people. He recognized, he said in a speech on 23 July 1968, "that the Palestinian people have risen to champion their own cause by themselves and to defend their rights by themselves." [294]

Having yielded the ground on ideology and tactics, the dictator had to give way to the more murderous aspect of revolutionary policy. The Fatah leadership had long wanted to draw the PLO into the general Palestinian movement, to nationalize it in a sense as an organization not merely intent upon destroying Israel, but more positively, a champion of Palestinian nationalism; above all, to remove it from Egypt's influence, which was incarnate in the charismatic Nasser. Therefore, the Central Committee of Fatah gave Arafat permission as "official spokesman and representative of Fatah "to negotiate with the PLO." From that day there commenced for Arafat what would become a long career as freedom fighter and diplomat, head of state (which did not exist, the PLO its proxy); and terrorist who had put aside conscience in pursuit of a high calling; a man who lived simultaneously in the two modes of violence and peaceful negotiation.

The Palestinian National Congress, formed the same year as the Palestine Liberation Organization (1964), had been as much Nasser's creature as was the PLO. Nasser alone decided who and how many might be represented in the PNC. One of Arafat's first acts was to request a recomposition of the Congress. The PLO leader, Hammuda (thus Nasser) agreed. By reason of this reorganization, thirty-eight seats would be assigned to Fatah, ten to the Movement (i.e., several groups not yet affiliated with Fatah). Of the remaining fifty-two seats, most were assigned to Fedayeen groups that were either intimately in league with Arafat or subject to Fatah influence. The few seats that remained were assigned to the PLO.

The original PNC had been composed of notables, important figures, some of whom had personal connections with Nasser; a sort of revolutionary club that almost always endorsed the dictator's policies. By assigning the seats to terrorist groups like Fatah, to militant trade union officials, and to militant students, a changed philosophy invested the PNC; in a sense it was transformed. When the Congress convened in July 1968, the Palestinian National Covenant was revised. The central purpose of the PLO, the destruction of Israel, remained, but a new doctrine was inserted in a permanent, even constitutional, sense. Armed struggle, the battle of armed groups, independent of any political direction, would work for the deliverance of oppressed peoples. Nasser, as it can be seen, by yielding to Arafat (or more exactly to Arafat's Fatah) had lifted the lid from a cauldron of frustration and violence that threatened to overwhelm him and was obviously now beyond his control. When the Congress met the next year Arafat was elected Chairman of the PLO in Nasser's presence. It was reported that Arafat wept openly. [295]

Unchained as it were, the PLO embarked upon a more violent career than before. Freed from Nasser's restraints, the organization became, in the eyes of its adepts, not merely the necessary instrument for Palestine's deliverance, but the "vanguard of the revolution." All subject peoples, from the Kurds in central Asia to the Mollucans in Indonesia, had a common destiny and a common engine for revolutionary progress: Armed Struggle. With calculation therefore, any terrorist act henceforth was meant to gain attention, the loss of life and property wholly irrelevant. In the next year and a half a number of airliners were abducted and forced to fly to Jordan, where the passengers became pawns in prolonged negotiations between the affected countries and the dedicated terrorists. The time came when even the paralyzed Hussein could no longer watch and wait for who could say what. His decision early in September to act at last against the Fedayeen in general, and the PLO in particular, came as the result of several developments, two unsuccessful attempts on his life among them. Pride had its place also. While reviewing the Legion one day, the king noticed that one soldier had attached to his radio antenna a brassiere, which fluttered in the wind as if it were the legion's standard; a stunning insinuation that the king, by his craven inaction, had converted the men of his famed legion into women.

On 17 September 1970 Hussein ordered his Bedouin troops to commence an attack on Fedayeen strongholds. It would go down in the annals of the Palestine Liberation Movement as "Black September." For eleven days the battle raged; at least 30,000 were killed.

Syria intervened on behalf of the Fedayeen finally, sending tanks into Jordan. In response the Israelis mobilized, and the Syrians withdrew. Remnants of the Fedayeen fled into Syria. Arafat went into hiding and eventually slipped out of Jordan in disguise, taking refuge in Cairo. Thereafter, Nasser played the role of mediator between Hussein and Arafat. On 27 September the two men signed a cease-fire agreement. The next day Nasser died from a massive heart attack. He was fifty-two years old. An estimated four million people lined the six-mile route from Al-Qubbah Palace to his final resting-place. Nasserism went to the grave with its founder.

With this most timely death of his nemesis, Hussein felt himself delivered. He renounced the agreement that had called for a continued existence of the PLO's presence in Jordan. The Legion now completed the work of driving the Fedayeen out of the country. Vowing revenge, the Fedayeen leadership created a secret assassin squad, calling it Black September. Shortly, Hussein's

Prime Minister, Wasfi al-Tal, was murdered at the entrance to the Sheraton Hotel in Cairo. The Egyptian authorities seized the assassins and had them tried for murder. They were acquitted, and crowds in Cairo turned out to celebrate them as heroes. Meanwhile, driven out of Jordan, the PLO set up its headquarters in Lebanon, still enjoying Syria's support.

ᗌᗌᗌ LEBANON: THE QUAGMIRE

Civil war in Lebanon stirred Western sensibilities much as Israel's unequal contest with the Arabs had affected the same opinion in 1947. A remote, mountainous country for the most part, Lebanon had been over many centuries a refuge for Christians in a sea of threatening Moslems. While security had never been certain, survival had never been in doubt.

The establishment of the French mandate in Syria, and subsequent enlargement of Lebanon to become Greater Lebanon, had a profound impact on the principal city, Beirut. In a short time, the French language, French cuisine, and French architecture made the city a pale imitation of Paris. In 1924 Lebanon became a republic, entirely separate from Syria. A patchwork creation, its exceptional fragility was predetermined by the way disparate regions had been joined together, producing what might be called an artificial society: multi-ethnic, multi-religious. The original Lebanese, descendants of the ancient Phoenicians, had been predominately Christian since the beginning of the Christian era. But the enlarged Lebanon, under French auspices, brought into the same polity a large number of Moslems.

The dominant group in Lebanon was the Maronite Christians, who observed Catholic ritual while denying the authority of the Pope. There was also a Greek Orthodox population, along with some Roman Catholics and Protestants, almost all living in Beirut. The Druze, a Moslem sect, occupied the high country and were historically the rivals of the Christians. The Moslems, almost half the population, were divided into two groups: Sunnis and Shiites.

The eventual solution for so much diversity was a simple political compromise: the president of the Lebanese republic would be a Christian; the prime minister, as speaker of the Assembly, would be a Moslem. The compromise worked tolerably well until the rise of Nasserism in the early fifties.

The creation of the United Arab Republic by Egypt and Syria prompted the Hashemite cousins, Hussein of Jordan and Feisal II of Iraq, to pronounce their own union: the Arab Federation. But this was no more than a statement on paper in defense of the imperiled monarchical principle. When the two kings decided to use both force and influence in support of the pro-Western government in Lebanon, they invited the wrath of the republican Nasserites. On 14 July 1958 an ambitious general, Abdul Kerim Kassem, and a small group of officers carried out a bloody coup at Baghdad, sending into the streets howling mobs who began to hunt down prominent government officials, resulting finally in the death of King Feisal as well.

The year before, Eisenhower had asked a joint session of Congress to support by military means any Middle Eastern country that seemed to be threatened by communism. This would be called the Eisenhower Doctrine, and on the doubtful premise that communism was stalking the Middle East (Lebanon its likely victim), the president sent the Sixth Fleet to Lebanese shores, landing a contingent of Marines at Beirut.

But an American show of force could do nothing for Lebanon, which was collapsing into anarchy for many reasons, international communism not one of these. The country's tragic plight was the result of being caught between Syria on one side and Israel on the other; finally to be overwhelmed by the arrival of the Fedayeen, who were nothing other than the instruments of the Syrian dictator, Hajif Assad. In the end, therefore, Lebanon's determined policy of neutrality toward the Israeli question since 1948 had not served to give it immunity from the effects of Arab nationalism. Powerless to prevent the Fedayeen from operating on its territory, the Lebanese were in a de facto fashion as much at war with Israel as the Syrians and the Egyptians. The arrival of the PLO under Arafat's leadership merely enlarged the crisis.

It has been said that cosmopolitan Beirut afforded the PLO a happy hunting ground, an ideal place for warriors of their ilk to enjoy the good life while engaged in nearly daily violence. Ensconced in a city that has been called "a carnival of death," Arafat began to behave like a head of state. [296] He issued passports and visas under the name of certain cooperating Arab states. [297] One of his colleagues, Farouq Qaddoumi, treated with foreign envoys; as many as 117 missions had arrived at PLO headquarters by 1981.

It was only axiomatic that communist governments would support the PLO. Fidel Castro severed relations with Israel in 1973, giving Cuba's recognition to the PLO. The next year Arafat opened an office in Havana. Thereafter his agents assisted Castro in the training of Latin American terrorists (i.e., patriots). A little later, eight more offices were established in South and Central America (one of these in Jamaica). [298] Subversive movements in some of these countries received money and arms by way of the PLO offices; so well endowed was the PLO that it could, in its diminutive way, play the role of arms merchant. Terrorist groups around the world received not only material support, but were encouraged to send volunteers to Lebanon for training and to participate in actions intended to lead to the destruction of Israel (to be accomplished, only incidentally, by the destruction of Lebanon).

Having achieved a condition of virtual sovereignty, the PLO soon developed extensive foreign relations: friends who could, and would, help. From the Soviet Union they enjoyed steady support in the UN, and eventually arms in abundance. Support from the Third World came early and was henceforth constant. From the Arab League Arafat expected both material and diplomatic support. But that body regularly disappointed him. Assad, who coveted Lebanon, looking upon the country as his own, tolerated with a reluctant sufferance the presence of the ever-growing, ever more influential PLO.

The PLO's relations with Saudi Arabia were clandestine, that archconservative country no more approving of Arafat's Armed Struggle than it had been of Nasser's republican socialism. Yet, the veritable seat of Islam could not be indifferent to the Jewish presence in Palestine, especially Israel's possession of Jerusalem, considered by Moslems to be the third most holy city in Islam.

Over the years, the Libyan dictator, Colonel Muammar Qadhafi, had been generous to the PLO, but was an unpredictable ally for Arafat. He was to Libya what Nasser had been to Egypt: a Pan-Arabist as ready to turn on his Arab rivals as he was to combat Western imperialism. Quixotic, vain, temperamental, Qadhafi's behavior and impulsive outbursts engendered a muted rivalry between two super egos, those of Arafat and himself. His methods were the same as those of the PLO: terrorism conducted on an international scale. The consensus, advanced without proof, is that he financed the Black September operation that resulted in the killing of eleven Israeli athletes at Munich in September 1972. It is more certain that in the years to follow, his operatives commandeered and blew up two airliners (a British plane in March 1974 and a TWA plane toward the end of that year.). There were kidnappings, half a dozen of these recorded and probably many more of a nature not notorious enough to earn space in Western newspapers.

Quadhafi had no faith in the notion of a popular Palestinian war, believing that only well-trained commandos, in conjunction with Arab armies, could defeat a state as well armed as Israel. [299] With his own revolutionary program, and oil-rich, he overtly dismissed the PLO by creating his own organization, calling it the National Arab Youth for the Liberation of Palestine; then creating still another: Arab Organization for National Liberation.

After Nasser's death, Assad and Quadhafi coveted, more than they could really claim, the fallen leader's mantle. Arafat profited from this rivalry, while at the same time exploiting the exigencies of the Lebanese civil war. His stature as spokesman for the Palestinian cause was immensely fortified in October 1974, when a large conclave of Arab leaders (twenty heads of state) met at Rabat, Morocco, and recognized the PLO as the "sole legitimate representative of the Palestinian people on any liberated Palestinian territory." The same month, the UN General Assembly voted overwhelmingly to recognize the PLO as the representative of the Palestinian people. (Only four delegations voted against the resolution: Israel, the United States, Bolivia, and the Dominican Republic.) The next month Arafat accepted an invitation to speak before the United Nations General Assembly. The Ford Administration grudgingly allowed the notorious terrorist to enter the U.S., characterizing him unofficially as an armed thug (an opinion shared by the American public, but perhaps not by the hippies and beatniks). Asked to remove the handgun strapped to his waist, symbol of his calling, Arafat refused. It was a time when a generation had come of age that offered only defiance to authority; resolved to change all things, do away with all restraints, refashion the world in fancied perfect terms, whether peacefully or violently did not matter; by reform or revolution (the difference between these two terms increasingly lost), by disturbed individuals as varied as San Francisco's "Flower Children," Red Guards, or Black Panthers. "Armed Struggle" had become a code word for valor, self-sacrifice, and righteousness. Arafat could not, of course, appear before the assembled delegates of the world unarmed. He was the darling of the Third World, a warrior out of necessity, and a peacemaker if the unjust powers of the world would but relent. I hold, he said (to paraphrase his histrionics), an olive branch in one hand and a pistol in the other.

The message in his brief address was hatred for Israel, Zionism more exactly. In a few words he traced the history of the PLO, showing how it had become a national organization, its legitimacy "intensified" by the support given to it by other national liberation movements. Ironically, he who had made a career out of terrorism now condemned the uses of terrorism. He denied that the PLO was, as so often charged, a terrorist organization: "those who call us terrorists wish to prevent world public opinion from discovering the truth about us and from seeing the justice on our faces."

At the end of his speech he received a prolonged ovation. A debate followed in which Israel was vilified, the representative from the USSR calling the Israelis "cruel and unscrupulous usurpers." The next year the General Assembly would pass a resolution branding Israel a racist state. [300]

In the years that followed, Arafat built a formidable military machine within the sanctuary that strife-torn Lebanon afforded him. A permanent revolutionary infrastructure was established in South Lebanon, centered in the Begaa Valley (called with grim humor, Fatahland). There the PLO could maintain itself indefinitely, at least as long as the civil war should continue, since it was a revolutionary organization that thrived on chaos and unchained savagery of the human breast, where pain was constant, brutality a near-indescribable fact of daily life, misery and anguish the lot for almost all—often as much for the predator as for the victims.

Syria's intervention at last decided the outcome of the civil war in Lebanon, as well as the PLO's fate. Still unhappy with the subordinate role Syria had endured under Nasser's overbearing sway, Hafiz Assad wished to play a large role, perhaps a decisive one, in resolving the Lebanese imbroglio. He had political skill enough; what he lacked was sufficient military power.

To say that Hafiz Assad ruled Syria with an iron hand is a cliché that does not quite reach the mark. Until coming to power, his personal life had been one of intrigue and violence; these qualities now invested his government. The Assad brothers, Hafiz and Rifat, by controlling an army of no more than 60,000 men, controlled the whole of the country with an inflexible authority. They were called with brutal jocularity, the "butcher brothers," Hafiz the Big Butcher and Rifat the Little Butcher.

It was imperative for Assad that Syria not be caught between a radicalized Iraq on one side and a radicalized Lebanon on the other, a likely event if the alliance between the PLO and the Sunni Moslems should result in reducing the Maronite community to the status of pawn. Israel's intervention in that case would be inevitable; and behind the Israelis stood their protector, the United States.

On the other hand, the prospect of the Maronites establishing a virtually autonomous state within Lebanon would be equally unacceptable to the Syrians. In short, Syria's domination of Lebanon, without occupying it and thereby facing a continuous guerrilla resistance from all sides, depended upon the use of force. [301] But not too much force, just enough to break up the alliance of the PLO and the Sunni Moslems, just enough to reduce the Maronite Christians to an impotent state. "Decisive military action in a country like Lebanon," Assad declared in a rare public address on 20 July 1976, was not possible because "the issue does not depend solely on might...". [302]

Diplomatic finesse, which Assad possessed in plenty, was part of the answer, but collaboration with the Americans was the key. The Nixon Administration presented itself as his willing foil, because "decisive military action" was denied it also.

Since the conclusion of the Yom Kippur War the Nixon policy had been that of honest broker. Henry Kissinger, first as Nixon's security advisor, then in the second administration as the president's secretary of state, became the prime mover of a policy characterized as "step-by-step," entailing negotiations with almost all parties involved. (Not with the PLO, however, viewed as a reprehensible terrorist organization.)

A general settlement of the multifarious issues that plagued the Middle East was as little congenial to Kissinger's thought as a reordering of the cosmos. In philosophical terms he was a conservative; temperamentally a pragmatist, one who eschews systems and ideologies. A student of Metternich, nineteenth-century Europe's equivalent of Machiavelli, he developed in his formative years a realism not far short of cynicism; as might have been expected of a Jewish youth fleeing with his family from Hitler Germany. His opus, *A World Restored*, gave him a brilliant reputation at a very young age. [303] The connections gained from his first success opened avenues for advancement that led him to the White House during the Nixon years.

A Machiavellian diplomat earns a certain reputation over time.

"Let me speak to you honestly, frankly, open-heartedly," said Le Duc Tho, the North Vietnamese envoy to the Paris Peace Conference in 1972. "You are a liar." [304] It is not likely Kissinger would have taken umbrage at this, since it was a professional appraisal more than a personal insult. In any case, he had already decided upon the qualities essential for successful statesmanship:

Statesmen must use cunning and patience. They must be able to manipulate events and people. They must play the power game in total secrecy, unconstrained by parliaments which lack the temperament for diplomacy. And they must also connive with the largest possible number of allies. They must not shy away from duplicity, cynicism or unscrupulousness, all of which are acceptable tools of statecraft. [305]

Fortified by such an outlook, and with intelligence well above average, Henry was able to confront the daunting challenges posed by the Middle East. Under his influence, the Nixon policy, *ad hoc* in its operational details (almost always the case with American foreign policy), did not seek a remedy for the region's age-old conflicts, but rather pursued a goal that was intensely personal for Kissinger. It would become Nixon's policy as well; mainly, it is thought, because the president became so preoccupied with the Watergate scandal that his secretary of state enjoyed an almost complete independence; not only in the conduct of foreign affairs, but in the formulation of policies. Still an émigré Jew emotionally, Kissinger obeyed that double standard the Zionists had always experienced: loyalty to two countries at once. He lived comfortably with the illusion that what is good for Israel is equally good for the United States, and carried it with him like a cause; a frank confession of serving Israel; "the survival and security of Israel," as he expressed it in 1976 in a speech he delivered at the Fiftieth Anniversary Jubilee Dinner of the Synagogue Council of America. [306]

"One day at a time," with patience, an infinite patience: these were the tenets of Kissinger's policy, which was neither brilliant nor imaginative. With the outbreak of the Yom Kippur War there began a tireless round of trips, visits, and audiences, soon called "shuttle diplomacy." His monotonous, phlegmatic reports of his progress, given on TV as a "talking head," reassured the American public that by tenacity, and over time, something worthwhile would happen in the Middle East.

It came down to this in a strange and unexpected way, that Syrian opportunism (as ruthless as that of the PLO) became joined with the humanitarian policies of the Americans, who could scarcely tolerate any longer the carnage that appeared on their television screens every day; and this spelled the beginning of the end. Ironically, American idealism was promoted by a diplomatic realist *par excellence*, Kissinger, who became the mediator and a messenger of peace, accepted at last by Assad, who could not countenance the ever-increasing influence of the PLO in Lebanon. After long negotiations, in July 1977, Syria and Lebanon, along with Arafat's second-in-command, Abu Iyad, entered into the Chtoura Agreement. By its terms Syria and Lebanon would restrain the Fedayeen and the PLO would remove its forces from the Israeli border.

With the Chtoura Agreement it seemed that the era of raids on Israel and an unbridled terror was over. Thereafter, the PLO maintained its position in South Lebanon with difficulty.

It cannot be said with fairness that Arafat was personally responsible for the murders, the bombings, the torture, and the kidnappings that attended the closing years of Lebanon's civil war. His control of the disparate factions in Lebanon was nominal, to say the least. The PLO was an organization in name only, existing as an organizational structure to be sure, but in practice an umbrella under which operated many groups, some of considerable size and longevity, others small and evanescent; all driven by different concepts of strategy and riven by dialectical disputes. Such unity as was possible depended upon Arafat's ability to cajole and to intimidate. Most important of all, he controlled the money, and to a large extent the flow of arms, especially the critical matter of munitions. Without him, the numerous factions were merely impotent floss in a revolutionary stream of action. His leadership was effective only when they were sufficiently united.

The apparent defection of Assad, counted only less heinous than Anwar Sadat's recognition of Israel in 1979, galvanized some Iraq militants who created their own PLO, commonly called the "Black Hand," whose actual title was Fatah Revolutionary Committee. The leader, Abu Nidal (nicknamed "Father of Struggle"), declared his organization was "the real Fatah." Small, about 200 zealots, the "Black Hand" was no match for Arafat's PLO or the Syrian army. Through salubrious maneuvers, however, and Arab dismay with Sadat's betrayal, Abu Nidal thought he could break up Arafat's PLO.

The advent of the Black Hand, along with the divisions within the Fedayeen and the PLO, went to Assad's advantage. He turned on his chief allies in Lebanon, the Christian Maronites, thus to cultivate the Moslems and the better to emasculate Arafat's PLO, which was too much a quasi-state in South Lebanon for his comfort. "You do not represent Palestine more than we do," he told Arafat at one point, "...and don't you forget one thing—there is no Palestinian people and there is no Palestinian entity—there is Syria." [307]

Syrian atrocities mounted in their struggle with the Maronites. Israeli air attacks on Beirut increased in proportion to Syria's attacks, these too being nothing less than atrocities. The PLO had become a cipher by now, and Arafat, as has been remarked, "little more than a figurehead." [308] Threatened up to death, as it seemed, he entered into cordial relations with Sadat, the man whom his organization a little earlier had vowed to kill. But Sadat could do nothing for him. His influence in the Arab world had been utterly lost by his decision to recognize Israel. [309] Among the Arab states Egypt had fallen into limbo, Sadat's alleged treachery having caused it to be expelled from the Arab League.

Although rendered almost impotent by political infighting, the PLO possessed a formidable military establishment consisting of at least 15,000 armed men. There had been assembled, thanks to the Soviet Union and China, the usual panoply of modern weaponry: long-range artillery, anti-aircraft guns, shoulder-held missile launchers, trucks, jeeps, tanks, munitions dumps, and gas and oil reserves. They were without aircraft, however, and this in time would become crucial. [310]

From the beginning Assad had encouraged the PLO to dig into the Begaa Valley, to serve as his surrogate in his undeclared war with Israel. It was a war by proxy, therefore, and the PLO caught between the hammer that was Israel, and the anvil, Syria. Begin, having come to power in the summer of 1977, almost simultaneously with the signing of the Chtoura Agreement, determined to destroy the PLO by methods of conventional warfare, through a full-scale invasion of Lebanon and military occupation of the country. The previous Israeli government, in pursuit of the terrorists, had been encroaching upon the frontier of Lebanon for over a year, sometimes as deep as six miles.

Begin's simplistic thinking allowed him to believe that if Arafat's organization should be destroyed, Palestinian nationalism would flutter and die, much as a candle is snuffed out. On this matter President Reagan saw eye to eye with Begin. However amiable his demeanor, Reagan was a pugnacious individual. For him the PLO was as much an enemy of the United States as was the Soviet Union. Through his agents he encouraged Begin (who needed little) to undertake a war in Lebanon that would result in the liquidation of the PLO. Thereafter, as Reagan and his secretary of state, Alexander Haig, believed, the Israelis would feel secure enough to negotiate a settlement of the Occupied Territories. [311] Ariel Sharon, Begin's defense minister, meditated on much more. The destruction of the PLO, yes, but Syria forced to withdraw from Lebanon; thereafter, the reconstruction of an independent Lebanon, friendly to Israel; with this, an end to the incessant raids perpetrated against Israel by the Fedayeen. Once its borders were secured, Israel would enjoy a perpetual possession of the Occupied Territories. [312]

On 6 June 1982 Israel sent troops into the Begaa Valley, calling it "Operation Peace for Galilee." The Syrians gave warning by radio. If Israel's actions were limited to striking Palestinian camps, Syria would not intervene. But if an Israeli occupation should take place, "Syria will certainly give the Palestinians and the Lebanese patriotic forces all the means necessary for checking the occupation and turning the occupier's life into an unbearable hell...".[313] The Israelis were unimpressed, and certainly undeterred. In 1976 they had drawn a line in the sand, so to speak, the so-called "Red Line," nine miles from the border in the vicinity of Nabatiyyah. They gave their own warning: should the Syrians cross over the line in defense of the Fedayeen they would do so at their peril.

Driving the Fedayeen out of South Lebanon required more than two months of hard fighting. Without air cover Arafat's force could not long resist the overwhelming power Israel had sent into Lebanon. Once the PLO leadership had taken refuge in Beirut, the city became besieged and the populace effectively hostages. Eventually, the United States envoy, Philip Habib, negotiated an agreement with the Lebanese government, the Israelis, and the representative of the PLO, Sa'ib Salam. Thereafter, an international force consisting of American, French and Italian troops served as an armed escort for the PLO as it left the country.

The exodus began on 21 August. In waves, and in several directions, more than 15,000 guerrillas started toward different countries willing to give them asylum.[314] Arafat and a small retinue found that only Tunisia would offer them sanctuary. And still once more it appeared that his career as a revolutionary had come to an end.

The interventionist policy of Begin and Sharon was a decided failure; Reagan's failure also. When terrorists later demolished the U.S. Marines' headquarters at Beirut on 23 October 1983, with the loss of more than 234 lives, the president ordered the withdrawal of his forces. The PLO (what was left of it after Arafat's departure) had now become fully dependent upon Syria, and Syria remained the paramount power in Lebanon. The civil war raged on while Israel had become bogged down in the Begaa Valley, a quagmire from which it could not withdraw, confronted by Shi'a militia men who were as redoubtable an enemy of Israel as Arafat's PLO had been. Palestinian nationalism was stimulated enormously by these events. It is thought by some that the uprising, Intifada, which occurred in the Occupied Territories a few years later, stemmed from this failed attempt to throttle the PLO. [315]

NOTES

252 Majid Khadduri, *Arab Contemporaries. The Role of Personalities in Politics* (The Johns Hopkins University Press, 1973), p. 43.

253 Jean Lacouture, *Nasser. A Biography*, trans., David Hofstadter (New York, 1973), p. 267.

254 Ibid., p. 130.

255 ANZUS: Australia, New Zealand and the United States; SEATO: the United States, Britain, France, New Zealand, Australia, the Philippines, Thailand, and Pakistan.

256 Dwight D. Eisenhower, *The White House Years. Waging Peace* 1956-1961 (New York, 1965), p. 33.

257 Eden's instability was recognized by his peers. See Robert Rhodes James, *Anthony Eden* (New York, 1986), chap. 11, *passim.*, and Leonard Mosley, *Dulles: A Biography of Eleanor Allen and John Foster Dulles and Their Family Network* (New York, 1978), pp. 404, ff.

258 Not only would this ruse be recognized by the international community at once; but technically, by terms of the Anglo-Egyptian Treaty of 1954 which had regulated the British withdrawal from the canal, the return of the British garrison was allowed only if Egypt should be attacked by another Arab state. An attack by Israel on Egypt was explicitly ruled out as an acceptable cause.

259 Mosley, p. 408.

260 Winston Burdette, *Encounter With the Middle East* (New York, 1969), pp. 96-97.

261 Gilbert, *Israel*, p. 318.

262 John W. Spanier, *Foreign Policy Since World War II*. 3rd ed. (New York, 1968), p. 127.

263 The decision taken earlier at Paris to wait until after the presidential election was obviously abandoned.

264 Eisenhower, *The White House Years*, p. 72.

265 Winston Burdette, pp. 186-87.

266 But not to be considered as such by any international agreement, and certainly not by Egypt and Saudi Arabia whose territories border the waterway.

267 Maxime Rodinson, *Israel and the Arabs*, trans., Michael Perl (New York, 1968), p. 78.

268 Gordon H. Torrey, *Syrian Politics and The Military*, 1945-1958 (Ohio State

University Press: Columbus, Ohio, 1964), pp. 378-79.

269 It was Ahmed's successor, the Crown Prince Mohamed al-Badr, who was driven from power in September 1962.

270 Of the approximately 46,339 square miles which made up historic Palestine, 35,468 square miles were taken to form Transjordan in 1922, an area about the size of Pennsylvania.

271 The Arab League was created to facilitate the cooperation of the several Arab states, and had nothing to do with the idea of Arab unity.

272 Martin Gilbert, *Israel*, op. cit., p. 352.

273 A revision of the Covenant in 1968 specified that the liberation of Palestine would be achieved by "Armed Struggle" (Article Nine).

274 But not the Grand Mufti, Haz al-Husseini, who believed that Palestinian independence was of little interest to Nasser.

275 Winston Burdette, p. 139.

276 Jillian Becker, *The PLO*, op. cit., p. 49.

277 Ibid., p. 54.

278 Ibid., p. 249.

279 Burdette, p. 128.

280 Lacouture, *Nasser*, p. 302.

281 Later, Nasser's apologists argued that the dictator's orders had been misunderstood, that he had not asked for the UN's withdrawal, but its deployment in such a way as to furnish him a "window" for action.

282 "The aggression [of Israel]," Hussein said later, "took us by surprise a year or a year and a half too early." Theodore Draper, *Israel and World Politics* (New York, 1978), p. 96.

283 Donald Neff, *Warriors for Jerusalem. The Six Days that Changed the Middle East* (New York, 1984), p. 174.

284 Draper, p. 97.

285 Neff, p. 181.

286 It is thought that Nasser could not have assembled more than 40,000 men. Israel had 320,000 ready for combat. M. Cherif Bassiouni, "The Misunderstood Conflict," *The Arab-Israeli Conflict*, ed., John Norton Moore, op. cit., p. 348.

287 Neff, p. 218.

288 Draper, p. 3.

289 The Israeli argument immediately after the war, and up to the present, holds that their actions were defensive. This fortified their further argument

that since they had not been aggressive, they might remain in the occupied territories until a general peace settlement had been achieved. The issue is usefully summarized in John Quigley, *Palestine and Israel*, pp. 163-167.

290 West Jerusalem had been in Israeli possession since the first Arab-Israeli war in 1947-48.

291 William Polk, *The United States and the Arab World*, op. cit., pp. 273-81, passim.

292 Seth P. Tillman, *The United States in the Middle East. Interests and Obstacles* (Indiana University Press, 1982), p. 187.

293 Ibid.

294 Becker, p. 68.

295 Ibid., p. 69.

296 Ibid., p. 117.

297 Ibid., p. 161.

298 Nicaragua, Panama, Jamaica Guyana, Mexico, Brazil, Columbia, Venezuela.

299 William B. Quandt, Fund Jabber, Ammosdy Lesch, *The Politics of Palestinian Nationalism* (Berkeley and Los Angeles, 1973), p. 116.

300 The resolution, number 3379, was far from being unanimous: 72 to 35 with 32 abstentions.

301 Moshe Aaoz, *Syria Under Assad*, p. 181.

302 Ibid.

303 Henry Kissinger, *A World Restored*. Metternich, Castlereagh and the Problems of Peace, 1812-1822 (Boston, 1957).

304 Stephen E. Ambrose, *Rise to Globalism. American Foreign Policy Since 1938*. 7th ed. rev. (New York, 1995), p. 224.

305 Alfred M. Lilienthal, *The Zionist Connection. What Price Peace?* (New York, 1978), p. 667.

306 Ibid., p. 664.

307 Itamar Rabinovich, *The War for Lebanon, 1970-1983* (Cornell University Press, 1984), p. 87.

308 Becker, p. 201.

309 As a result of Sadat's recognition of Israel, Egypt was expelled from the Arab League.

310 Up to the mid-seventies, the Peoples' Republic of China furnished about 75% of the war materièl to the PLO. After that the USSR became the principal supplier.

311 Ambrose, *Rise to Globalism*, p. 307.

312 Amos Perlmutter, *The Life and Times of Menachem Begin* (New York, 1987), pp. 375-76.

313 Ibid., pp. 186-87.

314 Tunisia, Jordan, North Yemen, South Yemen, Syria, Algeria, Iraq.

315 Patrick Seale, *Asad of Syria. The Struggle for the Middle East* (Berkeley and Lost Angeles, 1988), p. 418.

CHAPTER EIGHT

The Elusive Modus Vivendi

THE OCCUPIED TERRITORIES

he two world wars of the twentieth century made it possible for the Zionists to establish a sovereign state in Palestine. As a result of the First World War, a mandate was established in Palestine, allowing the Zionists, under the benevolent auspices of Great Britain, to compete effectively with the Arab majority for territory and advantage. World War II, because of the frightful ordeal inflicted upon world Jewry, created an almost universal climate of opinion favorable to the Zionists' winning their independence in 1947–48. This remarkable achievement was diluted only by the unexpected outcome of their success. The ideal of a Jewish state, religious at base, would fade away in half a century as a secular Israeli state became more and more a reality. The exclusive state, which might serve as a refuge for all the Jews of the world (an impossible dream, as even the ardent Zionists themselves had to acknowledge) did not materialize. Jewish nationalism (another dream, often evoked but never formed) became replaced by Israeli nationalism, eminently a reality. "The Zionist idea," Nahum Goldmann, former president of the World Jewish Congress wrote with evident regret, was "one of the great utopian programs of modern times." He believed, nonetheless, that it deserved the "world's acceptance and sympathy," even though it represented international lawlessness on a scale heretofore not imagined, "unique and unprecedented."

The Zionist demand for a Jewish state was in full contradiction with all the principles of modern history and international law. If this demand were to serve as a precedent, the Indians of North America could claim for themselves the United States, as could the descendants of other American natives in Mexico, Peru, and so on. [316]

For assimilated Jews anywhere in the world, Israel is a faraway place for which there is sympathy but no real attachment. They send money to support it as they might contribute to the welfare of a cherished relative. "When I visited Israel I admired it," wrote a New York Jew, "but from a distance. Moving there, on balance, would bring me to a more alien world than the one I am in now." He went on to say he was "pleased" that there was a Law of Return, thinking of it as "an available option," in the case of renewed persecution. "I am pleased that they can return to a parental home ... It is a family thing," a matter of being "nominally identified as one of the tribe." [317]

Ironically, a Jewish state, created at such enormous cost in human lives and treasure, had served as an instrument for the defeat of its main purpose. Israeli citizens in their majority became over time Jews who were Jews in name only. To save world Jewry from assimilation, and thus a loss of Jewish uniqueness, a state had been created where the result was the same after all; namely, a loss of that peculiar character so often called "Jewishness." While forces of assimilation everywhere in the modern world were diluting those qualities called Jewish, forces peculiar to Palestine (i.e., Israel) were accomplishing the same end. [318] "We face the stark reality," wrote a Jewish scholar, "that much of the Zionist impulse has collapsed in the face of the very goal it established initially—the creation of a Jewish state. The establishment of the State of Israel has created a milieu in which Jews live as a majority culture. Yet this has not inspired an increasing or even enduring sense of Jewish peoplehood, nor a belief in the unique purpose of the State of

Israel."[319] A Jew speaking Hebrew in Israel is, in quintessential terms, no different from a Jew speaking French in France, or a Jew in the United States speaking English. A secular style of life, with its multiplicity of profane values, embraces the Jew in Israel as much as it embraces Western Christians and Jews.

Both Israeli nationalism and Palestinian nationalism were forged through their mutual antipathy as well as their mutual desire to possess exclusively the same land. Palestinian nationalism, it has been observed, "owes its birth to Zionism, for it was the impact of Zionist colonization on the economic and social structure of the Palestinian people which brought Palestinian nationalism into being."[320]

In the context of emerging nationalism, the religious factor in Zionism, only moderately important in the beginning, simply withered enough to become insignificant in the life of the new nation.[321] Needless to say, the Israeli intelligentsia has examined Israel's social strata in minute detail, finding that half the population by this time is composed of "secular Jews." For all practical purposes these are non-Jewish Jews. Thirty percent of the society can be called "religious Zionists," modern orthodox Jews who have successfully melded the religious precepts of traditional Judaism with the demands (and the benefits) of modern society. Fifteen percent of the society is orthodox. Some part of that group (ultra-orthodox) is almost medieval in behavior, dress, outlook, and devotion to traditional Judaism. About a third of this category (judged to be 5 percent of the whole country) are fanatically messianic. They refuse to defend the state against aggression, and will therefore not serve in the military. Metaphysically entranced, they consider Israel to be a transient state of existence, merely a halting-place on the way to Redemption. Armageddon is not a fate to be feared, but rather to be anticipated with joy as serving for the final reunion with God.

The remaining 5 percent of Israeli society does not fit into any useful category for purposes of analysis, existing as a mixed bag: "nominal Jews," atheists, agnostics, homosexuals, social deviants (i.e., lost souls in Israeli prisons, incarcerated for all the reasons that misfits are always removed from society in any country).

A perpetual national insecurity, the paranoia of a beleaguered people, perpetuates a constant inquest: "Are you a Jew? Well, what kind of Jew? Are you a Zionist? Well, what kind of a Zionist?" "You turn on the television," said an Israeli, "and see they are arguing about the borders, about the boundaries, religion and state—nothing is ever settled here." [322] This remark has a particular relevance for the law. As Israel does not have a constitution, it does not have a civil code of law. In matters of law, custom prevails. In appearance, "the laws of Judaism are the law of the land." In practice, civil law proceeds from precedent which in turn flows from the eight Basic Laws (more particularly the Law of the Judiciary, passed by the Knesset in 1984). In practice, Israeli life proceeds by customs long established:

All government offices close on the Sabbath and on holy days. All public transportation halts. Stores, businesses, and places of public entertainment must be shut. Israel enters a kind of suspended animation every Friday evening and does not emerge from it until sundown on Saturday. Ships and commercial airliners that arrive in Israel on the Sabbath may not unload their passengers until Saturday night. In some ultra-Orthodox sections of the cities, anyone who drives a car on the Sabbath runs the risk of being stoned. Even the army is required to halt most activity on the Sabbath except in times of national emergency. The army, too, must observe the Jewish dietary laws. So also must El Al, the Israeli airline, and all other public institutions. Hotels must keep kosher kitchens. The raising of pigs is prohibited except in certain areas of the state that are inhabited by Christians. [323]

One might conclude that Israel is indeed a Jewish state, in appearance a theocracy. In reality, Halakah (religious law) is a formality widely acknowledged, but in practice violated daily, even hourly.

The religious factor in Palestinian nationalism is quite different from the Israeli. While in the latter case religious fundamentalism has been overwhelmed by modern secular forces, religious fundamentalism for the Palestinians remains a vital factor in their nascent nationalism. The force of this nationalism, reinforced by a fundamental religiosity, made the Israeli occupation of the West Bank and Gaza untenable from the start.

Most Israelis (Jewish Israelis) were naturally relieved to have won a perilous war in a mere six days. [324] At the same time, they were nearly stunned by the extent of their success. But, having seized the West Bank, the Gaza Strip, and the Golan Heights, they did not want to keep the territories they now occupied. [325]

The Jewish elite, both secular and religious, looked at the matter differently. Having, providentially as it seemed, regained still more of Eretz Israel, they were determined to keep it, despite the requirements of international law that the territories be returned to the rightful owners: the West Bank to Jordan, Gaza to Egypt, and the Golan Heights to Syria.

In a fairly brief time (about five months) the Security Council established a basis for peace: Resolution 242, passed by unanimous vote on 22 November 1967. Egypt, Israel, Jordan, and Lebanon accepted the resolution. Syria and the PLO rejected it. The main points were:

- Territory taken during the war could not be kept by the victors.
- A general settlement of the refugee question.
- Guarantees for the inviolability of territory.
- Withdrawal of Israeli forces from the Occupied Territories (but not all). [326]

Dr. Gunar V. Jarring, the Swedish ambassador to the Soviet Union, went to the Middle East as the personal representative of Secretary-General U Thant. In these first talks the Israeli government suggested that bilateral treaties might be negotiated between Israel and the other belligerents, and that the talks should commence with Egypt and Jordan. Those two countries demanded that Israel withdraw from the Occupied Territories prior to negotiating the treaties. Without refusing, Israel shifted the ground slightly, asking for direct talks between the several parties. Egypt and Jordan asked for indirect talks. Both sides declared a willingness "to implement Resolution 242." Thereafter the talks degenerated into disagreements over small points, and negotiations dragged on into 1969. Early in the spring of that year, Nasser, believing that the Israelis intended to stall indefinitely, began shelling Israel's fortified lines along the Suez Canal. Israel retaliated with its own artillery. These periodic exchanges, which amounted to a resumption of the war, continued up to January of 1970, when Israel initiated bombing raids over Egypt, whereupon Nasser journeyed to Moscow and got the Soviet government to send him SAM-3 ground-to-air missiles. Soon Soviet advisors arrived at Cairo. After that, Palestinian guerrilla raids on Jewish settlements increased. Israel responded by bombing the guerrilla sanctuaries in Jordan and Lebanon.

UN mediation having manifestly failed by this time, Great Power talks began. In November 1969 Secretary of State William Rogers made a comprehensive proposal. Tilting toward the Arab side, he declared that the status of Jerusalem could not be decided unilaterally, and, secondly, a solution to the Palestinian question was paramount if a general settlement was to be reached. This statement of policy, called sometime afterward the Rogers Plan, was not a plan in fact. Nixon took little interest in it, and Henry Kissinger, then national security advisor, supported by Alexander Haig, undercut a proposal too well-disposed to Arab interests.

Meanwhile, the intervention of the U.S., the USSR, Britain, and France resulted in a ninety-day cease-fire going into effect on 7 August 1970. This precipitated a new wave of hijackings on the West Bank and attacks on Jewish communal centers. Clashes occurred between the PLO and the Jordanian army. Syria then intervened on behalf of the Palestinians, and the United States government threatened to intervene in support of the king of Jordan. In the midst of this crisis, Nasser died. Free of the dictator's overpowering influence, Hussein finished driving the Fedayeen out of Jordan. Thereafter Arafat moved his headquarters to Lebanon.

Anwar el-Sadat, who succeeded Nasser as President of Egypt, continued his predecessor's policy of unremitting hostility toward Israel. Occasional Israeli overtures for a resumption of peace talks were spurned. Early in October 1973, on the eve of Yom Kippur, both Egypt and Syria were ready to resume the war.

As in 1967, the Israeli cabinet, led by Golda Meir, experienced a sense of dread as Syria and Egypt marshaled their forces. Again they considered the advisability of a preemptive strike, but finally rejected it. The usual Israeli explanation for this was their reluctance to strike first and thereby be pictured as the aggressor. But the fact is that Israeli defenses were thin and poorly organized. Time would be required to mount an offensive. In weakness, therefore, and indecision as well, they were caught unprepared, though information had come to them from their intelligence sources that an attack was imminent. Stronger than their enemies, they reckoned they could withstand the first attacks and, after that, commence a counter-attack that would result in an eventual victory. And so it was, the war lasting less than a month. It could not be a long war in any case, nor could either side win, since the rival superpowers hovering over their respective clients willed it so. The Soviets rushed additional arms to the Arabs, and the Americans replenished Israeli armaments up to the point of impasse when finally a cease-fire was arranged on 24 October.

The aftermath of another failed war against Israel produced in Egypt a decided defeatism. With hindsight Sadat declared that the war against Israel had been an intentionally limited one, "not all out" to win, but forceful enough to draw all interested parties to the peace table. In April 1977, he met with President Carter to explain the meaning of the "lost war." To the former, Sadat's démarche meant Egypt's abandonment of its formerly close relationship with the Soviet Union, and promised a general settlement of Middle Eastern questions. [327]

In November 1977 Sadat might have amazed the world, certainly his countrymen as much as the Israelis, when he went before the Egyptian parliament to say he would go to Jerusalem and negotiate a peace settlement. "I am willing to go to the ends of the earth for peace," he declared. "Israel will be astonished to hear me say how, before you, that I am prepared to go to their own house, to the Knesset itself, to talk to them." [328]

Sadat arrived in Jerusalem on 19 November, to be received with considerable pomp and circumstance. Menachem Begin, now premier, always Sadat's relentless and unforgiving enemy, extended his hand nonetheless, a sign of conciliation if not friendship. Crowds lined the streets, waving little Egyptian flags as Sadat was escorted to the Knesset.

Sadat's visit, however cordial, only revealed how impossible peace between Egypt and Israel seemed. His proposal, expressed as no more than a personal desire, was that Israel withdraw from all Occupied Territories and agree to the establishment of a Palestinian state. Since neither side could publicly acknowledge what amounted to an adulterous relationship, secret meetings commenced, first in Morocco and a little later in the south of England.

Scenting an opportunity, the Carter Administration offered to mediate. Unrealistically, Sadat persisted in the belief that Israel would accept the formation of a Palestinian state as well as withdrawal from the Sinai. But without any leverage he could only depend upon the benevolence of President Carter.

When finally the talks were moved to Camp David, the presidential retreat in the Maryland mountains, the negotiations became a colloquy between the three men. In the last analysis, however much he boasted about Israel's independence, Begin had to yield to Carter's relentless pressure, agreeing that Israel would remove all Jewish settlements in the Sinai and, most difficult for him to accept, that the building of Jewish settlements in the Occupied Territories must come to an end. However, he would not admit that Israel had an obligation to withdraw from the West Bank (Samaria and Judea). [329] In the final negotiations, he was able to have eliminated any reference to the critical words in UN Resolution 242: "Inadmissibility of territories acquired by war." In straightforward language, Israel had taken the West Bank by force and would keep it by right of conquest. This would have serious consequences for American statesmen in the future, when U.S. sentiment had changed enough to want to do something for the Palestinians.

The final draft of the agreement, "A Framework for Peace in the Middle East," written by Carter himself, was not intended to be a treaty, but rather a basis for further negotiations that would lead to a durable peace treaty between Egypt and Israel. In that regard, there was much vagueness in the language and a number of "understandings" which, in a matter of months, led to the realization that these were really misunderstandings. For example, Carter thought "a freeze" on the building of new settlements in the Occupied Territories would be permanent; but Begin understood that the freeze was to last only three months. Besides misunderstandings there were false hopes, as for example a treaty of peace between Egypt and Israel would cause Syria, Lebanon, and Jordan to follow suit. It was not to be. Like the later Oslo Accords, the Camp David Accords were sterile agreements. They would disappear in the same atmosphere of mistrust and duplicity that had shaped their composition.

Although the peacemaker, by forcing a treaty on Begin and Sadat, President Carter (who had earned the honor) would not receive the Nobel Peace Prize the next year. That prestigious award would go to Sadat and Begin, neither of whom, objectively speaking, deserved it. Ironically, while the Nobel Prize Committee paid tribute to the Camp David Accords, the UN General Assembly resolved, in a vote of eighty-eight to twenty-two (forty abstaining), to condemn the peace agreement between Egypt and Israel. Outraged, the PLO leadership meditated on the need to assassinate Sadat (it would in fact be accomplished by others). [330] Unable to get at the strong man of Egypt, they turned on important Palestinians in Gaza and the West Bank known to favor an accord between Israel and Egypt. Perhaps a dozen of these unfortunates were murdered; one says perhaps a dozen since there were others who died "under mysterious circumstances."

While protracted negotiations perpetuated the Israeli occupation, delaying a final peace treaty between Israel and Egypt by six months. Jewish settlers continued to move into the Occupied Territories, establishing themselves wherever Palestinian resistance was weak and Israeli authorities were lax or disposed to tolerate what were in fact illegal incursions. Carrying, in a manner of speaking, agricultural implements in one hand and the Torah in the other, the settlers, like American pioneers living in the presence of threatening Indians, survived as armed colonists in a world of alarmed and angry Palestinian Arabs. The need for security, as much as tradition, required that they live in small, guarded communities, practicing a collectivist way of life.

In defying the Israeli government and Israeli public opinion, they were motivated by powerful religious motives. To them the Six-Day War was a sign that the God of the Hebrews had delivered Eretz Israel to the Jewish people. The heavy and inscrutable doctrine of Redemption was examined again. Most influential of the theorists in this regard was Rabbi Zvi Y. Kook, who in his work continued a family tradition. His father, Rabbi Abraham Y. Kook, had elaborated a doctrine that could be called Religious Zionism. The son went a step further, shifting from a purely millenarian interpretation of Redemption to one that fused national sentiment with the old mystical notion that the Israelis, like their ancient forebears the Hebrews, moved according to God's will. Once upon a time they had taken the land of Canaan as the instruments of God's will. Similarly, by God's will, Samaria and Judea (the West Bank) had been restored to His chosen people.

By 1974 an informal colonization of the West Bank and Gaza was well under way. A movement, *Gush Emunim* (Block of the Faithful) appeared. GE, as it was called in time, represented a profound religious reaction to the secularism that had come to invest the State of Israel. It also promised to serve as a remedy for the intractable conflict between Orthodox Jewry and labor Zionism. Shortly, the adherents of GE organized themselves as a political party, their program to legitimize the settlement of the Occupied Territories.

The consensus of the Israelis after 1949, it is thought, was that the boundaries established by the cease-fire conventions were to be fixed eventually, representing both the limits of Israeli ambitions as well as the territorial limits of the State of Israel. [331] By 1974, that opinion was changing, the result of failed negotiations with the Arabs, the increasingly violent activity of the PLO, and the actual fact of settlement by religious zealots who now received support from the new religious party, Gush Emunim.

Those who filled the ranks of GE were young people for the most part. Many idealists had by then grown up within the folds of another religious party, the Mafdad (usually called the National Religious Party). The most extreme of them formed a sort of club, "Young Guard." Intensely patriotic, they were in fact chauvinists and religious zealots. Their influence on both the Israeli government and the general public was far out of proportion to their small numbers. Their intransigence may be seen in their determination to keep the Occupied Territories at all costs, even if death should be the price; their slogan: *Ye'Horeg Va'Al Ya'Avor* ("One should rather be killed than transgress"). [332]

The changing public attitude and the increasing number of settlements in the Territories had a profound effect upon the several right wing parties, drawing them together, their internal battles over small political points submerged by the larger question of what to do with the West Bank. Menachem Begin, who for years had worked to weld the factions together, now succeeded in fashioning a new coalition on the right, which was destined to have a long life and an important future. The *Likud*, as it was called, represented an association of nationalists and devout believers who fed upon Israeli fears and hopes in a number of ways. Samaria and Judea were reckoned to be more than a precious legacy. Once occupied they represented a barrier for the protection of the state. [333] A mountain range with an altitude of about 1200 feet in the north rises to approximately 2500 feet near Hebron. This peculiar geographical feature of the West Bank causes Israelis to call it the "wall." The State of Israel, by virtue of this analogy, might be called a fortress.

But it is really a state besieged, technically at war because peace cannot be achieved; a tiny country without a trustworthy ally, which might be overrun by the enemy in a matter of days. [334] From the beginning a continuous state of preparedness became the prerequisite duty of every Israeli government. Torn between the need to expand into Eretz Israel (the inherent ethos of Zionism), and the equal obligation to consolidate what had been won, Israel's every move on the diplomatic and military plane was ambivalent. To accept peace with its enemies meant the loss of Eretz Israel. To continue to seek redemption, a religious imperative, meant constant peril, perhaps an eventual national disaster. Israeli paranoia flowed from this particular contradiction from which they could not escape. Consequently, the indoctrination of Israeli youth became essential. The rituals in being inducted for military service had a profound effect upon young minds, without doubt. First, the draftee was made to climb to the summit of the massive mountain tabletop, Masada, to view the site where in 73 C.E., an estimated 960 Jewish defenders had committed suicide rather than surrender to the Roman legions—judged by the Israelis to have been a patriotic act and a source of eternal pride. Next, the recruit was escorted through the dim rooms of *Yad Va-Shem*, the memorial that is an eternal reminder of the Holocaust. After that, the swearing-in ceremony was performed near the Wailing Wall, which had its own self-evident significance.

While the right-wing factions enjoyed an ever-greater unity of purpose, the long tenure of the Labor Zionists was coming to an end. The aftermath of the October War merely hastened this evolution, producing a climate of emotions: relief and disorientation, above all widespread resentment against the labor leaders who, because of their unpreparedness, had left Israel open to invasion and a possible national disaster.

All this went to the advantage of the Likud, which was nothing less than a number of exalted right-wing factions welded together by religious ardor, national fervor, and a burning political ambition. Also, the Likud had won over a significant voting block, the

Sephardim. These were the second generation of Jews who had emigrated from Asian and African countries, dark-skinned, poor in many cases, considered to be a significant contrast to the light-skinned Sabra (the descendants of the Ashkenazi who had conquered the country and driven out most of the Arabs).

After thirty years in the political wilderness, now old and increasingly irascible, Begin's hour had come. In May 1977 he formed his first government.

To have Begin, erstwhile terrorist, at the head of the government was ominous from the Arab point of view. His record of ruthless and pitiless reprisals during the mandate period could be expected to be reproduced in the Occupied Territories, where the more violently disposed of the settlers could quite literally get away with murder.[335] Shortly after assuming power he toured the West Bank, promising the settlers that there would be more settlements. "Judah and Samaria," he declared, were "liberated," and not "occupied."[336]

It cannot be said that with age Begin had outgrown his proclivity for violence. To the contrary, at the head of the government, he could more easily gratify it through the actions of his surrogates in the Occupied Territories. One can reasonably believe that his youthful experience in Poland made him the man he became: dogmatic, domineering, paranoid, disposed to hate, this passion perhaps stronger than his lust for Eretz Israel.

The post-WWI period in Poland and Russia presents a picture of anarchy, complicated beyond description, without a pattern save for a single thread running through a torn fabric of violent events: the destruction of Jewish people by Reds, by Whites, by Cossacks, by armed bands, without a cause or redeeming feature to color an idea, but merely the craving for booty and the lust to kill. In Poland anti-Semitism was ancient and virulent, so endemic and so much a part of Polish culture, that one can say that if Polish Gentiles had been given the Nazis' situation, they would have adopted their own "final solution." Begin matured in this atmosphere. He arrived in Palestine in the fall of 1942, carrying with him a bitter memory and the spirit of vengeance, especially a hatred for the *goyim* (Gentiles), which was quickly transferred to another object, the Palestinian Arabs. Jabotinsky was his hero in the beginning, but the older man's luster diminished in his eyes as Begin became increasingly radical.

All policies of the previous labor government that gave tacit support to the settler movement had been approved by Begin. His personal policy now was to accelerate that process. Steeped in the Revisionist tradition bequeathed by Jabotinsky, he could not forget, much less forgive, the iniquitous British for giving Transjordan (more than half of Eretz Israel) to the Hashemites. So great was the feeling that for the whole of his long career he would never agree to meet King Hussein. To know this is to realize that for Begin and his ideological companions, the West Bank (Samaria and Judea, as they preferred to say) belonged to Israel and would never be returned to Jordan. In September 1977 Ariel Sharon, the minister of justice, proposed a plan that he called "Vision of Israel at Century's End." Two million Jews would be established in the Occupied (the Zionists said "Liberated") Territories by the year 2000. [337] The *de facto* annexation of the West Bank commenced with this strategy. A practice called the "sandwich" method was used to establish Jewish settlements in the midst of a numerically superior Arab population; usually choosing high ground, thereby allowing for better defense; but also a psychological posture, as they seemed to command the country they looked down upon. It was analogous to the way in which European settlers in North America (without direction from Washington, D.C., admittedly) had established enclaves within a region possessing a Native American majority. In time the arriving immigrants would overwhelm the indigenous population, which would have to move out or die out.

Ironically, Palestinians who had fled from the Zionists to the West Bank in 1947 now found themselves recaptured, once more under the alien authority they had tried to evade a generation earlier. They became inevitably what the Arabs who had remained in Israel were already—second-class citizens, politically enthralled and economically exploited.

It goes without saying that an occupied people have limited rights and are entirely dependent upon the whim and will of an arbitrary authority. Arabs who had become Israeli citizens were themselves subject to discrimination and civil disabilities. The Israeli Labor elite brought to the Occupied Territories the same arbitrary behavior that characterized their management of the Israeli population as a whole. The corruption inherent in factional politics, illegal and extralegal tactics, were reproduced endlessly in public administration. A generation of malfeasance was summed up by the frustrated judgment of a newly arrived immigrant to Israel: This poor country is being wracked by widespread law breaking and corruption, by kickbacks, swindles and dishonest manipulations of the laws. [338]

All of this was predetermined largely by the fact that a constitution had never been established for the State of Israel, perpetuating arbitrary government, and with that no legal means for the redress of grievances in cases of discriminatory legislation or abuses of power. Very early, the Zionists decided that a constitutional form of government would not be possible until the state was secure; but since the state was never in all these years secured, the foundation of all law in Israel rested upon a few fundamental decrees: the so-called Basic Laws. By the time of Begin's first administration there were eight of these. The most basic of them was (and is) the "Law of Return." Any Jew anywhere in the world, of whatever nationality, race, or ideology, may enter Israel and receive immediate citizenship. [339] Only the immigrant's authentic Jewishness must be certified. In brief, Herzl's original thought about Zion has been realized. Israel is uniquely a refuge for Jews. All the state's policies, domestic and foreign, are predicated on this one fact and a single belief: all the Jews in the Diaspora are citizens of the world and owe their ultimate fealty to the fatherland, Eretz Israel, to which they must move, if possible, and if that is not possible, to assist Israel in any way possible. It is a concept not unlike the Nazi idea of a universal German citizenship during the 1930's. In 1960 Ben Gurion put the matter before the World Zionist Congress in absolute terms: "Since the day when the Jewish state was established and the gates of Israel were flung open to every Jew who wanted to come, every religious Jew has daily violated the precepts of Judaism and the Torah by remaining in the Diaspora. Whoever dwells outside the land of Israel is considered to have no God." [340]

Closely connected to the notion of asylum was the undying dream: the recovery of all land that once, however briefly, fell under the authority of the ancient Hebrew kings. Thus, wherever that momentary influence of the past had left a Jewish impression, there any Jew may settle—if he dares. Hardly had the Law of Return begun to have its effects (massive immigration) when this flood tide was turned upon the land. The untoward victory of 1967 gave Israel control of a new territory for colonization. The presence of 500,000 Palestinian Arabs was not so much a deterrent to Israeli expansion as it was an embarrassing nuisance. One wonders if the average Jew, whether an Israeli or a Jew still abroad, did not accept Golda Meir's observation that there were no Palestinians; there were only "South Syrians." By such casuistry, readily endorsed by the Jewish intelligentsia, were Zionist expansionist designs fostered and justified anew.

A state under siege requires that both the citizens and the resident aliens be watched with equal care. Israelis abroad, and anyone associated with them, are subject to surveillance. This close scrutiny is imposed if even slight suspicions should be aroused about the individual's activity. The secret internal police, *Shin Beth* (also called *Shabak*) operates in coordinated ways with its external police (*Mossad*). It is an intimate association, as though the one were fingers and the other gloves. Either branch of this ubiquitous police force is little restrained by civil law. It is often charged that it acts as if a law unto itself. Israeli police do not know of "Miranda Rights." The men who are recruited to serve the state in this capacity are intelligent and disposed to be ruthless, unencumbered by the normal weaknesses of humankind: kindness, compassion and gentleness. Trained in methods of detection, abduction, arrest and interrogation, they are efficient, skilled, and have considerable knowledge of human frailties that may be exploited so as to achieve their ends. The ends are actually singular: security of the State of Israel.

The most ancient methods of interrogation are in fact the most modern: intimidation, physical violence (as for example, kicking, slapping, punching, hair pulling, and abuse of tender parts: the solar plexus, the back, the small bones, the genitals and the eyes). Most of the physical abuse is done without leaving noticeable scars, very often not even bruises; but pain and terror are achieved nonetheless. To give some credit to so brutal a regime, the employment of electric shock, it is rumored, rarely occurs, perhaps only when the security of the state is judged to be at risk.

The fate of those Arabs who remained in Israel entailed more than just becoming second-class citizens. They were treated as aliens in their own country, or rather, the country that had been theirs not so long ago. Considered dangerous to the new state, potentially traitors, they were watched closely and supervised with almost minute care. Permits were required before they might travel, specifying the route to be taken, the time estimated to make the journey, and an estimated time of return. Any infraction would result in arrest and fines or both. Pretty much the way in which the Nazis had ruled occupied peoples, the Israelis searched for (and found) Arabs willing to collaborate with them, informing on their fellow Arabs. In return they received favors. The best of these (or one may say the worst) went on secret payrolls. These onerous conditions would endure for more than ten years before some relaxation of military law took place.

In fundamental ways the concept "cold war" describes the relationship between Israel and its Arab enemies. Espionage, intelligence gathering, infiltration of clandestine groups, spying within the inner corridors of power of foreign governments (both friendly and implacably hostile ones), recalls the protracted duel between the U.S. and the former USSR. The more serious the terrorism the Israelis face, or merely imagine, the more deadly are the secret police in combating it. The justification for what is an evil condition is found in the circumstances under which Israel exists, and has existed since at least 1947: a state of siege.

Israel's methods with respect to law and order are fundamentally no different from those of its Arab rivals; not less nor more violent and uncaring for what is called in the West, human rights. Torture is practiced throughout the vast region. The uncomplicated Western mind cannot quite comprehend this mystery. That the Arabs, a little-advanced, almost primitive people should practice terror, perpetrate unspeakable atrocities, is understandable. [341] But the Jews, a product of Western culture, beneficiaries of the great ideas of the European Enlightenment, democratic people who are bearers of Western values, dedicated to both moral and material progress—that these Jews should not be different from the Arabs...what a puzzle!

While Israeli secret police maintain a surveillance over the underground resistance of Arabs who would subvert or overthrow the constituted authority of the state, the Israeli army and diplomatic corps secure it on the international plane, allowing Jewish capital to be expended on the work needed to transform the land. In one sense the result is beautiful and, from an aesthetic and economic point of view, laudable. Vineyards and orchards paint in bright colors what were once arid hillsides. On the lower levels of the terrain, irrigated gardens and nurseries bloom most of the year. All is the result of having brought life-giving water (and fertilizer) to a stony soil that was desiccated and infertile.

The other development is not so pretty. A burgeoning population in a small country, which seeks an ever-advancing standard of living, requires the amenities of the twentieth century as they are known in the West. Blacktop highways lace the land where once archaic roadways and more primitive footpaths adequately served a peasant population that walked from point to point and never journeyed far, and for the few among them who journeyed a great distance, the camel and the ass served for travel as well as the means for transporting simple goods. Today, freeways and divided highways allow one to cross the little country at high speed. Most destinations are measured in minutes, only a few in hours. A long day's journey is unknown. The country is exceedingly narrow, almost too confining to be a field of battle in modern warfare; but after independence the Israelis have never experienced a long war on their own territory. Their military aircraft are hardly aloft before they have passed over the borders of the country.

It is from the air, looking down before too great a height has been reached, that the most devastating picture is revealed. Ultramodern, aesthetically tasteless apartment buildings spill to the edges of what had been not very long ago small picturesque villages peopled by Arabs who had never heard the word "progress" or what it implies. "Urban sprawl," that distasteful term coined in the 1960s to describe a similar blight creeping over the American landscape, appears in Israel in its diminutive form. All this and more represent what is worst in the West (in Arab eyes), suspected by the Arab effendi who saw in the first Jewish immigrants an unacceptable future.

As one sees a bifurcated Palestine, organized as the State of Israel in part, the Hashemite kingdom of Transjordan in larger part, the juxtaposition of a simple infrastructure of the past with a modern, rampant, almost explosive superstructure of the present, strikes the imagination. Similarly, one sees the stark contrast between the newly arrived builders of Israel and the lethargic "native" population (to employ the Israeli expression for the Arabs who did not choose to leave Palestine). The movers and shakers who build the New Jerusalem, so to speak, live comfortably and not infrequently luxuriously. Their Semite brothers, on the other hand, survive in teeming quarters (the "Arab Quarter"), as in East Jerusalem, made up of cement corridors, box-like compartments, damp and usually malodorous because of inadequate sewage facilities. The contrast between wealth and poverty is staggering to the visitor who beholds the Third World, held fast within the framework of the First World as it is being fashioned by latter-day Zionists. Almost daily (except for those brief periods when a crisis in Palestinian-Israeli relations causes the latter to close the entry points), the frontiers are crossed by a labor force from the West Bank and the Gaza Strip seeking work, which cannot be found elsewhere. [342] It is the old story of a capitalized society relying on the energies of a society without capital: a considerable prosperity on the Israeli side, an immense poverty on the Palestinian side; with the usual result: envy and malice among those who have not; an unspoken guilt and disquietude among those who have much, and much to lose.

ᑲᑭ ISLAMIC REVIVAL

It is an intriguing question as to when a powerless people with a simple social structure may claim rights that only force can gain for them and only force can maintain for them thereafter. The establishment and development of the State of Israel encompasses all that this question implies. The scattering of the Palestinian Arabs and the eventual cognizance that they constituted a nation raised the same question. By 1967 the active elements of the Palestinian Diaspora were hammering on the door of world opinion, much as the Zionists after 1917 had insisted upon the rights of all Jews. As it developed, the Zionists were obliged to struggle for those rights, first by the usual practices of international politics: currying favor with the great and the mighty, and disseminating propaganda in strategic countries, to win the sympathy of masses of people who were perhaps occasionally interested but mostly indifferent. Through shameless tactics of terror, the murder of innocents, and theft of all kinds, did the Zionists in the first stages arm themselves for what they recognized would be a perilous struggle. In quite the same way did the Palestinian Arabs, dislodged from their country through no fault of their own, attempt to make the dream of a nation and a state a reality. It is the perversity one finds in this particular history that what the Jews did for themselves with pride and satisfaction, they then denied to the Palestinians because (as they averred) it would be a great wrong.

Once the Palestinian Liberation Organization was formed, the somewhat degrading term "refugee" gave way to the more hopeful expression, *d'idun* ("returnee"). Henceforth the question was not whether the returnees would recover their homeland, but only when. The allied question became how to accomplish it. "A new Zionism was born," wrote A. L. Tibawi. It was a yearning not unlike that of the Zionists for the restoration of a golden age. Palestinian writing, both literary and scholarly, reflected the hope and fantasies of the ordinary Palestinian. "They imagined," wrote a Palestinian author, al-Firdaws al-Mafgud, "paradise lost." [343]

The transition in the collective Palestinian mind from community as a nation to the more abstract notion of a nation-state paralleled the earlier Jewish experience. As the Zionists had reflected upon the need for a Jewish state, Palestinians began to consider not merely a return to the homeland, but the need for an organizing principle. Again, as the Fedayeen phenomenon had provoked a nationalist sentiment among the Palestinians, so did the interested Arab states promote the idea of a Palestinian state. A seminal work, written by an Egyptian journalist, Ahmad Baha' ad-Din, and published in 1968 with the title *The Proposal for a State of Palestine and the Controversy Surrounding It* gave the clue. The formation of a Palestinian state did not mean merely the return of the dispersed Palestinian Arabs to their lost lands. Very much like the Zionists' achievement earlier, the establishment of a Palestinian state would constitute a base of operations for the further gathering in of the Palestinian land and its people. Not to be forgotten, more than half a million Arabs remained effectively captives within the confines of the Jewish state. A large and discontented minority, many of them would forever long to return to the Palestine of their memory.

As the Arabs had never misunderstood, from the time that the Balfour Declaration was published, that the Zionists intended to take all of Palestine, so did it become clear to the Israelis that the Palestine movement would only come to an end when all of Palestine had been recovered by them. Ahmad ad-Din called his imaginary Palestinian state "a confrontation state" that would eventually absorb both Israel and Jordan—the whole of Palestine—for had not the British imperialists severed the East Bank from Palestine in

1920 and given it to the unworthy Hashemites?

In his analysis as in his hopes, Ahmad did not see a role for the Moslem Brotherhood. Despite the tolerance the Brotherhood enjoyed on the West Bank, namely freedom to criticize Hussein's government, the right to participate in elections and send representatives to the Jordanian Parliament, the Islamic movement declined to a surprising degree after 1949. By 1967 there were less than a thousand members, their representation in the Jordanian Parliament annually never more than four delegates.

The decline of the Brotherhood in Jordan may be attributed to the fate of their main idea, even their *raison d'être*: the creation of a purely religious society, *viz.*, Islamic society; at a time when another idea, Palestinian national identity and a desire for a secular nation-state, was becoming more and more appealing to more and more Palestinians.

The failure of the Moslem Brotherhood to go further in terms of popularity may be explained, finally, not by Israeli success in containing its activities on the West Bank and the Gaza Strip, but more vaguely in such terms as the appeal of nationalism to most Arabs, the desire of the Palestinians for independence, and the seductiveness of Western ways and examples. The manifest proof of this is to be seen just over the border in the Israeli standard of living, this to be contrasted with the squalid, hopeless life most Palestinians know; also, the ennobling ideas of self-rule and constitutional government, which promises an end to arbitrary and often brutal authority. To gain these things, a messianic vision entertained by the Brotherhood did not seem practical.

The idea of an Islamic State, though realized in Iran under the Ayatollah Khomeini, did not prosper in the Occupied Territories. This may be explained by the way in which Sunni and Shiite Moslems have reacted to the Western intrusion into a world overwhelmingly Moslem.

The basic rift in Islam, Sunni vs. Shiite, corresponds to the fundamental schism in Christianity: Orthodoxy vs. Catholicism. As Catholics trace the legitimacy of their faith back to Peter, Christ's favorite disciple, so do the Shiites claim an organic connection with Mohammed, going back to Ali, the Prophet's cousin (or son-in-law, since Ali married Mohammed's daughter, Fatima). Sunnis are orthodox Moslems. Shiites have in a number of significant ways departed from orthodoxy, resulting in disputes that are often arid and semantic. For example, while both Sunnis and Shiites accept the basic compilations of the Hadith (oral law), the Shiites attest to the validity of other compilations. Small points, though useful for purposes of polemical exchanges, but not important in sectarian disputes, are not numerous, only significant in terms of individual morality. For example, Shiites teach that a devout Moslem may deny his faith if faced by mistreatment, abuse, torture or death. A Sunni insists upon personal sacrifice in these cases.

The rivalry between the two sects is irrational and often vengeful, and goes back to the very foundations of Islam in 632, when Ali's grandson, Husayue, and his followers were killed by a rival family. Failing to gain the office of the Caliphate, the Shiites believed ever afterward, even when Arabs became subject to the Turks (the Sultan assuming the Caliphate), that they were the legitimate leaders of Islam.

To the Arabs, the intrusion of the Jews in the Middle East was a catastrophic event that could not be tolerated. To the Iranians (an almost wholly Shiite population and not Arab at all) the Jewish presence was far less important. The fate of Islam depended upon the elimination of *all* Western influences, of which the Jewish intruders were merely a part of the larger problem.

Shiite opinion on this question has been considerable, its influence explained by its geographical concentrations. Shiites make up 70 percent of the Gulf States' population, but all the ruling families of the six states comprising the Arab economic union (Gulf Cooperation Council) are Sunni. [344] In not a few cases they rule large Shiite minorities. In Bahrain Shiites are the majority, constituting one-fourth of Kuwait's population, and there are substantial minorities in Saudi Arabia, Quatar, and the United Arab Emirates.

For a long time, it was assumed by Westerners that the two Moslem sects reacted in fundamentally different ways to the western intrusion, i.e., the Sunnis adjusted to foreign ways without too much difficulty, while the Shiites resisted tenaciously. This may have been true for several decades, but the establishment of the sovereign State of Israel produced a changed attitude. Sunnis and Shiites drew increasingly close to one another, "amazing," wrote one author, "to ascertain." [345] "Today's problems," he wrote, "are reducible to a single question: how to cope with westernization." Such a pervasive, subtle, insidious nexus of influences acts like a drug. Moslems are "westoxificated" (*gharbzadaha*), addicted to things of the West.

The westernizing policies of Gamal Nasser and the Ba'ath parties of Syria and Iraq were repulsed by the Sunni and Shiite fundamentalists. They reacted bitterly, and sometimes violently, against modernizing regimes that were as violent as themselves. The Shah of Iran, a relatively humane man but not loath to use any means to stay in power was nonetheless overthrown in 1979. The Shiite Mullahs seized the power that he relinquished by abdication. A theocratic regime was installed, allegedly more cruel than his had been. To the Mullahs, the struggle was so fraught with peril that mercy had no meaning in what seemed a fight for life, the preservation of Islam. "Islam in the twentieth century," the Mullahs believe, "is facing a danger to its existence far beyond the scope and seriousness of any it has known in the past." [346] Fear of *gharb* (Arabic for the West) tinctures the thought of Islamic Revivalists. Gharb is where the sun sets, the Occident, "where darkness waits, swallows it; then all terrors are possible." [347] He did not fear the West's power, declared the Ayatollah Khomeini, "neither economic boycott nor military intervention. What we fear is cultural dependence and imperialist universities." [348] The key to Islam's salvation lies in the creation of an indoctrinated and regimented youth, who can carry the battle into the next generation so that it may in turn be "detoxificated." (They "hold the key to liberation from the fetters of westoxification." [349])

The Ayatollah Khomeini and his followers were the first religious zealots in modern times to seize a secular state and then exercise its sovereign powers so as to carry out a program of detoxification; in this case the elimination of all contaminating influences brought into Iran by the West. Both Sunni and Shiite writers had publicized this kind of program, teaching the doctrine that to control the state is to control the people; to control the people is to expose them to "the cure." [350] A regime dedicated to such purges may necessarily be more despotic than the one it has supplanted.

Even though Sunni and Shiite theologians and scholars were in basic agreement, it does not follow that the majority of Sunnis (perhaps not even a majority of Shiite Moslems) favored such a radical regime as the Ayatollah Khomeini brought into being. In fact, the convergence of Sunni and Shiite fundamentalism was interrupted, perhaps reversed, by the advent of the Khomeini revolution. Sunni intellectuals had written about a nebulous Islamic state. But, they offered no theories, only advanced images of a perfect society, one which would be obedient to Allah while following faithfully in the Prophet's footsteps. Similarly, the Ayatollah Khomeini, in his long exile, had entertained only an amorphous picture of a theocratic state. It is thought that his ideas about it were crystallized in 1970 while giving lectures to young Mullahs in Najf, Iraq. The next year there appeared his book, *The Islamic Government*. In the Islamic revolution he pictured, the *Ulama* would become a "revolutionary vanguard" led by the Ayatollah; which is very much like saying (in Western terms) the bishops would lead the priests in a holy war. In this context, Khomeini would, of course, be the pope. Once the powers of the state had been conquered, the Mullahs would perform a double function: their traditional spiritual duties, but also civic duties as any secular government would expect of them.

This break with tradition, the notion that a Mullah should be a civil officer (bureaucrat) shocked fundamentalist Sunnis. Khomeini justified it with a saying from the Hadith: "The Ulama are the heirs of the prophets"; Was not Mohammed a theocrat? Civil and military head of the Moslem State? And spiritual leader as well? It goes without saying that if a Westernized Arab government should be overthrown (perhaps Egypt), the Moslem Brotherhood would be inspired to follow the example of their Shiite brethren in Iran. Then would Israel's peril seem, more than ever before, the United States' also.

In these years, while the West Bank existed as a sort of refuge for the Brotherhood, in Egypt (its spiritual home) its legal existence had come to an end. Gamal Nasser, a pronounced Egyptian nationalist who had espoused Western social ideas, was anathema to the Brotherhood. The appeal of Arab nationalism, the heady vision of Arab unity, the promise of socialist doctrines, cooperation with the Soviet Union; all these represented secular forces that attenuated both the influence and the popularity of the Moslem Brotherhood in Egypt. Nasser's rise to power, with the attendant overthrow of the Egyptian monarchy and the rise of the Ba'ath Party in Syria, represented a series of defeats for the Brotherhood, resulting in a continuous decline in its membership—until 1967. Israel's remarkable victory that year, but more particularly the Israeli occupation of the rest of Palestine (except for Jordan on the East Bank), created among the Palestinians an environment of lost hope and bitterness, in which Moslem fundamentalism could flourish once more. To the Brotherhood, Egypt's defeat by Israel was "divine vengeance," the defeat of alien forces at work within Islam: nationalism, socialism, godless communism, the whole of that artificial ideology the Nassers of the Arab world had tried to impose upon Islam. The Pan-Arabian idea was presumed to be universal, but was not. Islam alone was universal. To the Brotherhood Nasser's defeat was poetic justice. Fraternizing with the West and its corrupting and contagious ideas, he had been defeated by the West through its agent, Israel.

Defeated and demoralized, Nasser (he would not live much longer), had seen his power and influence begin to wane. His attempts to extinguish the Brotherhood, rather like a vain effort to smother vapors, hardly dampened the energetic spirit of Islam. In the minds of the true believers there is but one world and one faith, as there is but one God.

The strength of the Brotherhood stemmed from its long tenure in Palestine, established there since at least 1935; above all its charitable and educational work among the refugees. [351] Possessing a network of influences, so well grounded as to be considered institutional, the Brotherhood's work of propaganda and proselytization continued without a letup. Week in and week out, year after year, the moral imperative was taught by the Brotherhood. True Believers should give away all: money, property, (the lives of their children, if need be), for the recovery of Palestine, for the removal of a curse imposed upon the land by the Jews, "the dirtiest and meanest of all races...defiling the most sanctified and honored spot on earth, a spot to which Allah sent a herald angel, and where the Prophet Mohammed made his midnight journey." [352]

In the theory held by the Brotherhood leadership, an Islamic transformation of Palestine would proceed Jihad, the Holy War for the destruction of Israel. Thus the importance of education (i.e., indoctrination) for every Palestinian. With the Islamic transformation of the Palestinians, Jihad would not be the perilous and lonely undertaking of a small beleaguered people, but rather a joint uprising of all Moslems. This was only the first stage of a chiliastic reverie. Islamic Revival would sweep over the whole of the still-unredeemed Moslem world.

Against this vast scheme of universal redemption, the ambition of the PLO seemed modest indeed: the liberation of some part of Palestine, with further progress in realizing the national ideal, the eventual recovery of the homeland, the establishment of a sovereign Palestinian state. These were ambitions not different from what the Zionists had dreamed upon a half-century earlier. Nonetheless, after 1967, collaboration between the PLO and the Brotherhood, unstated but real enough, commenced. The contrast between the partners was glaring. The Brotherhood operated within the mosque, citadel of Moslem certitude, with its powerful impact on the average Arab mind and conscience. The PLO operated in the streets and alleys, armed secular figures, hardly to be considered religious; realistic and ruthless gangs of young people whose brutality toward the enemy was not greater than toward their own kind should the weak among them lose heart and seem to betray the cause.

The penetration of the universities by the Moslem Brotherhood was long in its work and nearly imperceptible up to the late 1970s, when it seemed suddenly to blossom. [353] The proselytization of Palestinian students was a work of quiet persuasion, with neither political intent nor even much national sentiment attached to it. For the Moslem Brotherhood, as always, time seemed to be on their side in a struggle against the West that might last several generations, perhaps centuries. But such faith and patience did not belong to all the Believers. Within the Brotherhood a faction began to call for direct action, invoking Jihad, the holy war.

Jihad is one Arabic word that resonates in the Western world, yet its literal translation still leaves it a meaningless concept, so secular has Western society become in the past five centuries. "Between the realm of Islam and the realm of unbelief," it has been observed, "there is a canonically obligatory perpetual state of war which will continue until the whole world either accepts the message of Islam or submits to the rule of those who bring it." [354] Beginning with Mohammed, this mystique, a compound of theological certitude and religious fanaticism, had given control of the Middle East to the Arabs, then to the Turks. It survived the failure of two empires and surmounted the Western occupation after World War I, as vital today as in any time past.

Jihad appealed to the young who had already learned their lessons from the Brotherhood. Its appearance on the West Bank is determined exactly by a date and an event on that day. In July 1983, a Jewish student, Aaron Gross, was stabbed to death in downtown Hebron. "Islamic Jihad" soon issued a statement in which it claimed responsibility for the murder. The assailant or assailants were never found. There followed more attacks of this kind; finally a notorious assassination, the killing of an Israeli military officer in front of the Wailing Wall. This resulted in arrests and detentions; alleged torture, eliciting some information: the terrorists operated according to instructions sent from Jordan. They had been trained in Fatah camps. Islamic Jihad maintained "good relations with all the PLO factions."

This new breed of terrorists were found to be fearless, prepared to accept torture, and willing to give their lives in order to realize their goal. They would willingly drive vehicles loaded with explosives into selected buildings, aware that their mission was suicidal. It may be said that Islamic Jihad was a mindless terrorism, without an organization or a program; in a sense, it was a violent reflex action to the effects of a prolonged and often brutal military occupation, establishing a stereotype that contradicts the essential humanity of Islam. It also propelled more violently than before, and in an ultramodern form (the AKA assault weapon having replaced the dagger), Islamic Revival, which since the eighteenth century had been continuous resistance to "the imperialistic intrusion of the West and the advent of colonial dependency." [355]

Meanwhile, the Moslem Brotherhood, through its saintly work in public charity and education, stayed within the mainstream of traditional Islamic Revival. With the apparent collapse, perhaps the end, of the PLO at the close of the Lebanese debacle, it seemed the Moslem Brotherhood had won the long contest. "Armed Struggle," suddenly seemed to be a phrase without meaning. Meanwhile, Israeli settlers continued to spread out over the country, enjoying the clandestine support of the Israeli government in their illegal actions. Militant speakers in the Israeli Knesset spoke often of the "occupation problem," and a possible solution for it, *viz.*, to "transfer the Palestinians to the East Bank," and if this was not feasible, to find the Arabs another *watan badil* (homeland). Threatened in this way, the Palestinians learned again that the Arab states were reluctant to intervene on their behalf.

Underlying all these tensions and frustrations was the reality of an unwanted and increasingly arrogant military occupation. The Israeli government behaved like a colonial power, but without the redeeming features of most empire-builders: no subtly in managing the populations under their control, no attempt to win approval, or at least mere sufferance, from the influential sectors of the society they commanded.

Perhaps the Israelis could not have played an enlightened role under the circumstances of the time. But the harshness of the occupation regime, the policy of destroying the houses of poor people implicated or merely suspected of conspiracy against the military authority; imprisonment for small deeds; torture, more than any Israeli government would admit; confiscation of property, endless illegal and arbitrary mistreatment of Palestinian citizens ... such is a partial list of abuses by a military regime hardly responsible to any higher authority than its own.

The economic exploitation of the Occupied Territories, going largely to the advantage of the Israelis, were varied and widespread: the expropriation of Arab lands, grossly unfair allocation of water (for the benefit of the Jewish settlers, of course). The degrading poverty of a population without resources or capital had produced, after a twenty-year occupation, an "enraged proletariat." Not the agitation of radicals, but an abysmal condition of life presaged a general uprising; hence the argument given by the Arabs that "Israel's economic system was the real driving force behind the radicalization of the Palestinian public." [356]

In reality the economic stagnation on the West Bank was the end result of Israeli-Jordanian collaboration going back to 1963. In September of that year, Hussein had secretly received an Israeli agent, Dr. Yaakov Herzog, Director-General of the Prime Minister's Office. The understanding that followed was twofold: a joint effort to attenuate the Palestinian national movement at first, and, after 1967 when the West Bank became occupied by the Israelis, a joint economic exploitation of the territory. They held these points in common: the Palestinians did not exist as a distinct people, but were simply a part of the Arab nationality. The PLO was dedicated to the destruction of both Israel and Jordan. Yasser Arafat did not represent the Palestinians because there were no Palestinian people and because he was self-appointed, merely a violent demagogue. Finally, the idea of a Palestinian state was to be resisted, since it represented a threat to both Jordan and Israel.

Up to 1967, Hussein had "pursued" what has been termed "a policy of political fragmentation" toward the West Bank, "buttressed by economic backwardness that aimed to prevent the formation of large political parties or newly wealthy groups independent of its control who might challenge Jordanian rule." [357] Needless to say, the Israelis found Hussein's policy useful for their own purposes once they had taken control of the West Bank.

After 1967 Jordan enjoyed exceptional privileges, from the free circulation of the Jordanian dinar on the West Bank, to Jordan's participation in the management of local elections and municipal appointments. [358] One may speak of a diarchy therefore; an unequal one to be sure, as had been the Jewish Agency's collaboration with Great Britain during the mandate period.

The subterranean collaboration of Hussein and the Israelis, each able to claim no more than *de facto* possession of the same territory, was well known; universally detested by many Palestinians since they were the victims of this peculiar exploitation. Always, the king of Jordan was viewed as much a bloodsucker as any Israeli government.

The indifference of the Hashemites to the spirit of nationalism (or better to say, their obtuseness) is to be explained perhaps by their origins as members of the Arabian aristocracy. In his youth Hussein, like his grandfather, saw Arab nationalism (if he saw it at all) as an emanation of the past glories of Islam, that distant time when the Arabs ruled the Middle East.

The Hashemites had been for centuries the guardians of Islam's most holy shrine, the Kaaba, at Mecca. In 1922 they came into Palestine under the protection of the British Empire, at a time when the Saudis were overthrowing their authority in the Nejd. Receiving a desert wasteland from their patron, Great Britain, the Hashemites coveted the west bank of the Jordan, which offered some promise of prosperity. Abdullah annexed the territory in 1950, but the international community refused to officially sanction the extralegal possession of a territory to which no power and no country could make a legitimate claim, though the Israelis tried to do so with the argument that it was the "cradle of their civilization," Eretz Israel. The Palestinians claimed it also, on the grounds of national self-determination: the rightful owners, as the autochthonous people who had lived on the land from time out of mind.

After years of precarious existence as an essentially unformed state without formal borders, security for Israel had come to depend upon a single diplomatic strategy: to make a client of Transjordan, as Israel had the self-evident need to be a faithful client of the United States. (Israelis prefer the euphemism "ally.") Thus, the emergence of the Amman-Tel Aviv-Washington axis, constituting the matrix of American Middle East policy also, regardless of which political party controlled the White House. Unexpectedly, perhaps not generally perceived, Israel, a tiny state with scarcely any power, could collaborate with a superpower and usually determine the outcome of events in the Middle East, assuring self-preservation in the midst of many enemies, and resistance to the gathering storm of Islamic fundamentalism dedicated to destroying Western influences that corrupted traditional Moslem values.

The complicating factor was the Palestine national movement, making Israeli-American cooperation uncertain, often strained, and sometimes abortive. The Reagan peace plan, put forward only a few days after Arafat's expulsion from Lebanon, was only typical of several attempts by Washington to produce a general settlement of differences in the region. The main points of the plan were:

- Creation of an autonomous Palestinian state under the authority of the king of Jordan. (i.e., a federation of Transjordan and Cisjordan).
- The cessation of construction of Jewish settlements on the West Bank.
- Jerusalem to remain undivided, its eventual status to be determined through negotiations.
- U.S. support for Israel to continue, its commitment to its ally "iron clad."

In the proposed settlement no role was foreseen for the PLO. Naturally, the latter rejected the plan at once. The Israeli government also rejected it because, among other things, Jerusalem's future was non-negotiable, and no Israeli government wished to give a formal halt to the Jewish settler movement.

With the Reagan Plan a dead letter, the Saudis revived their own earlier plan. This was given much publicity, Prince Fahd (soon to be King Fahd) placing his plan before an Arab summit meeting at Fez. Basically, there were five points:

- Israel would withdraw to its pre-1967 borders.
- All Jewish settlements would be removed from the West Bank.
- Reparation would be paid to the Palestinian refugees.
- Jerusalem would become the capital of a Palestinian state.
- There would be a United Nations guarantee of the settlement.

The word *Israel* did not appear in the language of Fahd's plan since most Arabs believed that Israel "did not exist." On the other hand, the Saudi statesmen did not mention the PLO either.

Both the PLO and the Israelis rejected the Fahd plan. The Arab States would not endorse it either. The Fahd Plan was brought forward again the next year, this time with a proposal to bring the PLO into the settlement, but several of the Arab states insisted that recognition of Israel should not be included in the settlement.

In the aftermath of these failed plans, Arafat tried to establish a working relationship with his old enemy, Hussein. The latter gave perhaps no more than lip service to this. Finally, in April 1983 the King broke off negotiations with the PLO emissaries, declaring that the Palestinians would have "to save themselves and their land."

In need of a patron, and Hussein manifestly unavailable to them, Arafat and his companions had no choice but to return to the idea of Armed Struggle, but that meant the distasteful necessity of humbling themselves and returning under the authority of Assad, who still breathed the spirit of the Fedayeen (namely, destroy Israel at any cost).

The PLO was always an organization existing largely on paper, the factions forever at each other's throats, fratricidal relations of such shifting complexity as to be unrecorded. The point of interest is that a man as patient and as subtle as Arafat could use this kind of disunity for his own purposes. Also important to note is that while the doctrine of Armed Struggle had been disproved by the acid test of struggle in Lebanon, the popularity of the PLO in the Occupied Territories remained high.

By the 1980s a generation had grown up and been schooled in PLO doctrines. In this same time the Israelis had fostered rudimentary democracy in the Occupied Territories, conducted by secret ballot. On various occasions the PLO leaders would let it be known whom they favored, and most of the time these candidates won the municipal elections. Had a plebiscite been held, the Israelis would have learned (as all the rest of the world) that the policies of the PLO were those of the Palestinian masses. But since this diffuse opinion could not be consulted, notable Palestinians had formed the National Guidance Committee, the majority of its members sympathetic to the PLO. With this, the basis for a popular government in the Occupied Territories was possible and awaited the opportunity to take on a real political life.

A series of events beginning in late 1983 began to dissolve Israeli intransigence, at the same time eroding the United States' loyalty to its client. In December the UN General Assembly called for an international conference in order to consider a two-state solution to the Israeli-Palestinian problem. It was proposed that the PLO should represent the Palestinians in these negotiations; Israel should withdraw from the Occupied Territories, including East Jerusalem. But these overtures were unproductive—up to 1987.

⟳ INTIFADA

Every human eruption, whether reflecting the unplanned actions and hopes of many or the calculated aim of a few plotters, comes as a surprise, suggesting spontaneity. One day, an Israeli was stabbed to death in Gaza. The next day an Israeli truck collided with two vehicles carrying Arab working people. Several were killed in the accident. In the excitement it was the general opinion of the Palestinians that the Jewish trucker had rammed the Arab vehicles to avenge the death of the Jew who had been stabbed. Demonstrations occurred almost at once, in Gaza first, then erupting on the West Bank. A spontaneous uprising soon became a popular movement with a purpose. It was called *Intifada* (the throwing off).

These irrational actions were accompanied by equally irrational Israeli reactions. Shimon Perez suggested that perhaps Israel should demilitarize the Gaza strip. Taking the prime minister's offhand remark as evidence of Israel's weakening resolve to maintain the occupation, several Moslem notables met at the home of a retired schoolteacher, Ahmin Yasin. An organization was formed to exploit the situation. In this latest attempt to liberate the Occupied Territories, they called themselves *Harakat al-Macawama al-Islamiyii* (The Islamic Resistance Movement). Hamas would become the familiar acronym, derived from the capital letters of the movement's title, which means zeal and enthusiasm. With determination and much zeal, Hamas leaders endeavored to spur on a spontaneous uprising which, like all popular demonstrations, tended to play out in a few days. Without arms to speak of, and certainly no heavy weapons, in a small country almost devoid of cover for concealing guerrilla movements, the task they had assigned themselves must have seemed well-nigh impossible. Efficient and often ruthless, Israeli surveillance methods had made the individual efforts of Palestinian patriots vain ones for over twenty years.

Yasin, at fifty-one, was not the dedicated terrorist type, but rather a devout Moslem who had believed, almost romantically, one is obliged to say, that a spiritual regeneration of the Arab Palestinian populace would bring about their deliverance. Like most of the Palestinians, he had relied upon the Arab states and the PLO to do for the occupied people what they could not do for themselves. He was bold enough, however. Arrested in 1984 for carrying a weapon, he had received a thirteen-year prison sentence. He served only ten months before being released in a prison exchange agreement between the Israeli government and the PFLP-GC (Popular Front for the Liberation of Palestine—General Command).

Yasin understood very well, as did his companions, that any attempt to gather and store arms, or to even act openly in support of Intifada, meant a long term of imprisonment for the one apprehended. Expecting the worst, they decided to establish leadership in depth, calling it "virtual leadership." That is, leaders would emerge as fast as they were arrested and carried away. And therefore, as Hamas could not be extinguished by this strategy, Intifada would not die out. Resistance, to be effective, would be constant and it would be violent. It was not in keeping with the Arab mentality, it appears, or consonant with a history of the war with the Israelis (a struggle now forty years old), that Hamas would adopt a policy of pacific civil disobedience. Pacifism was for Thoreau and Gandhi in other times and places.

The practice of terror is effective over time, providing that those who engage in it are able to endure the injuries it inflicts upon themselves. In its violence and often-unspeakable atrocities, terror outrages the neutral observer, who insists upon a remedy. In the end, it wears down the nerve of those most directly affected by it. The Israelis had endured Palestinian/Moslem/Arab terror for forty years, for there was no way of escaping the punishment delivered to its border populations. Within the Occupied Territories their soldiers experienced nearly constant abuse, harassment and, occasionally, death. To turn the same injuries back on the Palestinians was simply to maintain a high level of terror—but this was precisely the aim of Hamas: to compel the Israelis to behave with the same brutality they condemned in Hamas and, worn down by these excesses, to conclude that continued occupation of Palestine was not worth the cost. In this same way the

Jewish terrorists in their time had driven the British out of Palestine. Hardly had Hamas organized, when the principal PLO factions came together, energized no doubt by the spectacle of an aroused people rising in revolt—was not the doctrine of Armed Struggle to be finally vindicated? This newest organization was named the United National Leadership of the Uprising (UNLU).

Intifada gave Arafat a new lease on his revolutionary life. After the ignominious retreat from Lebanon, no Arab country would offer him a safe haven. Eventually, the aging president of Tunisia, Habib Bourguiba, had provided him with accommodations in a small seaside village, Hammam el-Shat, about thirteen miles east of the Tunisian capital. These were temporary quarters—but there is a saying: "Nothing is so permanent as the provisional." Arafat and his lieutenants themselves believed that a generation might pass before the PLO could recover the power and influence it had enjoyed in Lebanon. [359] Living in shabby comfort at Hammam el-Shat, they characterized their headquarters as a "Government-in-Exile."

If he had nothing left of power and but little influence, Arafat still possessed a considerable reputation. Most important of all, he had a title: Chairman of the Palestinian Liberation Organization (in reality a titular leadership). He would not surrender the prerogatives that went with the title, however, and the numerous factions that comprised the PLO were too divided to be able to deny him his pretensions. They had possessed a "state" in Lebanon, lamented one of Arafat's colleagues, now they had neither territory on which to operate nor an office.

In the summer of 1983 the United Nations sponsored a conference at Geneva. Hoping to rebuild his shattered image, Arafat, with some of his lieutenants, journeyed there to speak. The armed struggle would go on, he declared to the assembled delegates. His remarks were enthusiastically applauded. But there was a hollow sound to the term "armed struggle" now, unpromising not only for the Palestinians, but for other oppressed peoples around the world. The outlaw spirit of the sixties, which had been driven by alienated youth, seemed to be spent by the end of the seventies. Arafat was getting old. (He turned fifty-four in the summer of 1983).

From Geneva he went to Sicily, then on to Lebanon, with what seems to have been the desperate notion that he could reassert his authority; to that end he was willing to defy Assad. He rejoined a remnant of the Fatah (about 6,000) camped near Tripoli, well aware of what Assad's reaction would be. On 3 November a Syrian bombardment of the camp commenced. Retreating into Tripoli, as always seeking a civilian population in which to hide, they brought the fury of Syrian artillery down on the town for several days. On 12 November the bombardment ended. Assad, it was rumored, had suffered a heart attack; and once more Arafat was saved from himself. He and his followers were given until 21 December to leave Lebanon. In due course, he and a company of 4,000 men and adolescent boys departed on several Greek ships, to be landed at three points: Tunis, Algeria, and North Yemen. In his last defiant remarks Arafat asserted that he would never give up armed struggle, and never recognize Israel. He returned to Tunis and what seemed to be certain oblivion. But, in time, the rivalry of Hamas and the PLO would give him another opportunity, one more promising than the Lebanese imbroglio a decade earlier.

Until the advent of Intifada the concept of Armed Struggle had been largely an abstraction to the PLO leaders. [360] The uprising of a suppressed people could hardly be pictured in real terms: Secondly, the sheer rising of a population against the military hardware of a determined oppressor means flesh against metal in an unequal contest that cannot be imagined nor accepted. Ultimately, there came to the minds of the Palestinian strategists a scheme that they called the Phased Plan. In a way, and probably unintentionally, it replicated the earlier successful plan of the Zionists to seize Palestine and oust the indigenous population. The first phase would bring about the establishment of an autonomous state, enjoying the approval of the international community. The return of the Palestinian Diaspora to the homeland would follow. The phases thereafter, as in the case of the Zionists earlier, would depend upon the exigencies that time and events always provide. Step by step, Israel would be absorbed by the new State of Palestine. What would or could be done with more than four million Jews was a question deferred because there was not an answer; just as the Zionists after 1919 had never found an answer as to how they could expel the Palestinians in their midst—until 1948, when the answer to that question revealed itself.

The contrast between the Machiavellian tactics of the Palestinian patriots on the one hand, and the otherworldly, albeit violent, methods of the Islamic Revivalists is something to conjure. After the UNLU had been established, Hamas and the PLO became incarnate in two personalities: Yasser Arafat and Ahmin Yasin. There had been a time when the two men were friends, young, idealistic, united by their ideas while living in Gaza. But they had separated, as did their separate experiences evolve in radically different ways. Yasin became drawn more closely to the Brotherhood, becoming a teacher and a pacifist. Arafat began a career of adventure, a hazardous and rootless existence, becoming a revolutionary finally; a terrorist in practice, that type of nationalist that had appeared again and again in Syria, Iraq, Egypt, Yemen; in Third World countries generally.

The idea of armed struggle came to both men, but in different ways; and, as in any revolution, as in any dovecote, the fine difference between two things makes all the difference. "The support which the Moslem Brotherhood gives to Yasser Arafat," remarked Yasin, "is in proportion to Arafat's support of the Islamic idea." Thus it remained simply a tactical question: how best to energize the masses so as to realize the goal desired by all Arabs: the destruction of Israel. The fundamental question could not be answered: Would the Palestinian state of the future be a secular one based on the western model or would it be an Islamic State fashioned more or less after the pattern offered by Iran?

In the duel between Hamas and the UNLU, both sides blanketed the territories with leaflets, a method of communication the Israeli authorities could not prevent entirely. [361] When the first anniversary of Intifada approached, the PLO moved to take control of the popular movement. Speaking to the Palestine National Council, which was meeting in Algiers (12–15 November 1988), Arafat announced his intention to proclaim the independence of Palestine. After the conference was over, the UNLU distributed its twenty-eighth leaflet. Entitled "Proclamation of Independence," it urged the Palestinians in Gaza and the West Bank to hold great public meetings for celebrating their independence. This same day the Palestine National Council declared the independence of Palestine, basing the validity of the declaration on United Nations resolutions 242 and 338.

Arafat was invited to speak to the UN General Assembly, but American Secretary of State George Schultz refused to grant him a visa, characterizing him as a terrorist. The General Assembly condemned the U.S. actions by a vote of 151 to 2, then voted to move to Geneva to continue their deliberations. In December, Arafat addressed the delegates, declaring that the PLO recognized the right of Israel to exist. "The PLO will," he said, "seek a comprehensive settlement among the parties concerned in the Arab-Israeli conflict, including the state of Palestine, Israel, and other neighbors, within the framework of the international conference for peace in the Middle East on the basis of Resolutions 242 and 338…".

Arafat's call to meet and treat all questions was spurned by the Israelis. Their ally and patron, the U.S., agreed; one did not negotiate with terrorists. Whereupon Arafat declared publicly that the PLO not only denounced terrorism, it renounced it. That was enough for the Bush Administration to reverse itself, much to the dismay of Israel, and agree to accept a dialogue with the PLO.

This breakthrough changed nothing in the Occupied Territories, where Intifada entered its second year with undiminished vigor and venom. Israelis in their great majority stood steadfastly against any dealings with the PLO and continued to insist that there would never be a Palestinian state on their borders.

The assumption of the Israelis that popular resistance would tire eventually, and the Intifada fade away, was perhaps a true estimate of things. The same assumption by the Hamas perhaps explains why they became ever bolder, ever more violent. Two soldiers, Avi Sasportas and Ilan Said, were abducted, then murdered. The Israeli government arrested three hundred suspects, among them Ahmin Yasin and Dr. Mahmoud Zahor. Thereafter they undertook the well-nigh impossible task of eliminating Hamas root and branch, which was rather like attempting to gouge the life and spirit out of a whole people, for Hamas had not been the cause of Intifada, but the direct result of it.

Sentenced to fifteen years in prison, Yasin remained the voice of Hamas nonetheless. The "virtual leadership" did not miss him or need him. Others would accept Yasin's sacrifice in their turn, and others after them. In a perverse way, the terror that had resulted in the death of two Israeli soldiers had the effect that had been sought: a resurgence of Intifada in response to Israeli reactions. The stage was set for a desperate pattern of assaults, reprisal, new assaults inviting more reprisals; a spiraling attrition for both sides, the only question, which side could endure the punishment the longest?

A meticulous surveillance over the years had given the Israeli authorities the names, and often the addresses, of several hundred of the more prominent members of Hamas. Those considered most dangerous were targeted for deportation, the rest arrested and imprisoned. A nameless fear ran through the Palestinian population, a widespread belief that this was the first step in Israel's often-rumored policy of "transfer," the implication being that the Occupied Territories would be emptied by degrees to make room for more Jewish settlers.

Saddam Hussein's occupation of Kuwait in July 1990 changed the Palestinian situation fundamentally. Hamas circulated a leaflet condemning American interference in a dispute it judged to be solely a quarrel between Iraq and Kuwait. But soon a second leaflet appeared, urging Saddam to withdraw from Kuwait. This shift in policy was probably the realization by the Hamas leadership that supporting Iraq would bring their subsidies from the Gulf

States to an end. [362] The PLO, in contrast to Hamas, expressed an unqualified support for Iraq, perhaps thinking of the Iraqi dictator as a future ally in the never-ending quest for the liberation of Palestine. Without much delay King Hussein joined the Palestinians in their support of Saddam. His was not an act of cowardice or of sincere support for the Iraqi dictator, but a frank recognition that his power (his throne and his dynasty in fact) was once more imperiled by popular Arab sentiment so strong he could not ignore it. But he would pay a price in due course for his realism.

In the Occupied Territories, the Gulf War (at once the greatest show on earth) seemed almost incidental where life and property were being destroyed daily. Intifada continued to beat fiercely in the Palestinian breast. Hamas terror, joined by that of the Islamic Jihad, continued without letup, earning Israeli reprisals just as regularly. On 8 October, Israeli police gunned down seventeen Palestinian worshippers at the al-Aqsa Mosque; a hundred more were wounded in the fusillade. As to be expected, Hamas retaliated, attacking Jewish settlers and their protecting police. As a result of this the Occupied Territories were placed under curfew. What had been previously a reservation patrolled by Israeli police and soldiers now became a prison. By such repression was Intifada throttled for the duration of the Gulf war. But with an end to the conflict, and the curfew lifted, the popular uprising started again. And then suddenly, astonishing to the world at large, Israeli representatives and their Arab counterparts found themselves talking face to face over the same table. The conference took place at Madrid on 30 October 1991, under the joint auspices of the U.S. and the USSR. At Israeli insistence no PLO delegation attended.

Historians may very well argue that it was Intifada that brought Israel to the peace table with a definite inclination to surrender some part of the Occupied Territories. The causes for the Madrid meeting were multiple, however, and complicated. The outcome of the Gulf War, the liberation of Kuwait, the humiliation of Saddam Hussein, and the isolation of those who had supported Saddam (an unforgivable betrayal from the U.S. point of view) all played a part in forcing a change of attitude on nearly every party involved in the Palestinian question. Not least among a number of factors was the advent of Perestroika in the Soviet Union, which betokened the end of the Cold War; thus the positive and cordial collaboration of the U.S. and the USSR in encouraging the belligerents to seek a permanent peace among themselves. Bush and Gorbachev agreed to serve as joint sponsors and were the first to speak when the conference opened.

From Madrid the delegations moved on to Washington. After that, a number of meetings took place between the Israelis and the Palestinian in several capitals of the world. Both the superpowers, having brought the antagonists together, left the diplomatic stage.

As prolonged negotiations reached a point of conclusion, the negotiators agreed that perfect secrecy was required. The talks were moved to a small village near Oslo. It was the Palestinians' good fortune, perhaps Israel's as well, that the Israeli Labor coalition had been reconstituted and the Likud forced back into a position of opposition. Something like a revolution had overtaken Labor Zionism. The failure of communism, then the dissolution of the Soviet Union, had a profound effect on Labor Socialists in Israel. The old social doctrines, socialist programs going back forty years or more, were now abandoned. Yitzhak Rabin, former warrior turned politician and premier, seemed to be transformed; he had become a peace-seeker. In this endeavor he was joined by his longtime political rival, Shimon Peres, who became foreign minister. Remarkably, the two men resolved that in not less than nine months they would gain an accommodation with the PLO that would provide for an autonomous Palestine. [363] By evacuating the Occupied Territories Israel would finally know the blessings of peace. But this proposition might have been made and realized any time in the previous twenty years. The fact was that such a volte-face as Rabin and Peres proposed would have to be carried against Israeli public opinion and, more particularly, against a rabid political opposition. To the Likud the evacuation of Samaria and Judea (West Bank) would be tantamount to treason. The party's history, its basic philosophy, rejected any accommodation with the Palestinian enemy. Therefore, not only was the world unaware of the Oslo talks, Labor's political opposition was kept in the dark as to what Shimon Peres and his colleagues were about. They were going to agree to give up some part of the Occupied Territories and expect to have in exchange peaceful relations with the Palestinians (the Arabs, more generally). Land for peace was the trade, and would become the Labor party's slogan.

The preliminary agreements were signed on 20 August 1993. A little later the same day Peres made an entry in his notebook. "How strange," he wrote, "that we Israelis are now the ones granting the Palestinians what the British had granted us more than seventy years ago, a 'homeland in Palestine'." [364] He did not seem to realize that with an air of noblesse oblige he and his fellow Israelis were giving back grudgingly only a fraction of what had been taken from the Palestinians in 1948. Had he reflected further he would have realized also that, while the British non-Jewish Zionists had made a homeland in Palestine available to the Jews in 1919, most of them had not wanted to see it evolve into a sovereign Jewish state. In quite the same way, the Palestinians expressed satisfaction with the prospect of receiving an autonomous status; but already they were thinking about the next step, which would lead to the establishment of a sovereign state with East Jerusalem as its capital.

For the Israelis, the assassination of Rabin in October 1995 by a Jewish extremist produced grave doubts about the validity of the Oslo Accords. In the aftermath of the murder, fear and irresolution created an environment in which the Likud factions could combine again. Supported by the ultra-nationalists and the religious extremists, Benjamin Netanyahu, a hard-liner and a vociferous critic of the Oslo Accords, won a bare majority of the votes, enough to establish a coalition government based on the right-wing parties in the Knesset. The Jabotinsky tradition was revived. Samaria and Judea, they vowed, would always be Jewish. Begin's often-repeated declaration was reaffirmed: "Now that we possess all of it, we shall not surrender another inch of territory." [365]

Jerusalem would be forever undivided, forever the capital of the Jews and none other. The unspoken policy, as much a hope as a policy, was that Palestinians might remain hopelessly divided among themselves, impotent, mired in poverty, and therefore not a threat to Israel.

NOTES

316 Seth P. Tillman, *The United States in the Middle East*, op. cit., p. 53.

317 Morris Grossman, "Exiled from Exile: Existential Reflections," *Diaspora*, ed., Etan Levine, op. cit., pp. 74-75.

318 Isaac Deutscher, *The Non-Jewish Jew and Other Essays* (New York, 1968), p. 40.

319 "Zionism and the Legacy of Exile," *Diaspora*, ed. Etan Levine, p. 291.

320 Simha Flapan, *Zionism and the Palestinians*, op. cit., p. 81.

321 The legal position taken by the Israeli Courts is Israel exists as a state (Jewish), but not a nation-state. World Jewry is the nation for which Israel serves a special purpose. See John Quigley, *Palestine and Israel*, op. cit., p. 129.

322 Robert Freedman, *From Beirut to Jerusalem*, op. cit., p. 289.

323 Silverberg, *If I Forget Thee, O Jerusalem*, op., cit., p. 185.

324 The ID cards carried by Israeli Arabs identify them Arabs by nationality. Legally speaking, because they are not Jews, they are not Israeli citizens.

325 Ofira Seliktar, *New Zionism and the Foreign Policy System of Israel* (Southern Illinois University Press, 1986), p. 156.

326 In the final revision of the resolution the article "the" was removed from the text, thereby allowing for the assumption that not all of the occupied territories has to be evacuated; thus giving Israel an opportunity to claim (perhaps annex) strategic areas which would give it security.

327 Jimmy Carter, *The Blood of Abraham* (Boston, 1985), p. 166.

328 Martin Gilbert, *Israel*, op. cit., p. 487.

329 Carter seems to have believed that Begin would accept some form of Palestinian autonomy. Carter, *The Blood of Abraham*, pp. 168-69.

330 Sadat was murdered by a member of the Islamic Jihad in October 1981.

331 Ofira Seliktar, *New Zionism and the Foreign Policy System of Israel*, p. 156.

332 David Weishurd, Jewish Settler Violence. *Deviance and Social Reaction* (The Pennsylvania State University Press, 1989), p. 23.

333 Mark A. Heller, *A Palestinian State. The Implications for Israel* (Harvard University Press, 1983), p. 14. Benjamin Netanyahu offers a chapter on the subject: *A Place Among the Nations*, op. cit., Chap. VII.

334 The repeated complaint of the Israelis is the United States' reliability as

an ally may be doubted, especially since its abandonment of South Vietnam: "I believe that at the point of testing, a weak Israel would elicit a great deal of American sympathy, but not much else." Netanyahu, *A Place Among the Nations,* op. cit., pp. 394-95.

335 A catalogue of this violence may be found in Weishurd, *Jewish Settler Violence.*

336 Ibid., p. 36.

337 Robert J. Friedman, *Zealots for Zion. Inside Israel's West Bank Settlement Movement,* op cit., p. xxvi.

338 Colin Shindler, *Israel, Likud and the Zionist Dream: Power, Politics and Ideology from Begin to Netanyahu* (London and New York, 1995), p. 80.

339 The law was revised after 1967, requiring one year's residence before citizenship would be granted.

340 Silverberg, p. 471.

341 Netanyahu's thesis. Ignoring the terrorism of his own party's past, he catalogues that of his enemies: Netanyahu, *A Place Among the Nations,* pp. 104-06.

342 It goes without saying that every week for a period of twenty-four hours, from Friday evening to the evening of the next day, the Sabbath effectively shuts down the economic life of Israel.

343 A.L. Tibawi, "Visions of the Return: The Palestinian Arab Refugees in Arabic Poetry and Art," *Middle East Journal,* 17 (1963), pp. 507-26; cited by Polk, *The United States and the Arab World,* p. 270.

344 The members are: Saudi Arabia, Bahrain, Kuwait, Oman, Quatar, the United Arab Emirates.

345 *Religious Radicalism and Politics in the Middle East,* eds., Emmanuel Sivan and Menachem Friedman (State University of New York, 1990), p. 40.

346 Ibid., pp. 40-41.

347 Fatima Mernissi, *Islam and Democracy. Fear of the Modern World.* Trans., Mary Jo Lakeland (Addison-Wesley Publishing Company, 1992), p. 13.

348 Robin Wright, *Sacred Rage. The Crusade of Modern Islam* (New York, 1985), p. 254.

349 *Religious Radicalism and Politics in the Middle East,* p. 4.

350 Ibid.

351 Abu-Amr Ziad, *Islamic Fundamentalism in the West Bank and Gaza. Muslim Brotherhood and Jihad.* (Indiana University Press, 1994), p. 6.

352 Ibid., p. 26.

353 Ibid., p. 136.

354 David K. Shipler, *Arab and Jew. Wounded Spirits in a Promised Land* (Times

Books, 1968), p. 170.

355 Bruce B. Lawrence, *Shattering the Myth. Islam Beyond Violence* (Princeton University Press, 1998), p. xiii.

356 *Intifada. The Palestinian Uprising—Israel's Third Front*, Ze'ev Schiff and Ehud Y'ari, eds., trans., Ina Friedman (New York, 1989), p. 93.

357 Charles D. Smith, *Palestine and the Arab-Israeli Conflict* (New York, 1988), p. 244.

358 Aaron S. Klieman, *Israel and the World After 40 Years* (New York, 1990), p. 227.

359 Neil C. Livingstone and David Halevy, *Inside the PLO* (New York, 1990), p. 24.

360 Quandt, Jabber, and Lesch, p. 114.

361 Beverly Milton-Edwards, *Islamic Politics in Palestine* (London, 1996), p. 148.

362 Ibid., p. 154.

363 Gilbert, *Israel*, p. 551.

364 Ibid, p. 563.365 Amos Perlman, *The Life and Times of Menachem Begin*, op. cit., p. 288.

The Endless Dialogue

itzhak Rabin suffered the same fate as Anwar Sadat: a violent death for having dared to make peace with the hereditary enemy. The Jewish ultra-nationalists and religious fundamentalists had opposed autonomy for the Palestinians from the beginning, believing (with good reason) that it would lead to new pressures for the creation of a sovereign Palestinian state. To perhaps half of the Israeli population, this would constitute an unacceptable threat to the country's existence.

The Likud factions, which inherited the Oslo Accords as well as its underlying philosophy (land for peace), considered the cession of the West Bank to the Palestinians to be nearly a treasonous policy; at the least, the basis for national suicide. Unwilling (and indeed unable) to repudiate the accords in any official way, they resolved nonetheless to defeat the terms of the agreement by taking measures of delay in implementing its provisions. Also, they resumed an ambitious building program in the Occupied Territories, including new construction in East Jerusalem, well aware that this would incite Palestinian extremists (Arafat's domestic opponents) to undertake acts of terror; and this would ostensibly justify Israeli fears that to surrender an inch to the Palestinians would only encourage them to demand another mile. The new premier, Benjamin Netanyahu, the leader of these extreme factions, reflected exactly in his stubbornness and his implacable hostility to the Oslo Accords, the Likud mentality.

Efforts by the Clinton Administration over several years to facilitate the fulfillment of the Oslo Accords were largely fruitless. In October 1998 both Arafat and Netanyahu were invited to Washington to discuss the delays, Netanyahu to explain Israel's temporizing policies, Arafat to explain why he could not contain the excessive actions of the Hamas. To ensure maximum privacy and confidence for the parties involved in the discussions, the meetings were moved to a plantation in Maryland called Wye. Clinton involved himself personally in these exchanges, which lasted for the better part of a week. The result was another set of agreements that merely promised that the Oslo Accords would be fulfilled. King Hussein, acutely ill, dying from cancer, attended the final sessions at Wye. Eloquently, he appealed for a reconciliation of the Jews and Arabs. In a long speech Arafat once more renounced terrorism ("no more confrontation"). Both Arafat and Netanyahu made final conciliatory remarks on the day the Wye Agreements were signed, and they shook hands in public view.

In the weeks that followed it was clear that nothing had changed. Another presidential visit to both Israel and the Occupied Territories during Christmas week of 1998 merely revealed that neither side would (or could) yield to the other anything of substance (though the leaders of the PLO did stand and raise their hands *en masse* to testify that the clauses of the Palestinian Covenant calling for the destruction of Israel were no longer valid).

Thereafter, Netanyahu continued the policy of temporizing and delay, his unchanging argument that so long as Arafat could not control the violent elements of his party, and the Palestinian society more generally, Israel would not resume withdrawing its occupying forces as called for by the Oslo Accords. Arafat countered Netanyahu's protestations by threatening unilateral proclamation of a sovereign Palestinian state in May 1999, when the life, the legal meaning, of the Oslo Accords would expire. Netanyahu promised retaliation in that event, the extent and ferocity of which Arafat could only guess and about which the

United States could only worry.

As the deadline for realizing the aims of the Oslo Accords approached in the early autumn of 1999, the religious and political bonds that had so far held the Likud factions together began to weaken, producing a mixture of trepidation and misgivings. Out of this welter of emotions surged the old pride, the most ancient ambition. Perhaps in another day, perhaps another decade, Eretz Israel would be regained. To leave the Occupied Territories was to forever abandon this hope. Finally, as collective intransigence took hold of the factions, bespeaking the end of Netanyahu's brief career as premier, he fell more fully than before under the spell of the most general fear that animated his heterogeneous party: namely, to yield to the Arab world would in the long run mean a national disaster for Israel, a fate more terrible than that which had visited the Palestinians a generation earlier.

Meanwhile, perhaps unexpectedly, Israeli public opinion began to recognize once more that a settlement must be accepted with the Palestinians (the Arabs more generally, since Syria remained Israel's avowed enemy). Netanyahu's decline in influence (complicated by serious ethical charges brought against him) produced a political crisis, out of which emerged another leader, Ehud Barak. Far more subtle and flexible that Netanyahu, Barak was, very much like Yitzhak Rabin, a warrior turned peacemaker, a military man whose essential pragmatism promised compromises. Without apparent political ambition, he would do what others before him could not, or would not, do. As if to underscore his resolve, and his willingness to risk his newly born political career, he ordered the withdrawal of all Israeli forces from Lebanon, immediately and without conditions. He initiated talks with Arafat also, and these led the Clinton administration to try anew for a general pacification of the Middle East through a comprehensive settlement of all questions that divided the Israelis and the Palestinians. Pourparlers in Washington led to a meeting of Clinton, Barak, and Arafat at Camp David. These hopeful events were facilitated by the sudden death of Assad, leaving Syria without an effective leader. In the crisis produced by Assad's disappearance a new leadership at Damascus might consider making sacrifices of a kind that were now being required of Arafat and Barak.

True to his reputation as one able to charm his listeners and at the same time cajole his interlocutors, Clinton expended some part of his political capital in a vain attempt to force compromises on each of the antagonists who sat at his table. Outwardly, the president behaved with an evenhanded concern toward his guests, perhaps even leaving the impression that he tilted in favor of the Palestinians. Indeed, for a period of two years, well before the Wye talks, the Clinton strategy had been one of befriending the Arabs, the better to disarm Arafat when the eventual concessions would be demanded of him. Surprisingly, for so sophisticated and Machiavellian a statesman as Arafat had become, he was long in recognizing that the American negotiators meant to use him for the eventual advantage of the American presence in the Middle East and Israel's part in that geopolitical ambition. [366] On the other hand, the American proposal seemed at once plausible and realistic: a joint possession of Jerusalem by both people; the Palestinians to take East Jerusalem, the Israelis West Jerusalem; sovereignty over the whole city to remain with the latter. Predictably, Arafat refused. Just as predictably Barak agreed, leaving the onus on Arafat.

The failure of the Camp David talks could only be considered inevitable. What might well be called the sacred cow of Middle East politics had finally been confronted directly: Jerusalem. The Wye talks had considered nothing more than a timetable for Israel's final withdrawal from the Occupied Territories (the United States to furnish an adequate security in those last stages). By contrast, the Camp David talks foundered on the seemingly intractable question of Jerusalem's future status. Embittered, Arafat returned to Gaza. As for Barak, he had staked his political career on making some gains that would placate the Palestinians, yet not alienate his own constituency.

While Arafat had gained nothing also, he had lost nothing, save time; for he was getting old and showing signs of frailty. Yet, there was not another Palestinian in view who could supplant him, nor claim to have the capacity to hold the clashing factions together for the never-ending quest to regain all that had been lost in 1948. Once more, Arafat threatened to proclaim a Palestinian state on 17 September 2000. Thereafter he undertook an arduous tour of the world's capitals, seeking support from those numerous countries that had always been sympathetic to the Palestinian cause. However, pressure from the international community did not materialize. An enormous meeting of the world's leaders at the UN discussed the Arab-Israeli conflict (as well as other crises), but nothing came of it. With impotent friends aplenty (the actual history of his career), Arafat remained isolated, his people more frustrated and vengeful than at any time in the past. Not expecting, as usual, more than lip service from the Arab states, Arafat remained dependent upon American largesse, and the uncertain patronage of an American president whose motives were quixotic and narcissistic. Always, for Clinton, success in political matters was meant to redound to his personal credit, only secondarily for the gratification of any laudatory policy he might embrace. He could dream of the impossible: a solution that would allow the Palestinians to rule themselves in sovereignty while living autonomously in East Jerusalem, acknowledging Israel's sovereignty over the city. The achievement would cast such luster on the tarnished president that his tawdry affair with a vulnerable young woman, like his impeachment, would slip ever deeper into the shadows of forgetfulness. The ultimate crown for this success might well be the Nobel Prize for peace.

The seventeenth of September came and went, without the proclamation of a Palestinian state. In the meantime Israeli withdrawal from the Occupied Territories had come to a halt (Barak's withdrawal of Israeli forces from Lebanon an almost uneventful action). Through the remainder of the year 2000 Barak and Arafat continued to meet. The hovering American president could add little to what were in effect sterile conversations.

Early in October, Netanyahu (having been cleared of the charges

327

brought against him), seemed ready to seek control of the State of Israel again; thus to prepare his people for another year, or another decade, or perhaps the remainder of the century, in the never-ending need to gird the Israeli state for survival in the midst of its eternal enemies.

As if to announce the revival of the Likud, and to affirm its intransigence, Ariel Sharon, the Palestinians' abiding *bête noir*, elected to enter the Mosque of Omar on a Friday afternoon. His appearance among devout Moslems in prayer was likened to the one who pours gasoline on a fire already lit. A veritable explosion occurred, mad panic and rage. The riots that followed were reminiscent of those that occurred at the same place in 1929; but now much more dangerous, perhaps more difficult than before to stop. In a few days, Clinton, for the United States, and Hosni Mubarak, for Egypt, offered to meet with Arafat and Barak at Sharam-el-Sheikh. Forgotten now were vast plans for a Middle East peace settlement; there was only one question to be raised: how to stop the tumult that had come with the failure of the Palestinians and the Israelis to deal with Jerusalem's eventual status. Forgotten also was the likely fact that both parties to the conflict had not changed their fundamental positions, which alone made a genuine peace impossible: the Palestinians would never forget that they had lost their country to an alien power that relied for its strength upon aid from Western countries. In every generation there would be some, perhaps many, who would think only of how they might regain what was rightfully theirs. Aware of this, the Israelis could only reflect on how they might save themselves, alone and without help, at some future time.

The desperate condition of a small country when imperiled cannot be exaggerated, perhaps not imagined. In case of war, Israel has scarcely any territory to yield in exchange for time. If invaded in any depth, the national territory and all the cities involved would be ravaged at once, a possibility that seems to haunt the Likud leadership. [367] If a state is large enough, it can withstand terrible punishment, even a decimation of its population, and over time can recover from the bloodletting. But the loss of territory for a small state means almost certain annihilation at worst, captivity at best. There is no place in so small a country where an uprooted population can take refuge. In such an event (to speak of poetic justice), a given Israeli generation would experience the disorganized flight, terror, and destitution a generation of Palestinians suffered in 1948.

A hostile Palestinian state on Israel's borders, supported by sympathetic Arab allies, would mean a continuous threat of extinction for the Israelis. It can be seen that the effort to establish a Jewish majority in the former Samaria and Judea after 1967 was as much a matter of military calculation as it was a religious obsession.

The only solution for Israel's security needs, as it seemed to most of their strategists, was to retain Samaria and Judea (the "Wall"), and promote massive immigration from the Diaspora in order to counter the numerical superiority of the Palestinians (not only the Arabs within Israel, but the Palestinians on the West Bank—approximately one million by 1990).

The idea of "transfer," i.e., the forcible expulsion of the Palestinians from Eretz Israel, had by 1990 become another vain hope, almost as fanciful as the idea that eight million Jews might be encouraged to emigrate to Israel; this a notion almost as bizarre as the original fantasy of the Zionists that had brought them to Palestine in the first place. Nonetheless, Netanyahu insisted upon its feasibility. "For Israel's Jewish population to grow," he wrote in 1988, "to constitute more than half of the world's Jews is no longer impossible, and may not be very far away." [368]

The magnitude of this "renewed Zionism" and the imperious necessity for Israel to keep most of the West Bank as a consequence, made the resistance of the United States to the colonization of the Occupied Territories seem like a betrayal to many Israelis, as Great Britain's resistance to Jewish immigration during the mandate period has been considered ever since an unforgivable "betrayal."

While the iniquities of the latter cannot be forgiven by the Israelis, the errors of the United States can be overlooked, or at least tolerated, because of American naiveté (it is thought) and an apparent misunderstanding of what Jewish immigration means in macro-historical terms; but more especially because of a tendency of the Americans to swallow Palestinian propaganda uncritically: "The first real sign that the Arab campaign to harness Washington to its anti-immigration agenda has worked." [369]

The peoples of the Middle East have experienced insoluble dilemmas for thousands of years, which brings to mind one of the region's most enduring stories, that of the Gordian knot, which could not be untied until one day Alexander the Great solved the problem by the simple expedient of cutting it in two. In this regard, the power of arbitration that presently is the unique possession of the United States, at a time when it is not inhibited by a power equal to itself, while enjoying an immense trust from a congeries of nations large and small, provides a window of opportunity through which a statesman of vision might slip and cut the Gordian knot: *viz.*, the separation and pacification of the quarreling siblings. For many years the world community of nations has wished for a solution to the problem, one favorable to the Palestinians while not injurious to the Israelis. Any just solution supported by the United States could be carried through the United Nations with ease, and imposed thereafter upon the siblings in a brief period of time. There lacks only on the part of the United States a will to arbitrate and the wisdom of its statesmen to realize at last that unswerving support of Israel (wrong or right) over the decades has been a fruitless policy.

The key for solving the Israeli-Palestinian conflict may be found in the original partition of Palestine in 1922, when the Hashemite family were installed as rulers over a small, fictitious country made up mostly of sterile desert. Today, the ambition and pride of a petty dynasty, gratified in 1922, could be easily sacrificed. Given the rapid progress of democratic practices at the beginning of a new century no institution seems more irrelevant, more costly while being less useful, than monarchy. The few that survive are truly vestiges of an earlier innocent, and indeed ignorant, time in human development.

"Your Highness" is an expression as empty sounding and meaningless as royal absolutism or divine right monarchy.

The Oslo Accords gave the deathblow to any hopes King Hussein might have harbored that eventually, out of the vicissitudes of war and politics in the Middle East, he could regain control of the West Bank. Diplomatically and morally isolated, he never recovered from his decision to support Saddam Hussein during the Gulf War. In 1994, contrite and ever more conciliatory in his pronouncements, he made his penitential journey to Washington, last stage on the way to Jerusalem, where he would finally (because nothing else was left to him) recognize the State of Israel, thereby acknowledging also, if only by implication, that the West Bank belonged to the Palestinians and not to himself.

Each generation lives with the errors bequeathed to them by their predecessors. But on occasion the opportunity arises when an escape from the toils of the past is possible. Had Hussein's magnanimity been equal to the image he presented in public at Wye in 1998, he might have abdicated the position the British had conferred upon his family in 1922. By allowing the Jordanians (the majority of them Palestinians in reality) to choose, they would doubtless merge their territory with that of their compatriots on the opposite bank. [370] Then would the Palestinian national movement have received its benediction, making inevitable the establishment of a sovereign Palestinian Republic, perhaps with Amman as its capital and Gaza its chief seaport. One may wonder too if at that point the United Nations would not have been willing to enforce the resolution voted in 1950 for the internationalization of Jerusalem: spiritual center of the world's three great monotheistic religions. But, as Hussein (and his successor also) could not surrender the pretension of being grand as the head of a small state, the Israelis could not summon the courage to renounce the Holy City, precious artifact from their ancient past. Against such intransigence the international community was reluctant to act, largely because there did not exist an incentive such as the dominant world power might have offered the whole body of the United Nations. In

331

that hypothetical case the arbiter (i.e., the United Nations) would have resolved: Tel Aviv is an adequate capital for a small country like Israel, Amman is an appropriate capital for a Palestinian commonwealth, and Jerusalem belongs to the world. Of course, had this come to pass, given Israel's uniqueness as a state, and its anomalous situation in the Arab world, it would have been incumbent upon the UN to provide the former with an international guarantee for its continued existence.

At present, few perceive that the world's humanity races toward increasing integration; social, racial, and ethnic amalgamation, as one country after another slips into the mainstream of ever wider and deeper modernization. The age-old plight of the unwanted, disliked, and often-feared Jew is by now a legacy of the past. Increasing secularization, which inevitably accompanies modernization, means that religious values (while still vital in spiritual terms) will impinge less profoundly on a given state or society in the future. The need for a Jewish haven, once sought at so enormous a price, does not any longer seem to be the imperative that it was for Jews and Christians a generation ago.

Bibliography

Acheson, D. *Present at the Creation*. (London, 1970)

Aldington, Richard. *Lawrence of Arabia* (London: Collins, 1955)

Alus, Naji. *Arab Resistance in Palestine 1917-1948* (Arabic text) (Beirut: Dar al-Taliah, 1970)

Ambrose, Stephen E. *Rise to Globalism. American Foreign Policy Since 1938.* 7th ed. rev. (New York, 1995)

Antonius, George. *The Arab Awakening* (London: Hamish Hamilton, 1955)

Ashavar, Bernard. *The Tragedy of Zionism. Revolution and Democracy in the Land of Israel* (New York, 1985)

Barkai, Haim. "The Kibbutz: An Experiment in Microsolialism," *Israel, the Arabs and the Middle East*, Ivisky Hower and Carl Gershman, eds. (Bantam Books: New York, 1972)

Becker, Jillian. *The PLO*

Begin, M. *The Revolt* (Tel Aviv, 1951)

Bell, J. Bowyer. *The Long War. Israel and the Arabs Since 1946* (Englewood Cliffs, NJ, 1969)

Bell, J.B. *Terror out of Zion* (New York, 1977)

Beller, Steven. *Herzl* (London, 1991)

Ben Gurion, David. *Israel. A Personal History* (New York and Tel Aviv, 1971)

Ben Gurion, David. *My Talks with Arab Leaders* (Jerusalem, 1972)

Bentwich, Norman D. *England in Palestine* (London: Kegan Paul, 1932)

Brandeis, Louis D. "The Jewish Problem," *The Curse of Bigness. Miscellaneous Papers of Louis D. Brandeis*, Osmond K. Frankel, ed. (Port Washington, NY, 1965)

Bullock. A. *The Life and Times of Ernest Bevin* (London, 1960, 1967) 2 vols.

Burdette, Winston. *Encounter With the Middle East* (new York, 1969)

Carter, Jimmy, *The Blood of Abraham* (Boston, 1985)

Cattan, Henry. *Palestine, The Arabs and Israel* (London: Longmans, 1969)

Cohen, Aharon. *Israel and the Arab World* (New York, 1970)

Crossman, R. *Palestine Mission* (London, 1947)

Dalton, H. *Memoirs: High Tide and After* (London, 1967)

Davis, John H. *The Evasive Peace* (London, 1968)

Deutscher, Isaac. *The Non-Jewish Jew and Other Essays* (New York, 1968)

Dobson, Christopher. *Black September* (London: Robert Hale, 1974)

Donner, Fred McGraw. *The Early Islamic Conquests* (Princeton University Press, 1981)

Draper, Theodore. *Israel and World Politics* (New York, 1978)

Eban, Abba. *My People. The Story of the Jews* (New York, 1968)

Eddy, W. A. *FDR Meets Ibn Saud* (New York, 1954)

Eden, Anthony. *Full Circle* (Boston, 1960)

Eisenhower, Dwight D. *The White House Years. Waging Peace 1956–1961* (New York, 1965)

Elon, Amos. *The Israelis. Founders and Sons* (New York, 1972)

Epp, Frank H. *Whose Land is Palestine? The Middle East Problem in Historical Perspective* (Grand Rapids, MI, 1970)

Flapan, Simha. *The Birth of Israel. Myths and Realities* (New York, 1987)

Flapan, Simha. *Zionism and the Palestinians* (London: Croom Helm, 1979)

Frank, Gerald. *The Deed* (New York: Simon & Schuster, 1963)

Frankel, Jonathon. "The Crisis of 1881–82 as a Turning Point in Modern Jewish History," *The Legacy of Jewish Immigration: 1881 and Its Impact*, David Berger, ed. (Brooklyn College Press, 1983)

Ganin, Z. *Truman, American Jewry and Israel, 1945–1948* (New York, 1979)

Garcia-Granados, J. *The Birth of Israel* (New York, 1949)

Gilbert, Martin. *Exile and Return. The Struggle for a Jewish Homeland* (New York, 1978)

Golan, Galia. *The Soviet Union and the Palestine Liberation Organization: An Uneasy Alliance* (New York: Praeger, 1980)

Gordon, David C. *Lebanon: The Fragmented Nation* (London: Croom

Helm, 1980)

Hadawi, Sami. *Bitter Harvest: Palestine Between 1914–1979* (New York: The New World Press, 1967)

Heller, Mark A. *A Palestinian State. The Implications for Israel* (Harvard University Press, 1983)

Heniger, Joseph. "Pre-Islamic Bedouin Religion," *Studies on Islam*, Merlin L. Swartz, ed. (Oxford University Press, 1981)

Herzl, *Complete Diaries*, Raphael Patai, ed., Harry Zohn trans. (New York, 1960)

Herzog, Chaim. *The Arab-Israeli Wars* (London: Arms & Armour Press, 1982)

Hitti, Philip K. *History of the Arabs* (London: Macmillan, 1940)

Horowitz, D. *State in the Making* (New York, 1953)

Hurewitz, J.C. *Diplomacy in the Near and Middle East* (Princeton, NJ: Van Nostrand, 1956) 2 vols.

Hurewitz, Jacob C. *The Struggle for Palestine* (New York: Norton, 1950)

Hyams, Edward. *Terrorists and Terrorism* (New York, 1974)

Hyamson, Albert M. *Palestine Under the Mandate, 1920–1948* (London: Methuen, 1950)

James, Robert Rhodes. *Anthony Eden* (New York, 1986)

Jiryis, Sabri. *The Arabs in Israel*, Inea Bushag, trans. (New York and London, 1976)

Jones, Martin. *Failure in Palestine. British and United States Policy after the Second World War* (London and New York, 1986)

Kedourie, Elie. *England and the Middle East: The Destruction of the Ottoman Empire, 1914–1921* (London: Bowes & Bowes, 1956)

Kedourie, Elie. *Islam in the Modern World and Other Studies* (London: Mansell, 1980)

Khadduri, Majid. *Arab Contemporaries. The Role of Personalities in Politics* (The Johns Hopkins University Press, 1973)

Khalidi, Walid, ed. *From Haven to Conquest: Readings in Zionism and the Palestine Problem Until 1948* (Beirut: Institute for Palestine Studies, 1971)

Khouri, Fred J. *The Arab-Israeli Dilemma*, 2nd ed. (Syracuse University Press, NY, 1976)

Kiernan, Thomas. *Yasser Arafat. The Man and the Myth* (New York, 1976)

Kimche, Jon, and David Kimche. *A Clash of Destinies: The Arab-Jewish War and the Founding of the State of Israel* (New York: Praeger, 1960)

Kimche, Jon. *The Second Arab Awakening.* (New York: Holt, Rinehart & Winston, 1970)

Kirk, G. E. *A Short History of the Middle East From the Rise of Islam to Modern Times* (London: Methuen, 1966)

Kissinger, Henry. *A World Restored. Metternich, Castlereagh and the Problems of Peace, 1812–1822* (Boston, 1957)

Kissinger, Henry. *Years of Upheaval* (London: Weidenfeld & Nicolson, 1982)

Klieman,, Aaron S. *Israel and the World After 40 years* (New York, 1990)

Lacouture, Jean. *Nasser. A Biography*, trans., David Hofstadter (New York, 1973)

Laffin, John. *The PLO Connections* (London: Corgi, 1982)

Lash. *Eleanor. The Years Alone* (New York, 1972)

Lawrence, Bruce B. *Shattering the Myth. Islam Beyond Violence* (Princeton University Press, 1998)

Lenczowski, George. *The Middle East in World Affairs* (Ithaca: Cornell University Press, 1952)

Lewis, Bernard. *Islam in History* (New York: Open Court, 1972)

Lilienthal, Alfred M. *The Zionist Connection. What Price Peace?* (New York, 1978)

Livingstone, Neil C. and David Halevy. *Inside the PLO* (New York, 1990)

Ma'oz, Moshe. *Syria and Israel: From War to Peacemaking* (Oxford: Clarenden Press, 1995)

Mackey, Sandra. *Passion and Politics, The Turbulent World of the Arabs* (New York, 1992)

Manson, T. W. *The Teaching of Jesus* (New York, 1931)

Manuel, Frank E. *The Realities of American-Palestine Relations* (Washington, DC, 1949)

Masalha, Nur. *Expulsion of the Palestinians. The Concept of "Transfer" in Zionist Political Thought, 1822–1948* (Washington DC, 1992)

McDowall, David. *Palestine and Israel. The Uprising and Beyond* (Berkeley and Los Angeles, 1989)

Meinertzhagen, R. *Middle East Diary 1917–1956* (London: The Cresset Press, 1959)

Mernissi, Fatima. *Islam and Democracy. Fear of the Modern World.* Trans., Mary Jo Lakeland (Addison-Wesley Publishing Company, 1992)

Meyer, Alfred G. *Communism*, 2nd ed. (New York, 1962)

Meyer, Michael A. *Ideas of Jewish History* (New York, 1974)

Milton-Edwards, Beverly. *Islamic Politics in Palestine* (London, 1996)

Mosley, Leonard. *Dulles: A Biography of Eleanor Allen and John Foster Dulles and Their Family Network* (New York, 1978)

Neff, Donald. *Warriors for Jerusalem. The Six Days that Changed the Middle East* (New York, 1984)

Newby, Gordon Darnell. *A History of the Jews of Arabia. From Ancient Times to their Eclipse under Islam* (University of South Carolina Press, 1988)

Palestine Papers, 191701922: Seeds of Conflict, Doreen Ingrams, ed. (London, 1972)

Parkes, James W. *A History of Palestine From 135 A.D. to Modern Times* (New York: Oxford University Press, 1949)

Patai, Raphael. *The Seed of Abraham. Jews and Arabs in Contact and Conflict* (University of Utah Press, 1986)

Pearlman, Maurice. *The Mufti of Jerusalem* (London: Victor Gollancz, 1947)

Peretz, Don. *Israel and the Palestine Arabs* (Washington DC: The Middle East Institute, 1958)

Perlmutter, Amos. *The Life and Times of Menachem Begin* (New York, 1987)

Poliakov, Leon. *The History of Anti-Semitism*, Richard Howard, trans. (New York, 1965)

Polk, W.R., Samler, D. M. and Asfour, E. *Backdrop to Tragedy: The Struggle for Palestine* (Boston: Beacon Press, 1957)

Polk, William R. *The United States and the Arab World*, 3rd ed. (Harvard University Press, 1975)

Porath, Y. *The Emergence of the Palestinian-Arab National Movement*, Vol. 1,

1918–1929. Vol. 2. 1929–1939 (London, 1974, 1977)

Pryce-Jones, David. *The Face of Defeat: Palestinian Refugees and Guerrillas* (London: Weidenfeld & Nicolson, 1972)

Quandt, William B., Fund Jabber, Ammosdy Lesch. *The Politics of Palestinian Nationalism* (Berkeley and Los Angeles, 1973)

Quigley, John. *Palestine and Israel. A Challenge to Justice* (Duke University Press, 1990)

Rabinowicz, O. K. *Winston Churchill on Jewish Problems* (London, 1956; New York, 1960)

Rodinson, Maxime. *Israel and the Arabs*, trans. (New York, 1968)

Rodison, Maxine. *Israel: A Colonial-Settler State*, David Thorstad, trans. (New York, 1973)

Rose, N. A., ed. *The Gentile Zionists* (London, 1973)

Rubinstein, Amnon. *The Zionist Dream Revisited. From Herzl to Gush Emunim and Back* (New York, 1984)

Russell, D.S. *The Method and Message of Jewish Apocalyptic. 200 B.C.–A.D. 100* (Philadelphia, 1964)

Saaka, Dr. Saul. *Blood in Zion. How the Jewish Guerillas Drove the British Out of Zion* (London and Washington, 1995)

Sachar, Howard. *A History of Israel* (New York, 1976)

Said, Edward W. *The Question of Palestine* (New York, 1979)

Sakran, F. C. *Palestine Dilemma: Arab Rights Versus Zionist Aspirations* (Washington: Public Affairs Press, 1948)

Sanders, Ronald. *Shores of Refuge. A Hundred Years of Jewish Immigration* (New York, 1988)

Schama, Simon. *Two Rothschilds and the Land of Israel* (London: Collins, 1978)

Schiff, Ze'ev and Ehud Y'ari, eds. *Intifada. The Palestinian Uprising—Israel's Third Front.* (New York, 1989) trans., Ina Friedman

Schindler, Colin. *Israel, Likud and the Zionist Dream: Power, Politics and Ideology from Begin to Netanyahu* (London and New York, 1995)

Seale, Patrick. *Asad of Syria. The Struggle for the Middle East* (Berkeley and Los Angeles, 1988)

Segev, Tom. *1949: The First Israelis* (New York and London, 1986)

Seliktar, Ofira. *New Zionism and the Foreign Policy System of Israel* (Southern

Illinois University Press, 1986)

Shadid, Mohammed. *The United States and the Palestinians* (London: Croom Helm, 1979)

Shimoni, Gideon. *The Zionist Ideology* (Brandeis University Press, 1995)

Shipler, David K. *Arab and Jew. Wounded Spirits in a Promised Land* (Time Books, 1968)

Shurer, Emile. A History of the Jewish People in the Time of Jesus, Naham V. Glatzer, ed. (New York, 1961)

Shwadran, B. *The Middle East, Oil and the Great Powers* (New York, 1973)

Silverberg, Robert. *If I Forget Thee O Jerusalem: American Jews and the State of Israel* (New York, 1970)

Simons, Hugh J. *British Rule and Rebellion* (Edinburgh & London: Blackwood, 1937)

Sivan, Emmanuel, and Menachem Friedman, eds. *Religious Radicalism and Politics in the Middle East* (State University of New York, 1990)

Slutsky, Y. *History of the Hagana* (in Hebrew). Vol. 3 (Tel Aviv, 1975)

Smith, Charles D. *Palestine and the Arab-Israeli Conflict* (New York, 1988)

Snetsinger, J. *Truman, The Jewish Vote and the Creation of Israel* (Stanford, 1974)

Spanier, John W. *Foreign Policy Since World War II.* 3rd ed. (New York, 1968)

Steinsaltz, Adin. *The Essential Talmud* (New York, 1976)

Stewart, Desmond. *Theodore Herzl* (New York, 1974)

Thompson, J. A. *The Bible and Archaeology* (Grand Rapids, Michigan, 1965)

Tillman, Seth P. *The United States in the Middle East. Interests and Obstacles* (Indiana University Press, 1982)

Torrey, Gordon H. *Syrian Politics and The Military, 1945–1958* (The Ohio State University Press, 1964)

Toynbee, Arnold. *A Study of History*, D.C. Somerville, ed. (Oxford University Press, 1946)

Trever, Albert A. *History of Ancient Civilization.* Vol. I, *The Ancient Near East and Greece* (New York, 1936)

Truman, H. S. *Memoirs*. Vol. 2, *Years of Trial and Hope* (New York, 1956)

Weishurd, David. *Jewish Settler Violence. Deviance and Social Reaction* (The Pennsylvania State University Press, 1989)

Weizmann, Chaim. *Trial and Error. The Autobiography of Chaim Weizmann* (New York, 1959)

Wilson, Harold. *The Chariot of Israel. Britain, America and the State of Israel* (New York and London, 1981)

Wright, Robin. *Sacred Rage. The Crusade of Modern Islam* (New York, 1985)

Ziad, Abu-Amr, *Islamic Fundamentalism in the West Bank and Gaza. Muslim Brotherhood and Jihad.* (Indiana University Press, 1994)

9/02